Preserving Privacy in On-Line Analytical Processing (OLAP)

Advances in Information Security

Sushil Jajodia
Consulting Editor
Center for Secure Information Systems
George Mason University
Fairfax, VA 22030-4444
email: jajodia@gmu.edu

The goals of the Springer International Series on ADVANCES IN INFORMATION SECURITY are, one, to establish the state of the art of, and set the course for future research in information security and, two, to serve as a central reference source for advanced and timely topics in information security research and development. The scope of this series includes all aspects of computer and network security and related areas such as fault tolerance and software assurance.

ADVANCES IN INFORMATION SECURITY aims to publish thorough and cohesive overviews of specific topics in information security, as well as works that are larger in scope or that contain more detailed background information than can be accommodated in shorter survey articles. The series also serves as a forum for topics that may not have reached a level of maturity to warrant a comprehensive textbook treatment.

Researchers, as well as developers, are encouraged to contact Professor Sushil Jajodia with ideas for books under this series.

Additional titles in the series:

SECURITY FOR WIRELESS SENSOR NETWORKS by Donggang Liu and Peng Ning; ISBN: 978-0-387-32723-5

MALWARE DETECTION edited by Somesh Jha, Cliff Wang, Mihai Christodorescu, Dawn Song, and Douglas Maughan; ISBN: 978-0-387-32720-4

ELECTRONIC POSTAGE SYSTEMS: Technology, Security, Economics by Gerrit Bleumer; ISBN: 978-0-387-29313-2

MULTIVARIATE PUBLIC KEY CRYPTOSYSTEMS by Jintai Ding, Jason E. Gower and Dieter Schmidt; ISBN-13: 978-0-378-32229-2

UNDERSTANDING INTRUSION DETECTION THROUGH VISUALIZATION by Stefan Axelsson; ISBN-10: 0-387-27634-3

QUALITY OF PROTECTION: Security Measurements and Metrics by Dieter Gollmann, Fabio Massacci and Artsiom Yautsiukhin; ISBN-10: 0-387-29016-8

COMPUTER VIRUSES AND MALWARE by John Aycock; ISBN-10: 0-387-30236-0

HOP INTEGRITY IN THE INTERNET by Chin-Tser Huang and Mohamed G. Gouda; ISBN-10: 0-387-22426-3

CRYPTOGRAPHICS: Exploiting Graphics Cards For Security by Debra Cook and Angelos Keromytis; ISBN: 0-387-34189-7

PRIVACY PRESERVING DATA MINING by Jaideep Vaidya, Chris Clifton and Michael Zhu; ISBN-10: 0-387- 25886-8

BIOMETRIC USER AUTHENTICATION FOR IT SECURITY: From Fundamentals to Handwriting by Claus Vielhauer; ISBN-10: 0-387-26194-X

Additional information about this series can be obtained from
http://www.springer.com

Preserving Privacy in On-Line Analytical Processing (OLAP)

by

Lingyu Wang
Concordia University
Canada

Sushil Jajodia
George Mason University
USA

Duminda Wijesekera
George Mason University
USA

 Springer

Lingyu Wang
Concordia University
Concordia Institute for Information
  Systems Engineering
Montreal, QC
Canada H3G 1T7
wang@ciise.concordia.ca

Sushil Jajodia
George Mason University
Mail Stop 5B5
Suite 417, Research I Bldg.
4400 University Drive
Fairfax, VA 22030-4444
jajodia@gmu.edu

Duminda Wijesekera
George Mason University
Mail Stop 5B5
Suite 417, Research I Bldg.
4400 University Drive
Fairfax, VA 22030-4444
dwijesek@gmu.edu

Preserving Privacy in On-Line Analytical Processing (OLAP)
by Lingyu Wang, Sushil Jajodia, Duminda Wijesekera

ISBN-13: 978-1-4419-4278-4

e-ISBN-10: 0-387-46274-0
e-ISBN-13: 978-0-387-46274-5

Printed on acid-free paper.

9 8 7 6 5 4 3 2 1

springer.com

To my wife Quan, with love.
- Lingyu

To my wife, Kamal.
- Sushil

To Devika and Olindi, for the past and hopes beyond.
- Duminda

Preface

Information is of strategic and operational importance to any organization. With rapid advancements in computer and network technology, it is possible for an organization to collect, store, and retrieve vast amounts of data of all kinds quickly and efficiently. Databases of today no longer contain only data used for day–to–day data processing; they have become information systems that store everything—vital or not—to an organization.

Aggregation and derivation are important and desirable effects of collecting data and storing them in databases. Aggregation is the combining of information from various sources. Derivation goes one step further; it uses different pieces of data to deduce or create new or previously unavailable information from the aggregates.

Unfortunately, aggregates and derived data pose serious problems since new information can be derived from available information in several different ways. If the concerns related to security are not properly resolved, security violations may lead to losses of information that may translate into financial losses or losses whose values are obviously high but difficult to quantify (e.g., national security). At the same time, these large information systems represent a threat to the privacy of individuals since they contain a great amount of detail about individuals. Admittedly, the information collection by an organization is essential for conducting its business; however, indiscriminate collection and retention of data represents an extraordinary intrusion on privacy of individuals.

Privacy protection is both a personal and fundamental right of all individuals. Individuals have a right to expect that organizations will keep personal information confidential. One way to ensure this is to require that organizations collect, maintain, use, and disseminate identifiable personal information and data only as necessary to carry out their functions.

This book addresses the problem of disclosure in on-line analytical processing (OLAP) systems. These systems are designed to help analysts in gaining insights to the large amount of data stored in enterprise data warehouses. OLAP systems heavily depend on aggregates of data in order to hide insignificant details and hence to accentuate global patterns and trends. As the underlying data model, a data cube can nicely organize multi-dimensional aggregates formulated using dimension hierarchies inherent to given data.

It is critical that data cubes be analyzed for possible inference or derivation problems. This book first provides a good understanding of the ways such inference problems may arise. Armed with this understanding, the book then takes steps to eliminate these problems. Following a review of past research in statistical databases, the book shows how existing methodologies can be borrowed for developing security measures in OLAP data cubes. These measures produce improved results than by their counterparts in statistical databases, but they also inherit certain limitations from the latter. Taken such limitations as a lesson, the book discusses several novel methods that finally demonstrate a promising way to completely eliminate threats to privacy in OLAP systems.

Fairfax, VA,   *Lingyu Wang, Sushil Jajodia, Duminda Wijesekera*

Contents

1

Introduction

1.1 Background

Electronic privacy is drawing more and more attention nowadays, as evidenced by cover stories in media [31] and initiatives of governments [70]. Public surveys also reflect strong concerns about potential privacy breaches. The results of recent public opinion polls show that 86% of respondents want a web site to obtain opt-in consent before collecting personal information, and 81% of respondents worry that companies may misuse the collected private data [10]. Privacy is relevant to the business, too. Privacy concerns cause consumers to routinely abandon their shopping carts when too much personal information is being demanded. The estimated loss of internet sales due to such privacy concerns is as much as $18 billion according to analysts [36]. A failure to protect customers' privacy will eventually become the breach of laws due to upcoming privacy legislation, such as the Health Insurance Portability and Accountability Act (HIPAA) enacted by the U.S. Congress in 1996.

One of the efforts in reducing the privacy concerns of internet consumers is the platform for privacy preferences (P3P) project by WWW Consortium, which allows a web site to provide machine-readable privacy policies [19]. The web browser of a consumer can thus determine if the provided privacy policies may satisfy the consumer's privacy preferences by comparing the two in an automated way. However, P3P only helps companies in making promises, but it does not enforce them to keep those promises [23]. Unfortunately, keeping one's promises is usually easier said then done. Privacy breaches may occur in various ways after personal data have been collected and stored in the enterprise's data warehouses. The data may be intentionally misused by the company for profits, violating the privacy policies under which the data have been collected. Such intentional misuses can be addressed by privacy legislation. The data may also be stolen by attackers that infiltrate the system through exploiting existing vulnerabilities. Such outsider attacks can be addressed by defensive mechanisms such as firewalls and intrusion detection systems.

More challenging threats are usually from the insiders who need limited accesses to the data. For example, a company may want to study the shopping preferences of its customers to facilitate upsale. The company invites a third party analyst for this purpose. Without sufficient security mechanisms safeguarding the data, the analyst may obtain and later misuse the personal information about the customers. Such disclosures of sensitive information is undesired, because it may lead to privacy breaches of individuals and consequently causes damages to the company's interest. On the other hand, companies collect data not just to occupy hard disks. They need to analyze the data and extract useful knowledge from it. Hence, the data in appropriate formats should be readily available to authorized users. How to prevent privacy breaches caused by inappropriate disclosures of sensitive information while not adversely impacting the availability of data to legitimate users is the main topic of this book.

Among various ways of data analysis, OLAP (On-line Analytic Processing) is one of the most popular techniques. OLAP helps analysts to extract useful knowledge from a large amount of data. It allows analysts to gain insights to different perspectives of the data. This is achieved by aggregating data along multiple dimensions. Aggregations at different levels can be organized into a *data cube* [37]. Looking at coarser aggregations, an analyst may obtain general patterns and global trends. Upon observing an exception to established patterns or trends, the analyst may drill down to finer aggregations to catch those outliers. This interactive exploration can repeat over different portions of the data cube until a satisfactory mental image of the underlying data has been successfully constructed.

Similar to any technology, OLAP is also a double-edged sword. Without sufficient security components, an OLAP system may become a powerful tool in the hands of malicious users in threatening the privacy of individuals. Unfortunately, most of today's OLAP systems lack effective security measures to preserve privacy. Existing security mechanisms can at best alleviate the privacy breaches caused by inappropriate disclosures of sensitive information, but they cannot completely remove the threat. Several security mechanisms that are especially relevant for preserving privacy in OLAP are discussed as follows.

- *Data sanitization* aims to remove sensitive information about individuals by deleting explicit identifiers, such as names and SSN from data. The sanitized data is then deemed *anonymous* and made available to users. However, data sanitization has long been recognized as insufficient for preserving privacy by itself [34, 56, 60]. Re-identification is possible by linking seemingly non-identifying information to widely available data. For example, an individual may be identified through his/her DOB, sex, and zip code, if the combination of those values matches a unique record in the public-available voter list [60].

- *Access control* denies unauthorized accesses to protected data. Access control techniques in traditional data management systems, such as relational databases, are quite mature. However, directly applying the access control technique in relational databases to OLAP meets two difficulties. First, the data model of OLAP is different from the relational model used by relation databases. The difference in the data models makes it difficult to express and enforce the security requirements for OLAP. Secondly, access control in relational databases is unaware of another kinds of threat to privacy, malicious *inferences* of sensitive information, which OLAP is more vulnerable to. Data analysis with OLAP heavily relies on statistical aggregations (such as MAX, MIN, SUM, COUNT, and so on) such that desired general patterns can be accentuated and extracted. However, the aggregation process does not completely destroy the sensitive information in data. The remaining vestiges of sensitive information, together with other knowledge obtained through out of bound channels, make malicious inferences possible. As a simple example, Bob can infer the amount of Alice's commission from the amount of their total commission, given that Bob knows his own commission. Access control cannot capture such an inference, as the total salary is a seemingly innocent aggregation to access control.

- *Inference control* has attracted tremendous interests in statistical databases and census data from 1970's. However, the complexity results of inference control are usually negative in tone [15] for on-line systems. Most restriction-based methods adopt a *detecting-then-removing* approach. The detecting of complex inferences usually demands complicated computations over entire collection of data and the bookkeeping of all answered queries. Such a requirement may lead to prohibitive on-line performance overhead and storage requirements. Even at such a high cost, a detecting method typically applies to only limited cases with abundant unrealistic assumptions. Many proposed methods require the assumption of a single type of allowed aggregation (for example, only SUM is allowed); they assume a fixed sensitivity criterion for determining whether the information disclosure caused by queries is sensitive (for example, only the disclosure of exact values is sensitive and that of approximated values is not); they suppose that users do not have the outbound knowledge about the data type of sensitive values (for example, all sensitive values must assumed as unbounded real numbers). The aforementioned assumptions are rarely met in practice, which partially explains the fact that most commercial products have no support of inference control at all.

This book investigates the privacy threats in OLAP applications and provides solutions to remove such threats. We shall describe how adversaries may potentially steal sensitive information from an OLAP system and thus breach the privacy of individuals. We shall study the feasibility of detecting such privacy breaches in the special settings of data cubes. We shall propose a series of methods for removing malicious inferences from OLAP data cubes. In developing the security measures, we shall also take into consideration their effect to the availability and performance of OLAP systems.

1.2 Problem Statement

As discussed in Section 1.1, the main purpose of this book is to understand and provide a solution to the privacy threats in OLAP applications. More specifically, the following questions are to be answered.

First, *how can privacy be breached in OLAP?* OLAP is of course not initially designed for breaching privacy. Instead, its initial purpose is for extracting useful trends and patterns from a large collection of data stored in data warehouses. We thus need to understand potential ways of misusing OLAP for stealing sensitive data and thus causing a breach to privacy. Such misuses may include unauthorized accesses to and malicious inferences of sensitive data. These misuses are well understood in traditional data management systems, such as relational databases, statistical databases, and census tables. However, the data model of those applications vary from the data cube model used by OLAP. The difference in data models brings to the old threats with new characteristics in the special settings of OLAP systems. Therefore, the key challenge with respect to the first question is to reveal the new aspects of the old problems.

Second, *how can existing methodologies be applied to preserve privacy in OLAP?* The problem of improper disclosures of sensitive information has been studied before in traditional data management systems, and accordingly many security techniques have been proposed to deter such inappropriate disclosures. Therefore, the second issue is to investigate the feasibility of applying available techniques to OLAP systems. A review of related work is given in next two chapters. Among the relevant research areas, *access control* and *inference control* are the most closely related. The settings of existing research are usually different from and more general than that of OLAP systems. Hence, the results of the former will usually still apply to the latter but can be improved by exploiting the unique characteristics of the latter. It would have been unnecessary to invent new techniques, if the improved results of existing research were satisfactory for OLAP systems. Therefore, the key challenge with respect to the second question is to show convincingly that known techniques usually do not suffice the requirements of preserving privacy in OLAP.

Third, *how can novel methods be developed to effectively preserve privacy in OLAP systems at a reasonable cost?* With a thorough understanding of the threats as well as the limitations of existing methods, the book will focus on devising new methods as a solution to the problem. As mentioned before, the two major threats to privacy in OLAP systems are unauthorized accesses and malicious inferences of sensitive data. Accordingly, the solution to privacy preserving in OLAP must also combine access control and inference control to remove both threats. At the same time, providing security should not adversely reduce the usefulness of an OLAP system. More specifically, an ideal solution to preserving privacy in OLAP should meet following objectives:

Security The sensitive data stored in underlying data warehouses should be guarded from both unauthorized accesses and malicious inferences. Such a definition of security considers not only the information a user can directly obtain from an OLAP system, but also those that he/she can derive by exploiting the relationship among data as well as external knowledge. Hence, a solution must provide provable security in the face of threats ranging from direct attempts in accessing protected data to indirect inferences in deducing protected data from combined results of a large amount of seemingly innocent queries.

Adaptability The security provided by a solution should not depend on any assumption about specific settings of OLAP systems. OLAP applications may vary in the type of supported aggregations, the external knowledge adversaries may possess, and the criteria used to decide whether a disclosure is sensitive. These factors are underlying the study of the privacy preserving problem. A generic solution is the one that can cover different combinations of such factors without the need of significant modifications.

Efficiency The performance of an OLAP system should not be adversely affected by privacy preserving methods. The name of OLAP itself indicates the interactive nature of query-answering in such systems. Most queries should be answered in a matter of seconds or minutes. A significant portion of the OLAP literature has been devoted to meeting such stringent performance requirement and to make the interactive analysis of large amount of data a reality. A privacy-preserving solution will not be acceptable if it causes too much delay to answering queries. Hence, a desired solution is computationally efficient, especially during the processing phase of a query after it has arrived in the system.

Availability Data should be readily available to legitimate users with sufficient privileges. Restricting all accesses brings full security but also renders OLAP systems useless. Although it is usually infeasible to maximize the availability of queries while at the same time meeting the security requirement, a solution must nonetheless place security upon justifiable restrictions of accesses. The restriction is justifiable in the sense that the removal of any restriction will either lead to the compromises of security or make the task of providing satisfiable security computationally infeasible.

Implementability The implementability aspect says that incorporating the solution into an existing OLAP system should not demand significant modifications to the existing infrastructure of a system. A solution should take advantage of any query-processing mechanisms and security mechanisms that are already in place. Such a solution incurs much less effort in its implementation than the one that requires fundamental modifications to the system.

The main challenge of the stated problem arises from the inherent trade-off between above-mentioned objectives. Having both provable security and justifiable availability in varying settings of OLAP systems usually demands complicated on-line computation that is expensive and hard to implement. As mentioned before, existing security measures are not satisfactory for OLAP partly because they fail to meet one or more of these objectives. For example, data sanitization and access control may be good in most of the aspects but they do not provide sufficient security since they are vulnerable to re-identification and malicious inferences. Some existing inference control methods may provide provable security and reasonable availability, but they cannot be adapted to different settings of OLAP systems and are computationally expensive and difficult to implement. These failures of existing methods motivate us to further investigate the problem of privacy preserving in OLAP and to propose novel solutions such that a balance among the above objectives can be achieved.

1.3 Overview

This book answers the aforementioned questions. That is, to understand the problem of preserving privacy in OLAP, to investigate the limitation of applying existing methods, and to provide novel solutions to overcome the limitations. The rest of this section first provides an overviews of the three parts and then elaborates on each of them.

- The first part of the book first devises a framework for studying the privacy problem in OLAP data cubes. Based on such a framework, we explore various kinds of privacy breaches caused by the disclosure of sensitive data. We show that known threats of unauthorized accesses and malicious inferences in relational databases remain to be possible, if not exasperated, in the special settings of OLAP data cubes. We also show that malicious inference is a severer and more challenging threat to the privacy of OLAP in contrast to unauthorized accesses. Such insights create a foundation for deriving solutions to the problem later in the book.

- The second part of the book attempts to extend some existing approaches in inference control to the special settings of OLAP. We consider two of the most influential methods, *cardinality-based inference control* [29] and *inference control by auditing* [16]. We borrow the intuitions and apply them to OLAP data cubes. We aim to improve the results by exploiting the special characteristics of OLAP data cubes. The results are not fully satisfactory; however, these attempts justify the needs for developing novel approaches and also provide critical insights to later discussions.

- The third part provides novel solutions to the problem, which aims to achieve a desired balance between the various objectives outlined in Section 1.2. The solutions prevent both unauthorized accesses and malicious inferences of sensitive data in data cubes; the solution remains effective in different settings of OLAP systems; the static solution has negligible on-line performance overhead, and the dynamic version improves availability at a cost of small increases in performance overhead; the solutions provide good (optimal in some cases) availability of data while achieving provable security; the solution is built upon popular architectures of OLAP systems and takes advantage of existing security mechanisms for easy implementation.

1.3.1 Overview of Basic Concepts

We shall closely follow the data cube model originally proposed by Gray et al. (a brief review of the data cube model is given in next chapter) [37]. However, to simplify discussion, we replace the relational terms with more concise notations, such as vectors and matrices. For example, dimensions of data cubes are regarded as sets of attributes, and attributes are sets of values from fixed integer domains. Tuples of relational tables are thus vectors of integers, and cuboids of data cubes are sets of such vectors. A dependency relation organizes attributes of each dimension into a dependency lattice. Therefore, a *data cube* is simply a collection of sets of integer vectors organized along the dependency lattice. Such simplified notations allow us to more conveniently describe and focus on the security problems.

Authorization *objects* (or simply objects) define what are not allowed to be accessed by subjects. In relational tables objects can be tables, records of a table, and fields of a record. An analogous partition can be defined on data cubes along one or more dimensions. A data cube can also be partitioned along the dependency lattice. This gives an additional opportunity for finer authorization. We define objects in data cubes with two functions, *Slice*() and *Below*(), which corresponds to the partitioning of data cubes along dimensions and dependency lattices, respectively. The two functions are combined through intersection to describe an object in data cubes. The cells included by any object are said to be *protected*.

Queries describe what is requested by subjects. Because of the dependency relationship between attributes, values that depend on others can be computed from the latter. Therefore, queries are defined in such a way that not only the explicitly requested cells are deemed as part of (the result to) a query, but those that derivable from the requested ones are also regarded as part of the query. At the same time, a query may select any portion of the data cube. Hence, a query is the dual concept to object defined with two functions, *Slice*() and *Above*(). The cells that are included by any query are said to be *requested*.

Unauthorized accesses are intersections between answered queries and objects. If any protected cell of a data cube is requested by a query, then answering the query will cause unauthorized accesses to the data cube (or more specifically, to that cell). Preventing unauthorized accesses through restrictions on queries is relatively straightforward. Indeed, in this book we do not explicitly address unauthorized accesses, but we make the restrictions required to prevent malicious inferences a superset of those required for preventing unauthorized accesses. Hence, unauthorized accesses are always absent in the result of inference control. Moreover, we shall use the cost of preventing unauthorized accesses as a benchmark for any proposed methods, because such threats must be removed before any security can become possible.

Malicious inferences are the deterministic inferences that enable a subject to learn about the value of protected cells from answered queries and external knowledge, in the absence of unauthorized accesses. Malicious inferences thus depend on several factors. First, they depend on the answered queries and objects, which are the set of cells that cause the inference and the set of protected cells to be inferred, respectively. Second, inferences depend on the set of allowed aggregation functions, such as SUM, MAX, MIN, AVERAGE, etc. Third, the sensitivity criterion that determines whether an information disclosure is deemed as unacceptable. Finally, inferences also depend on the external knowledge a subject may possess before asking queries.

Malicious inferences occur in various forms. The detection of straightforward ones is easy, while that of the sophisticated ones can be complicated or even infeasible. A single aggregation may cause an one-dimensional inference, if among the aggregated values all but one are known from external knowledge. Multiple aggregations computed from overlapping sets of values can lead to more sophisticated inferences. For the case of SUM-only queries, linear algebra techniques can be used to infer protected unbounded real [16]. With the external knowledge that such values are bounded real or integers, linear programming or integer programming techniques can be used for inferences [45, 47]. Different type of aggregations over the same set of values can also be combined to obtain inferences, such as the case of mixed SUM/MAX queries [13]. In both the case of SUM-only queries over integers and the case of mixed SUM/MAX query over unbounded real, detecting malicious inferences are intractable [13, 45]. This book will show that most of those inferences can be easily adapted to OLAP with the queries restricted to be collections of data cube cells.

1.3.2 Adapting Previous Approaches to Data Cubes

The first method to be addressed is the *cardinality-based inference control* (a brief review of the method is given in Chapter 3) [29]. Dobkin et al. give a lower bound on the number of sum queries that may cause malicious inferences. Any set of answered queries whose size is below this bound will not cause any inference. The method provides provable security under certain assumptions. Moreover, it is efficient in the sense that only the *number* of answered queries matters, whereas which specific queries are answered is irrelevant. That is, the result is based on the *cardinality*. Such an approach to inference control is desirable because cardinalities can be easily obtained and maintained.

Although the result certainly applies to the special case where queries are limited to collections of data cubes cells, the direct application is not satisfactory because the original result is derived for arbitrary queries in statistical databases. It does not consider the special structures of data cubes. For example, in data cubes if we view the cells as queries, then no overlap exists between the query sets of any two cells in the same cuboid, and the intersection between the query sets of any two cells in different cuboids yields another cell. Such characteristics are unique to data cubes, and they should be exploited to improve the existing results (that is, a tighter bound).

There is another difference between statistical databases and data cubes. In statistical databases, both queries and external knowledge about known values may vary. In contrast, the structure of data cubes only depends on the number of dimensions and the size of each attribute domain. Once such parameters are fixed, the structure of a data cube is fixed. The only thing that may vary is thus which cells are known to adversaries from outbound channels. Hence, instead of considering the cardinality of the set of answered queries, we must consider the number of known cells. The value in known cells is of no interest to inference control, because we can no longer withhold such a value from the adversary no matter what that value might be. We thus model the known values as *empty* cells. Apparently, inferences become more likely with more empty cells (that is, known values). Such a connection between the cardinality of empty cells and inference leads us to study the issue: *Can we derive an upper bound on the number of empty cells, under which any given data cube is guaranteed to be inference-free.*

The second method we shall consider is *inference control by auditing* (a brief review of the method is given in Chapter 3) [16]. Chin et al. propose to audit and keep checking all answered SUM queries for inferences. The queries are represented using a binary matrix with each protected value corresponding to a column of the matrix and the query set of each query (and its answer) to a row. The main result says that inferences are possible if and only if the reduced row echelon form (RREF) of such a matrix includes at least one unit row vector (that is, a row vector that contains exactly one 1). The result is usually regarded as a milestone in the literature since it provides both provable security (because the condition is sufficient) and maximal availability (because the condition is necessary). Notice that the maximal availability is only provided for strictly sequential queries. Obtaining the RREF of a $m \times n$ matrix takes time $O(m^2 n)$. A better result of $O(mn)$ is obtained for the special case of one-dimensional range queries (that is, queries that sum over continuous ranges in a sequence of values) [14]. Another interesting extension is that by regarding each protected value as a vertex and each query that sums exactly two values as an edge, inferences are impossible if and only if the vertices and edges form a bipartite graph [16].

Directly applying the auditing method to data cubes incurs unacceptable performance penalty. The complexity of the method $O(m^2n)$ becomes prohibitive because m (that is, the number of queries) and n (that is, the size of data cubes) are usually very large in an OLAP application. Moreover, the auditing process is invoked after queries arrive, and hence answers to queries must be withheld until the auditing finishes. Such delay in answering queries makes an OLAP system less useful, because OLAP analysis is expected to be an interactive process. On the other hand, the special structure of data cubes implies that the auditing method can be more efficient in the special settings of OLAP. Chin has shown that the complexity of the auditing can be reduced to $O(mn)$ if users are limited to one-dimensional range queries [14]. Data cube cells can be considered as multi-dimensional range (MDR) queries. Hence, a natural question arises: *can restricting users to MDR queries yield more efficient auditing methods?* Moreover, Chin's result on the queries that sum exactly two values (or sum-two queries in short) implies a promising direction towards answering this question. That is, if we can find the connection between MDR queries and sum-two queries, then a more efficient method might exist to determine whether the former causes inferences.

1.3.3 A Lattice-based Solution

The attempts to extend existing methods to data cubes do not yield a fully satisfactory solution. The cardinality-based approach has a low complexity but yields poor availability since the cardinality can only determine the existence of inferences in some extreme situations. The study of MDR queries yields a method for controlling inferences in data cubes with the complexity $O(mn)$, and the method provides reasonable availability. However, both methods only allow SUM-only queries, and extending them to address other queries is not straightforward. On the other hand, the study sheds light on the nature of the problem and provides important insights for proposing novel solutions. First, inferences can be divided into two categories, that is the *one-dimensional* inferences caused by aggregations over disjoint sets of values and the *multiple-dimensional* inferences caused by multiple overlapping aggregations. Second, attempting to detect multiple-dimensional inferences is the root cause of high complexity and other limitations of existing methods.

Based on such observations, we propose to prevent multiple-dimensional inferences instead of detecting them. More precisely, we seek to restrict queries in such a way that an adversary can never find multiple aggregations over overlapping sets of values for a multiple-dimensional inference. In another word, we eliminate the source of multiple-dimensional inferences. Hence, we do not need the costly detection of multiple-dimensional inferences. Although one-dimensional inferences still need to be detected, the detection can be easily realized through a one-pass scan, because intuitively one-dimensional inferences do not help each other. Moreover, the effectiveness of such a scan is independent of the specific settings of OLAP systems, such as aggregation functions and sensitivity criteria.

The first solution is static in the sense that the restriction on queries only depends on the objects and is fully computed off-line (that is, before the system receives any queries). The restriction satisfies the desired properties of provable security (that is, neither malicious inferences nor unauthorized accesses are possible) and reasonable availability (that is, removing any of the restrictions without breaching security is computationally infeasible). The static nature of this solution implies a trivial implementation simply by pre-computing all answerable cells and then restricting users to only the answerable cells. However, it also implies potential impacts on the availability because optimal restrictions usually depend on actual sequences of queries, which cannot be easily predicted. This issue motivates us to study the next solution.

The second solution is dynamic in the sense that the restriction on queries is not determined beforehand but instead is derived based on actual queries. More specifically, a profile of the answered queries is used to determine which cells are further answerable without losing the security. While more queries arrive, this profile is continuously updated to reflect all answered queries. Security is guaranteed even if a user is able to combine all the answers for inferences. Availability is maximized in the sense that a query is answered if only possible (that is, without breaching the security). Although such a query-driven approach unavoidably brings more online performance overhead, we show that such overhead is comparable to that of computing the results of queries, and hence is reasonable. By properly encoding the profile of answered queries, the solution can be easily implemented within existing OLAP architectures.

OLAP and Data Cubes

This chapter reviews On-line Analytical Processing (OLAP) in Section 2.1 and data cubes in Section 2.2.

2.1 OLAP

Coined by Codd et. al [18] in 1993, OLAP stands for On-Line Analytical Processing. The concept has its root in earlier products such as the IRI Express, the Comshare system, and the Essbase system [67]. Unlike statistical databases which usually store census data and economic data, OLAP is mainly used for analyzing business data collected from daily transactions, such as sales data and health care data [65]. The main purpose of an OLAP system is to enable analysts to construct a mental image about the underlying data by exploring it from different perspectives, at different level of generalizations, and in an interactive manner.

As a component of decision support systems, OLAP interacts with other components, such as data warehouse and data mining, to assist analysts in making business decisions. A data warehouse usually stores data collected from multiple data sources, such as transactional databases throughout an organization. The data are cleaned and transformed to a common consistent format before they are stored in the data warehouse. Subsets of the data in a data warehouse can be extracted as data marts to meet the specific requirements of an organizational division. Unlike in transactional databases where data are constantly updated, typically the data stored in a data warehouse are refreshed from data sources only periodically.

OLAP and data mining both allow analysts to discover novel knowledge about the data stored in a data warehouse. Data mining algorithms automatically produce knowledge in a pre-defined form, such as association rule or classification. OLAP does not directly generate such knowledge, but instead relies on human analysts to observe it by interpreting the query results. On the other hand, OLAP is more flexible than data mining in the sense that analysts may obtain all kinds of patterns and trends rather than only knowledge of fixed forms. OLAP and data mining can also be combined to enable analysts in obtaining data mining results from different portion of the data and at different level of generalization [39].

In a typical OLAP session, the analyst poses aggregation queries about underlying data. The OLAP system can usually return the result in a matter of seconds, even though the query may involve a large number of records. Based on the results, the analysts may decide to *roll up* to coarser-grained data so they can observe global patterns and trends. Upon observing an exception to any established pattern, the analysts may *drill down* to finer-grained data with more details to catch the outliers. Such a process is repeated in different portions of the data by *slicing* or *dicing* the data, until a satisfactory mental image of the data has been constructed.

The requirements on OLAP systems have been defined differently, such as the FASMI (Fast Analysis of Shared Multidimensional Information) test [58] and the Codd rules [18]. Some of the requirements are unique to OLAP. First, to make OLAP analysis an interactive process, the OLAP system must be highly efficient in answering queries. OLAP systems usually rely on extensive pre-computations, indexing, and specialized storage to improve the performance. Second, to allow analysts to explore the data from different perspectives and at different level of generalization, OLAP organizes and generalizes data along multiple dimensions and dimension hierarchies. The data cube model we shall address shortly is one of the most popular abstract models for this purpose.

The data to be analyzed by OLAP are usually stored based on the relational model in the backend data warehouse. The data are organized based on a *star schema*. Figure 2.1 shows an example of star schema. It has a *fact table* ($timeID, orgID, commission$), where the first two attributes $timeID$ and $orgID$ are called *dimenions*, and *commission* is called a *measure*. Each dimenion has a *dimension table* associated with it, indicating a dimension hierarchy. The dimension tables may contain redundancy, which can be removed by splitting each dimension table into multiple tables, one per attribute in the dimension table. The result is called a *snowflake schema*, as illustrated in Figure 2.2.

Fig. 2.1. An Example of Star Schema

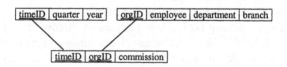

Fig. 2.2. An Example of Snowflake Schema

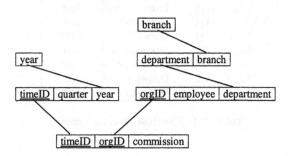

Popular architectures of OLAP systems include *ROLAP* (relational OLAP) and *MOLAP* (multidimensional OLAP). ROLAP provides a front-end tool that translates multidimensional queries into corresponding SQL queries to be processed by the relational backend. ROLAP is thus light weight and scalable to large data sets, whereas its performance is constrained because optimization techniques in the relational backend are typically not designed for multidimensional queries. MOLAP does not rely on the relational model but instead materializes the multidimensional views. MOLAP can thus provide better performance with the materialized and optimized multidimensional views. However, MOLAP demands substantial storage for materializing the views and is usually not scalable to large datasets due to the multidimensional explosion problem [57]. Using MOLAP for dense parts of the data and ROLAP for the others leads to a hybrid architecture, namely, the *HOLAP* or hybrid OLAP.

2.2 Data Cube

Data cube was proposed as a SQL operator to support common OLAP tasks like histograms (that is, aggregation over computed categories) and subtotals [37]. Even though such tasks are usually possible with standard SQL queries, the queries may become very complex. For example, Table 2.1 shows a simple relation *comm*, where employee, quarter, and location are the three dimensions, and the commission is a measure. We call *comm* a *base relation* since it contains the ground facts to be analyzed.

Suppose analysts are interested in the sub-total commissions in the two-dimensional cross tabular in Table 2.2 (other possible ways of visually representing such subtotals are discussed in [37]). The inner tabular includes the quarterly commission for each employee; below the inner tabular are the total commissions for each employee; to the right are the total commissions in each

employee	quarter	location	commission
Alice	Q1	Domestic	800
Alice	Q1	International	200
Bob	Q1	Domestic	500
Mary	Q1	Domestic	1200
Mary	Q1	International	800
Bob	Q2	International	1500
Mary	Q2	Domestic	500
Jim	Q2	Domestic	1000

Table 2.1. The Base Relation *comm*

year; at the right bottom corner is the total commission of all employees in the two years.

	Alice	Bob	Mary	Jim	total(ALL)
Q1	1000	500	2000		3500
Q2		1500	500	1000	3000
total(ALL)	1000	2000	2500	1000	6500

Table 2.2. A Two-dimensional Cross Table

The sub-totals in Table 2.2 can be computed using SQL queries. However, we need to union four GROUP BY queries as follows:

```
SELECT employee, quarter, SUM(commission)
FROM    comm
GROUP BY employee,quarter
UNION
SELECT 'ALL', quarter, SUM(commission)
FROM    comm
GROUP BY quarter
UNION
SELECT employee, 'ALL', SUM(commission)
FROM    comm
GROUP BY employee
UNION
SELECT 'ALL','ALL', SUM(commission)
FROM    comm
```

The number of needed unions is exponential in the number of dimensions. A complex query may result in many scans of the base table, leading to poor performance. Because such sub-totals are very common in OLAP queries, it is desired to define a new operator for the collection of such sub-totals, namely, *data cube*.

A data cube is essentially the generalization of the cross tabular illustrated in Table 2.2. The generalization happens in several perspectives. First, a data cube can be n dimensional. Table 2.3 shows a three-dimensional data cube built from this new base table. Based on the ALL values, the data cube is divided into eight parts, namely, *cuboids*. The first cuboid is a three-dimensional cube, usually called the *core* cuboid. The next three cuboids have one ALL value and are the two-dimensional planes. The next three are the one-dimensional lines. The last cuboid has a single value and is a zero-dimensional point.

The second perspective of the generalization is the aggregation function. The aggregation discussed so far is SUM. In general any aggregation function, including customized ones, can be used to construct a data cube. Those functions can be classified into three categories, the *distributive*, the *algebraic*, and the *holistic*. Let I be a set of values, and $P(I) = \{p_1, p_2, \ldots, p_n\}$ be any partition on I. Then an aggregation function $F()$ is distributive, if there exists a function $G()$ such that $F(I) = G(\{F(p_i) : 1 \le i \le n\})$. It is straightforward to verify that SUM, COUNT, MIN, and MAX are distributive.

By generalizing the function $G()$ into one that returns an m-vector, the algebraic aggregations have a similar property like that of the distributive ones, that is $F(I) = G(\{F(p_i) : 1 \le i \le n\})$. For example, Let $G() = <SUM(), COUNT()>$, then $AVERAGE$ is clearly an algebraic function. However, a holistic function like MEDIAN cannot be evaluated on $P(I)$ with any $G()$ that returns a vector of constant degree. The significance in distinguishing those three types of aggregation function lies in the difficulty of computing a data cube. Because the cuboids in a data cube form a hierarchy of aggregation, a cuboid can be more easily computed from other cuboids for distributive and algebraic functions. However, for a holistic function, any cuboid must be computed directly from the base table.

The third perspective of the generalization is the dimension hierarchy. For the data cubes shown in Table 2.2 and Table 2.3, each dimension is a two-level pure hierarchy. For example, the employee dimension has basically two attributes, employee and ALL (ALL should be regarded as both an attribute and its only value). In general, each dimension can have many attributes, such as the example in Figure 2.1. The attributes of a dimension may form a lattice instead of a pure hierarchy, such as day, week, month, and year (week and month are incomparable). The attribute in the base table is the lower bound of the lattice, and ALL (regarded as an attribute) is the upper bound. The product of the dimension lattices is still a lattice, as illustrated in Figure 2.3. This lattice is essentially the schema of a data cube.

The lattice structure has played an important role in many perspectives of data cubes. For example, materializing the whole data cube usually incurs prohibitive costs in computation and storage. Moreover, materializing a cuboid does not always bring much benefits to answering queries. In Figure 2.3, the

employee	quarter	location	commission
Alice	Q1	Domestic	800
Alice	Q1	International	200
Bob	Q1	Domestic	500
Mary	Q1	Domestic	1200
Mary	Q1	International	800
Bob	Q2	International	1500
Mary	Q2	Domestic	500
Jim	Q2	Domestic	1000
Alice	Q1	ALL	1000
Bob	Q1	ALL	500
Mary	Q1	ALL	2000
Bob	Q2	ALL	1500
Mary	Q2	ALL	500
Jim	Q2	ALL	1000
Alice	ALL	Domestic	800
Alice	ALL	International	200
Bob	ALL	Domestic	500
Mary	ALL	Domestic	1700
Mary	ALL	International	800
Bob	ALL	International	1500
Jim	ALL	Domestic	1000
ALL	Q1	Domestic	2500
ALL	Q1	International	1000
ALL	Q2	International	1500
ALL	Q2	Domestic	1500
Alice	ALL	ALL	1000
Bob	ALL	ALL	2000
Mary	ALL	ALL	2500
Jim	ALL	ALL	1000
ALL	Q1	ALL	3300
ALL	Q2	ALL	3000
ALL	ALL	Domestic	4000
ALL	ALL	International	2500
ALL	ALL	ALL	6500

Table 2.3. A Three-Dimensional Data Cube

core cuboid must be materialized because it cannot be computed from others. However, if any of the cuboids with one ALL value has a comparable size to the core cuboid, then it may not need to be materialized, because answering a query using that cuboid incurs similar costs as using the core cuboid instead (the cost of answering a query is roughly proportional to the size of the cuboid being used). Greedy algorithms have been proposed to find optimal materialization of a data cube under resource constraints [40].

Fig. 2.3. The Lattice Structure of Data Cube

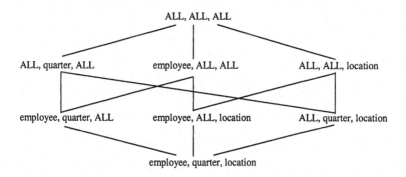

Even if the whole data cube needs to be computed, the lattice structure can help to improve the performance of such computations. For example, if the computation is based on sorting the records, then the core cuboid can be sorted in three different ways (by any two of the three attributes). Each choice will simplify the computation of one of the three cuboids with one ALL value because that cuboid can be computed without additional sorting. However, computing the other two cuboids will require the core cuboid be re-sorted. Based on estimated costs, algorithms exist to make the optimal choice in sorting each cuboid, and those choices can be linked to form pipelines of computation so the needs for re-sorting cuboids can be reduced [2].

Inference Control in Statistical Databases

Inference control has been extensively studied in statistical databases and census data for more than thirty years, as surveyed in [1, 28, 80]. The proposed methods can roughly be classified into *restriction-based* techniques and *perturbation-based* techniques. Restriction-based inference control methods prevent malicious inferences by denying some unsafe queries. The metric used to determine the safety of queries includes the minimal number of values aggregated by a query [28], the maximal number of common values aggregated by different queries [29], the approximate intervals that can be guessed from query results [47, 46, 50, 48, 49, 52, 53, 51], and the maximal rank of a matrix representing all answered queries [16]. Perturbation-based techniques add random noises to sensitive data [69], to answers of queries [7], or to database structures [64].

Among the restriction-based inference control methods, *Cell suppression* and *partitioning* most closely relate to our discussions. Cell suppression is used to protect census data released in statistical tables [21, 22]. Cells containing sensitive COUNTs are first suppressed according to a given sensitivity criterion. Possible inferences of the suppressed cells are then detected and removed using linear (or integer) programming-based techniques. While such a detection method is effective for two-dimensional cases, it is intractable for three or more dimensional tables even of small sizes [22, 25]. *Partitioning* first defines a partition on the set of sensitive data, it then restricts queries to aggregate only complete blocks in the partition [15, 81]. As a variation of partitioning, *microaggregation* replaces clusters of sensitive values with their averages [54, 80]. In partitioning and microaggregation, partitions are defined without considering the rich hierarchies inherent to data cubes, and hence the results may contain many clusters of values that are meaningless to OLAP users. Moreover, it may demand significant modifications of OLAP systems in order to handle the specially designed partitions of data and to restrict queries based on such partitions.

Parallel to our study, perturbation-based methods have been proposed for *privacy-preserving in data mining* [3, 72, 11]. Random noises are added to sensitive values to preserve privacy, while the statistical distribution can be approximately reconstructed from the perturbed data to facilitate data mining tasks. The problem of protecting sensitive data in OLAP is different from that in data mining. The knowledge discovered by data mining, such as classifications and association rules, depend on the distribution models of data. In contrast, OLAP users heavily depend on ad-hoc queries that aggregate small, overlapping sets of values. The precise answers to such queries are not obtainable from distribution models alone, even if the models can be successfully reconstructed. As suggested by the literature of statistical databases, having both significant noises in sensitive data and unbiased consistent answers to ad-hoc queries is usually infeasible. The methods proposed in [4] can approximately reconstruct COUNTs from perturbed data with statistically bound errors, so OLAP tasks like classification can be fulfilled. However, potential errors in individual values may prevent an OLAP user from gaining trustful insights into small details of the data, such as outliers. The methods discussed in this book are not based on perturbation. While all queries are not answered as a result of security requirements, the answer is always precise. *Secure multiparty computation* allows multiple distrusted parties to cooperatively compute aggregations over each other's data [71]. Cryptographic protocols enable each party to obtain the final result with the minimal disclosure of their own data. This problem is different from inference control, because the threat of inferences comes from what users know, not from the way they know it.

The *k-anonymity* model enables sensitive values to be released without threatening privacy [60, 61, 17]. Each record has the same identifying values as $k - 1$ others, and hence any attempt of linking an individual in the physical world to (the sensitive values in) such records will end up with at least k indistinguishable choices. While inference control typically hides sensitive values through aggregation, this dual approach releases those sensitive values but make them anonymous. Unifying the two models in our framework comprises an interesting future direction. Very recently, an information theoretic approach characterizes insecure queries as those that bring a user with more confidence in deducing the existence of sensitive records [55]. However, the author noted that such a metric of security is ineffective for queries with aggregates, as it will deem any query as insecure as long as it aggregates a sensitive value.

The need for security and privacy in data warehouses and OLAP has long been identified [8, 65, 66]. However, significant efforts still need to be made. This is partly evidenced by most of today's commercial OLAP products. They typically have only limited support of access control to prevent authorized accesses to sensitive information, and they provide practically no control over malicious inferences of such information [65].

On the other hand, relational databases have mature techniques for access control, at table, column and cell level [20]. In relational databases, access control regulates direct accesses to sensitive data using various models. The discretional access control (DAC) uses owner-specified grants and revokes to achieve an owner-centric control of objects, such as a relational table or a tuple (attribute) in the table [38]. The role-based access control (RBAC) simplifies access control tasks by introducing an intermediate tier of role that aggregates and bridges users and permissions [62]. The flexible access control framework (FAF) provides a universal solution to handling conflicts in access control policies through authorization derivation and conflict resolution logic rules [43].

Many existing research efforts are more or less related to the problem of privacy preserving in OLAP. Even though these results may not be directly applied to data cubes with satisfactory outcomes, they nonetheless lay a solid foundation from which our discussions stem. The rest of this section reviews some of the related work in more details. Following chapters will then focus on several promising approaches [76, 77, 78, 74, 75, 73, 79].

3.1 Query Set Size Control and Trackers

The aggregate of a single value can trivially disclose that value, and the aggregate of a small number of values may also seem to be insecure. Hence, the first efforts in inference control aim to prohibit such aggregates. More specifically, the subset of records satisfying a query is called the *query set* of the query. *Query set size control* denies any query whose query set includes less than k records, where n is a pre-determined threshold. If the database has totally n records, then the query set size control needs to also prohibit a query whose query set is greater than $n - k$, because its complement includes less than k records and violates the control.

However, instead of the complement of a query with respect to the database, one can form its complement with respect to another query (or more than one queries). This intuition leads to a series of attacking methods, namely, *trackers* [26, 27]. For example, consider the simple relation *comm* shown in Table 3.1, and suppose the query set size control is in place with $k = 2$. The following query has a singleton query set (whose only member is the first record), and hence is denied.

```
SELECT SUM(commission)
FROM    comm
WHERE   employee='Alice' and quarter='Q1' and location='Domestic'
```

However, considering that the WHERE clause is the conjunction of three conditions, one can instead ask the following two queries. The query set of both queries is between k (two) and $n - k$ (seven). Both queries will thus be allowed. Subtracting the result of the second query from that of the first query leads to the inference of the first record. We can similarly infer any query asking for the aggregation of less than k records.

employee	quarter	location	commission
Alice	Q1	Domestic	800
Alice	Q1	Interational	200
Bob	Q1	Domestic	500
Mary	Q1	Domestic	1200
Mary	Q1	International	800
Bob	Q2	Interational	1500
Mary	Q2	Domestic	500
Jim	Q2	Domestic	1000

Table 3.1. A Relation *comm*

```
SELECT  SUM(commission)
FROM    comm
WHERE   quarter='Q1' and location='Domestic'
```

```
SELECT  SUM(commission)
FROM    comm
WHERE   employee<>'Alice' and quarter='Q1' and location='Domestic'
```

The above tracker apparently depends on the records to be inferred, and each inference requires finding a different tracker. A better way is to find a universal tracker and pad it to any record (or query) to be inferred. For example, in Table 3.1 we can form the tracker with the selection condition `employee='Mary' or employee='Jim'`. Because the tracker's query set has four records, the following two queries will both be allowed.

```
SELECT  SUM(commission)
FROM    comm
WHERE   employee='Mary' OR employee='Jim'
```

```
SELECT  SUM(commission)
FROM    comm
        employee<>'Mary' AND employee<>'Jim'
```

Adding the results to the two queries together gives us the total commission in the table. Next, without loss of generality, suppose we want to infer the first record. We ask the following two queries.

```
SELECT  SUM(commission)
FROM    comm
WHERE   (employee='Alice' AND quarter='Q1' AND location='Domestic')
        OR (employee='Mary' OR employee='Jim')
```

```
SELECT  SUM(commission)
FROM    comm
WHERE   (employee='Alice' AND quarter='Q1' AND location='Domestic')
        OR (employee<>'Mary' AND employee<>'Jim')
```

The first query pads the first record with the tracker, and the second query pads it with the complement of the tracker. Adding the result to the two queries and then subtracting the value from the total commission that we have computed earlier leads to the inference of the first record. Similarly we can infer any query asking for the aggregation of less than k records. Because the inference pads the query to be inferred with both the tracker and the complement of the tracker. In order for such two queries to be allowed, the size of the tracker must meet a more stringent condition, that is it must be between $2k$ and $n - 2k$. However, more complicated trackers may relax this condition [63]. Trackers are indeed examples of the more general linear system attack we shall discuss shortly. However, the study of trackers nonetheless demonstrates the ineffectiveness of the query set size control.

3.2 The Star Query Model

Kam and Ullman studied a particular model of sum queries [44], which we shall refer to as the *star query* model. To illustrate the model, consider encoding Table 3.1 as follows. Assuming the domain of the attribute employee has four values, it can thus be encoded with two bits. Similarly, the attribute quarter and location can each be encoded with one bit. Suppose we round the commissions to integers, then the commission attribute can be mapped to the set of integers (further assume a commission can be either positive or negative).

We can thus consider the database as a function $f() : \{0, 1\}^4 \to I$, where $\{0, 1\}^4$ denotes all binary strings of length four and I denotes the set of integers. The database includes sixteen records, each of which has two parts, a binary string and an integer. A *star query* is any string in $\{0, 1, *\}^4$, where $*$ is a special symbol that *matches* both 0 and 1. The query set of a star query includes any record whose binary string matches the star query. For example, the query set of a star query 100* includes two records whose binary string is 1000 and 1001, respectively. The result to this query is computed as the summation of the integer part of these two records.

Another database can be obtained by transforming the given one as follows. If the binary string of a record has even number of 1's, we add one to the integer part of that record; we subtract one, otherwise. It then follows that the new database yields the same answer to any star query with exactly one *. For example, the result to 100* is computed from two records whose binary strings are 1001 and 1000. In the new database, these two records have their integer parts added one and subtracted one, respectively, yielding the same result to 100* as the original database does. The existence of another database yielding the same query result shows that it is impossible to infer the integer part of any record with star queries with exactly one *.

Because any query with more than one * can be answered using results to the queries with one *, we can now conclude that no inference is possible with star queries that have at least one * [44]. However, this result critically depends on a few assumptions. First, the range of the function $f()$ must include all integers. If the adversary has additional knowledge about those values, then it may be possible to infer a record. For example, if the range of $f()$ is known to be $[0, d]$ for some integer d, and the query 100* returns the result $2(d - 1)$ or 0, then we can certainly deduce both records. An interesting special case is when the range of $f()$ is binary. It is shown that only two databases may be free of inferences no matter how many bits are used to encode the database.

Another assumption is that the adversary has no prior knowledge about any of the 2^n records, where n is the number of bits the database is encoded with. Chin pointed out that this assumption may rarely hold in practice [12], because many of the records may not appear in the database and such absence may be known to the adversary. For example, Table 3.1 only has eight records, whereas $2^n = 16$. To remove this assumption, assume any record may already be known by the adversary, and it can thus be ignored from further consideration (that is, regarded as absent from the database). However, this is actually equivalent to considering a fixed collection of records and allowing arbitrary queries instead of star queries.

3.3 Key-Specified Queries

Key-Specified queries can have any subsets of the database as their query sets. With key-specified queries, the inference of a record is trivial if singleton query set is allowed, or if query sets can include both even and odd number of records. Hence, we shall only consider queries whose query sets include even number of records. In the collection of such *even queries*, any query whose query set has more than two records can be answered using queries whose query set has exactly two records, namely, *sum-two queries*. By such decomposition, we only need to consider sum-two queries for inferences. The sum-two queries can be conveniently represented as a simple undirected graph, called *query graph*, with each record as a vertex and each query set as an edge.

Chin shows that the collection of sum-two queries (and hence the collection of even queries) leads to inferences if and only if the query graph contains an odd cycle [12]. The if part of the result can be illustrated as follows. Let $x_1, x_2, \ldots, x_n$, where n is any odd number, be the values of the records that form an odd cycle in the query graph. We can then infer the first value as:

$$2x_1 = (x_1 + x_2) - (x_2 + x_3) + (x_3 + x_4) - (x_4 + x_5) \ldots + (x_n + x_1)$$

For the only if part, a query graph without odd cycles is a bipartite graph whose vertices are 2-colorable (with no edge connecting vertices of the same color). We can thus add an arbitrary value to the records in one color while subtract the same value from those in the other color, and the result to every query will remain unchanged. One implication of this result is that if a set of sum-two queries causes inferences, finding its maximum subset that does not cause inferences is NP-hard because it corresponds to finding the maximum bipartite subgraph in any graph.

Instead of restricting users to even queries, Dobkin, Jones, and Lipton study the case when the size of the overlap between query sets is restricted [29]. More precisely, given the values $x_1, x_2, \ldots, x_n$ to be inferred, all queries have their query sets include *exactly* k of these values, and no two query sets can have more than r values in common. Moreover, l of the values are already known to the adversary. The question is then that how many such queries are required to infer any unknown value. That is, we want a lower bound on the number of queries that may lead to inferences.

The upper bound is given as $1 + (k - (l + 1))/r$ [29]. Without loss of generality, suppose we want to infer x_1. We first must ask a query whose query set includes x_1. However, the query introduces k values among which $k - l$ are unknown. In order to infer x_1, we must *cancel* the other $k - (l + 1)$ unknown values by asking more queries. Because any query may have at most r values in common with the first query, we will need to ask at least $(k - (l + 1))/r$ queries. Hence, totally $1 + (k - (l+1))/r$ queries are required for the inference.

To illustrate the discussion, consider the following example where $l = 0$ (no previously known values) and $r = 1$ (no two queries can have more than one value in common) [29]. We place the $(k - 1)k$ values $x_1, x_2, \ldots, x_{(k-1)k}$ in a two-dimensional cross tabular as shown in Table 3.2, and we place $x_{(k-1)k+1}$ in the last row. We then ask totally $2k - 1$ queries whose query set are shown as corresponding rows or columns in the table. It can be verified that all query sets include k values and no two query sets have more than one value in common. However, the value $x_{(k-1)k+1}$ can be inferred by adding up the last $k - 1$ queries and subtract from the result the first k queries (that is, $x_{(k-1)k+1} = (\sum_{i=k+1}^{2k-1} Q_i - \sum_{i=1}^{k} Q_i)/k$).

Assuming $r = 1$, $l = 0$, and the values $x_1, x_2, \ldots, x_n$ to be distinct, De-Millo, Dobkin, and Lipton study inferences caused by MEDIAN queries [24]. A MEDIAN query returns the MEDIAN of the query set, but it does not disclose which record has that value. The key result is that an inference is always

	Q_1	Q_2	$\ldots$	Q_k
Q_{k+1}	x_1	x_2	$\ldots$	x_k
Q_{k+2}	x_{k+1}	x_{k+2}	$\ldots$	x_{2k}
$\ldots$	$\ldots$	$\ldots$	$\ldots$	$\ldots$
Q_{2k-1}	$x_{(k-2)k+1}$	$x_{(k-2)k+2}$	$\ldots$	$x_{(k-1)k}$
	$x_{(k-1)k+1}$	$x_{(k-1)k+1}$	$x_{(k-1)k+1}$	$x_{(k-1)k+1}$

Table 3.2. An Example of $l = 0$ and $r = 1$

possible with no more than $4k^2$ queries. The result is based on the fact that for any k, there always exists an $m(m \leq 4k^2)$ satisfying the following. That is, we can find m subsets of $x_1, x_2, \ldots, x_{m-1}$ satisfying that no two subsets have more than one value in common. Considering these m subsets as query sets, then we can ask m MEDIAN queries about the first $m - 1$ values. By the pigeon hole principle, at least two of these queries must have the same answer. The overlap between the two queries thus leads to the inference of a record. An interesting aspect is that the result only requires each query to return (any) one of the values in the query set, and hence does not depend on specific aggregation functions.

3.4 Linear System Attack and Audit Expert

The trackers discussed in Section 3.1 can be generalized into the *linear system attack* based on the following model given by Chin and Ozsoyoglu [16]. Given sensitive values $x_1, x_2, \ldots, x_n$, any SUM query on those values can be modeled as an equation $\sum_1^n a_i x_i$, where $a_i = 1$ if x_i is in the query set and $a_i = 0$, otherwise. A collection of m queries thus form a linear system $AX = D$, where A is an $m \times n$ binary matrix, $X = (x_1, x_2, \ldots, x_n)$, and D is the vector of query results. For example, the second tracker discussed in Section 3.1 can now be modeled as the linear system in Table 3.3.

$$
\begin{pmatrix}
0\,0\,0\,1\,1\,0\,1\,1 \\
1\,1\,1\,0\,0\,1\,0\,0 \\
1\,0\,0\,1\,1\,0\,1\,1 \\
1\,1\,1\,0\,0\,1\,0\,0
\end{pmatrix}
\times
\begin{pmatrix}
x_1 \\ x_2 \\ x_3 \\ x_4 \\ x_5 \\ x_6 \\ x_7 \\ x_8
\end{pmatrix}
=
\begin{pmatrix}
3500 \\ 3000 \\ 4300 \\ 3800
\end{pmatrix}
$$

Table 3.3. SUM Queries Represented As A Linear System

An inference using the tracker can then be modeled as a sequence of elementary row operations on the matrix A (that is, multiplying a row with a non-zero number, swapping two rows, adding a row to another multiplied by a number). For Table 3.3, an inference of the first value x_1 is possible by adding the last two queries and subtracting from the result the first two queries. This can be modeled as the elementary row operations shown in Table 3.4.

$$
\begin{pmatrix} -1 \\ -1 \\ 1 \\ 1 \end{pmatrix}^T \times \begin{pmatrix} 0\,0\,0\,1\,1\,0\,1\,1 \\ 1\,1\,1\,0\,0\,1\,0\,0 \\ 1\,0\,0\,1\,1\,0\,1\,1 \\ 1\,1\,1\,0\,0\,1\,0\,0 \end{pmatrix} = \begin{pmatrix} 1 \\ 0 \\ 0 \\ 0 \\ 0 \\ 0 \\ 0 \\ 0 \end{pmatrix}^T
$$

Table 3.4. A Linear System Attack

To determine whether any given queries may lead to an inference, we need to answer the question: Does there exist a sequence of elementary row operations that transform A into a unit row vector (that is, a vector with one 1-element and all others being 0's)? Chin and Ozsoyoglu show that this can be determined by first transforming A into its reduced row echelon form (RREF) through a special sequence of elementary row operations, that is the Gauss-Jordan elimination [42]. For example, the matrix A in Table 3.3 has an RREF as shown in Table 3.5.

$$
\begin{pmatrix} 1\,0\,0\,0\,0\,0\,0\,0 \\ 0\,1\,1\,0\,0\,1\,0\,0 \\ 0\,0\,0\,1\,1\,0\,1\,1 \\ 0\,0\,0\,0\,0\,0\,0\,0 \end{pmatrix}
$$

Table 3.5. A Matrix in Its Reduced Row Echelon Form

The key result is that any matrix A can be transformed into a unit row vector through a sequence of elementary row operations, if and only if its RREF includes such a vector. The if part is trivial, because the Gauss-Jordan elimination itself is a sequence of elementary row operations. The only if part can be proved by contradiction. To illustrate, consider the RREF in Table 3.5. A unit row vector whose 1-element is in the first, second, or fourth position clearly cannot be a linear combination of those four rows in the matrix. A unit row vector whose 1-element is in other positions cannot, either. Because any linear combination of the four rows will have at least one non-zero element in the first, second, or fourth position. The above result is essentially a precise model for inferences of unbounded real values using SUM-only queries.

The result also leads to a method for checking whether a new query, taken together with queries answered before, will cause inferences. A straightforward but inefficient approach is to keep all answered queries and re-computing the RREF when each new query is received. For m queries on n values, the Gauss-Jordan elimination takes time $O(m^2 n)$. Considering that the elementary row operations on a matrix is associative, a better approach is to incrementally updates the RREF for each newly answered query. *Audit Expert* maintains the RREF of a matrix that corresponds to the set of queries answered so far. A query is denied when adding it to this set causes an inferences. Because the RREF of a matrix only includes linearly independent rows, the total number of rows must be no greater than the rank of matrix. For queries over n values, this rank cannot be greater than n. After a new row is added to the matrix, the RREF of the new matrix can thus be computed in $O(n^2)$ time.

Chin, Kossowski, and Loh later show that the auditing can have a better performance for a special class of queries, namely, *range queries* [14]. Assuming an arbitrary but fixed order on the sensitive values $x_1, x_2, \ldots, x_n$, a range query can be specified by two integers $1 \leq i \leq j \leq n+1$ and its query set is $\{x_l : i \leq l < j\}$. If we model any collection of range queries as a linear system $AX = D$, then all the row vectors of A will have consecutive 1-elements. For example, the matrix A in Table 3.6 depicts four range queries on seven values.

$$\begin{pmatrix} 1 & 1 & 0 & 0 & 0 & 0 \\ 1 & 1 & 1 & 1 & 0 & 0 \\ 0 & 0 & 1 & 1 & 1 & 1 \\ 0 & 1 & 1 & 1 & 1 & 0 \\ 0 & 0 & 0 & 1 & 1 & 0 \end{pmatrix}$$

Table 3.6. Range Queries Represented by A Matrix

Instead of transforming the matrix A into its RREF, the Audit Expert maintains a *range basis* consisted of linearly independent row vectors having consecutive 1-elements. Whenever two vectors start or end at the same position, we replace the one having more 1-elements with its difference from the other vector. For example, the second row vector in the matrix in Table 3.6 can be *shortened* by subtracting the first row vector from it, and then subtracting the result from the third row vector will result in another shorter row vector, and so on. When this process terminates, no two row vectors will have a common start or end position, and final result is clearly a range basis. Table 3.7 shows the range basis for the matrix in Table 3.6.

$$\begin{pmatrix} 1 & 1 & 0 & 0 & 0 & 0 \\ 0 & 0 & 1 & 1 & 0 & 0 \\ 0 & 0 & 0 & 0 & 1 & 1 \\ 0 & 1 & 1 & 0 & 0 & 0 \\ 0 & 0 & 0 & 1 & 1 & 0 \end{pmatrix}$$

Table 3.7. A Range Basis

The key result says that any row vector having consecutive 1-elemnents can be represented as a linear combination of the range basis, if and only if it is the summation of some row vectors in the range basis [14]. Hence, if a unit row vector can be obtained by transforming the range basis through elementary row operations, then that unit row vector must already appear in the range basis. This shows that checking range queries for inference can be based on the range basis, instead of the RREF of the original matrix A. For example, Table 3.7 shows that no inference is possible with the four ranges queries depicted in Table 3.6. In addition, a query whose query set is $\{x_2, x_3, x_4, x_5\}$ can be answered, because its corresponding vector is the summation of the last two row vectors in the range basis.

Instead of using a matrix, a range basis can be represented in an efficient way. For example, consider the range basis in Table 3.7. The 1-elements of the first three row vectors form a partition on the interval $[1, 6]$, and those of the last two form another partition on $[2, 5]$. The range basis can thus be represented in terms of the two partitions as $(1, 3, 5, 7), (2, 4, 6)$. Suppose a new query with the query set $\{3, 4, 5\}$ is received. The starting position 3 of the new query belongs to the first partition, whereas the ending position 5 belongs to the second partition. Answering the new query thus will update the range basis by merging the two partition into a finer partition $(1, 2, 3, 4, 5, 6, 7)$. This implies that the new query will cause inferences to all the values, and hence cannot be answered. It is shown that updating the range basis and checking for inferences like this has a time complexity of $O(n)$ and requires $O(n)$ storage [14].

Alternatively, Audit expert can be applied in a *static* mode, as studied in [9]. That is, instead of checking queries for inferences, we can pre-define what queries can be answered. Given n records, the rank of the matrix A must be no greater than $n - 1$ in order to keep the database free of inferences. When the rank is $n - 1$, the RREF of A can be of the form $[I|B]$, where I is an $(n - 1) \times (n - 1)$ identity matrix and B is a column vector whose elements are either 1 or -1. Under the constraint that no inference is possible, the objective is to maximize the number of answerable queries, namely, the usability.

The key result says that the maximal usability is $\left(\frac{n}{\lfloor n/2 \rfloor}\right)$, and this is achieved when the aforementioned vector B has almost equal number of 1's and -1's (more precisely, the number of 1's and -1's are: $n/2$ and $n/2 - 1$ when n is even, and either both $(n-1)/2$ or $(n-)/2$ and $(n+1)/2$ when n is odd, respectively). However, this result assume no queries have been answered before. If certain answered queries must be taken into account, then deciding the maximal usability is shown to be NP-complete [9].

3.5 Intractbility of Inference Control

As discussed above, Audit Expert denies a query if and only if it causes an inference. In contrast, query set size control discussed in Section 3.1 cannot prevent inferences caused by trackers or linear system attacks, whereas controlling the overlap between query sets, as discussed in Section 3.3, may restrict queries that do not cause any inference. Audit Expert thus has the advantage of providing *precise* inference control. However, Audit Expert makes a few simplified assumptions whose removal will greatly complicate inference control. First of all, Audit Expert only considers SUM queries, which enables it to model inference based on linear algebra. Other types of aggregations, such as MAX and MIN, have very different algebraic properties from that of SUM. Inferences caused by these aggregation functions thus need completely different models. Section 3.3 has discussed a special case of MEDIAN and other order statistics.

Chin studies the general case of MAX (or similarly MIN) queries [13]. As discussed in previous section, the inference caused by SUM queries has a natural linear algebra-based model. The inference caused by MAX queries has a different model. Chin summarized operations that can be used to transform any given set of answered MAX queries to a standard form. These operations are analogous to the elementary row operations by which the RREF of a matrix is obtained for SUM queries. Suppose the values in $X = \{x_1, x_2, \ldots, x_n\}$ are all distinct, the transformations *decompose* queries sets through set intersection and set difference operations and derive the maximum value for the results.

For example, suppose following four queries are answered:

1. $MAX(\{x_1, x_2, x_3\}) = 600$
2. $MAX(\{x_2, x_3, x_4\}) = 600$
3. $MAX(\{x_3, x_4, x_5\}) = 700$
4. $MAX(\{x_3, x_5, x_6\}) = 700$
   We can make following inferences from the answered queries, as illustrated in Figure 3.1:
5. $MAX(\{x_2, x_3\}) = 600$ by line 1 and 2

6. $MAX(\{x_1, x_4\}) < 600$ by line 1 and 2
7. $MAX(\{x_3, x_5\}) = 700$ by line 3 and 4
8. $MAX(\{(x_4, x_6\}) < 700$ by line 3 and 4
9. $MAX(x_5) = 700$ by line 5 and 7
10. $MAX(\{x_2, x_3\}) = 600$ by line 5 and 7
11. $MAX(x_6) < 700$ by line 6 and 8
12. $MAX(\{x_1, x_4\}) < 600$ by line 6 and 8

Fig. 3.1. Inferences Caused by MAX Queries

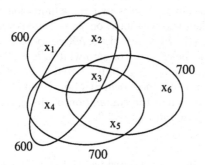

The above transformation can be generalized into six cases based on whether a maximum value is known (for example, line 1) or it is known to be less than some value (for example, line 6), and also based on the relationship between the two queries [13]. By repeatively applying these operations, any set of answered queries can be transformed into a collection of queries whose query sets form a partition on the involved values. In the above example, the sets in line 9 through line 12 clearly form such a partition on $X = \{x_1, x_2, \ldots, x_6\}$.

The key result is that if the maximum value of any $S \subseteq X$ can be derived from the answered queries, then S must be a superset of some set in the aforementioned partition. In another word, this partition actually corresponds to the smallest possible subsets of X about which the maximum values can be derived from the answered queries. It then follows that an inference is possible if and only if the partition does not include a singleton set. In the above example, the partition includes two such sets (line 9 and 11), and the value of x_5 and the upper bound of x_6 are thus inferred. It is shown that updating the partition and checking for inferences for a new query takes linear time in the size of that query and requires linear storage in the number of involved values.

Chin shows that the combination of MAX and MIN is easy to dealt with because an upper bound tells nothing about the lower bound, unless they coincide. Hence, the key result is that a collection of MAX and MIN queries causes inferences if and only if (1) the set of MAX queries (or the set of MIN queries) does so by itself, or (2) one of the MAX queries has the same answer as one of the MIN queries. The first case can be checked by the aforementioned method in linear time and storage. For the second case, assuming all values are distinct, the two queries must have exactly one value in common, and this value is thus inferred as the answer to both queries.

Chin then shows that auditing the combination of SUM and MAX (or MIN) is intractable because it is no easier than the NP-complete *partition* problem [13], which is to determine whether there exists any subset of $A = \{a_1, a_2, \ldots, a_n\}$ whose summation is half the summation of A. The instance of the auditing problem is constructed on $2n + 2$ unknown values as follows. The same answer a_i to the SUM and the MAX query on $\{x_i, x_{n+i}\}(1 \le i \le n)$ restrict x_i and x_{n+1} to be either a_i or zero while allowing them to swap their values. Similarly, x_{2n+1} and x_{2n+2} are restricted to be either zero or half the summation of all the a_i's. An additional SUM query on $\{x_1, x_2, \ldots, x_n, x_{2n+1}\}$ whose answer is equal to half the summation of the a_i's then completes the construction, as illustrated in Figure 3.2.

Fig. 3.2. Inferences Caused by SUM and MAX Queries

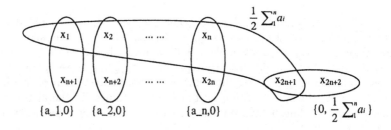

From the above construction, it can be concluded that an inference is possible if and only if the a_i's has a partition, and hence determining the inference is NP-hard [13]. The only if part holds because if the a_i's do not have any partition, then x_1 through x_n must be zero and x_{2n+1} must be half the summation of the a_i's. This is the only solution that will yield the answer to the last query mentioned above. For the if part, the same solution applies and in addition two other solutions are possible. That is, because the a_i's have a partition, we can let x_1 through x_n to be any one of the two sets in the partition. The three solutions provide at least two possible values for x_1 through x_{2n+2}, so no inference is possible.

The result basically announces the intractability of inference control in general, because any case more general than the combination of SUM and MAX is likely to be infeasible as well, whereas in practice a database system rarely restricts users to one or two type of aggregations. Kleinberg, Papadimitriou, and Raghavan enhanced the result from another perspective [45]. That is, the auditing problem is coNP-complete if the sensitive values are known to be binary by the adversary. Moreover, they show that the problem remains to be coNP-complete even if all the query sets can be represented as two-dimensional ranges.

4

Inferences in Data Cubes

4.1 Introduction

As discussed in Chapter 2, the characteristics that distinguish OLAP systems from general-purpose databases include restricted forms of queries, high efficiency in answering such queries, and relatively less frequent updates of data. OLAP users are more interested in well-formed queries, such as multi-dimensional range query [41]. These queries usually convey information about general properties. Hence, they better serve the needs of OLAP users in discovering universally applicable knowledge. Although OLAP queries usually involve the aggregation of a large amount of data, they are to be answered in merely a few seconds. Such a fast response is achieved through comprehensive pre-processing and the materialization of multi-dimensional views from which the answer to queries can be more easily derived. Although initially proposed as a relational operator, data cubes can serve as a popular model for organizing multi-dimensional aggregates to facilitate the fast computation of OLAP queries.

Because OLAP systems focus on restricted forms of queries rather than arbitrary queries, a natural question to ask is: *Can privacy still be breached through inferences with queries of such restricted forms?* It is a natural conjecture that the restrictions on queries will reduce the threat from inferences since compromising general-purpose databases usually requires arbitrary queries or even key-specified queries. The so-called Tracker [26] and the linear system attack [29] both depend on queries about arbitrary subsets of sensitive values. Such arbitrary queries are usually meaningless to OLAP users, and hence restricting those queries rather than well-structured queries may lead to better availability. However, the question is whether such restrictions are helpful in preventing inference control or at least in alleviating it.

Unfortunately, the answer is *no*. This chapter will show that although more sophisticated mechanisms are required, it is usually possible to make inferences with legitimate OLAP queries. We find trackers composed of only range queries to subvert the restrictions on small query sets. Even when only the range queries involving even numbers of values are allowed, we can still construct such trackers. The results demonstrate that the privacy breaches caused by inferences remain to be an important issue in OLAP systems. By showing how easy a compromise is and how serious the threat can be, we motivate the study of various inference control methods in following chapters. The discussion also provides a better understanding of the inference problem in OLAP data cubes.

The rest of the chapter is organized as follows. Section 4.2 introduces our notations for the chapter. Section 4.3 studies the inference caused by unrestricted range queries. Section 4.4 discusses compromising with restricted range queries. Section 4.5 concludes the chapter.

4.2 Preliminaries

This section introduces our notations. We have discussed the basic concepts of OLAP data cubes in Chapter 2. Now we review these concepts through a motivating example. Figure 4.1 shows a base relation. The attributes *Year* and *Name* are dimensions and the attribute *Adj* is the measure.

Year	Name	Adj
2002	Alice	1000
2002	Bob	500
2002	Mary	-2000
2003	Bob	1500
2003	Mary	-500
2003	Jim	1000

Fig. 4.1. Relation *Salary_Adjustment*.

A data cube constructed from the base relation *Salary_Adjustment* is shown as the cross-tabular in Figure 4.2. The aggregation function is SUM. The first column and the first row of the table is the dimension *Year* and *Name*, respectively. The values of the measure *Adj* are shown in the middle of the table. Each value in the last column and the last row (but not both) gives the aggregation $SUM(Adj)$ for the corresponding row and column, respectively. The value at the last column and row is the aggregation $SUM(Adj)$ for all the values of *Adj* in the table.

The SUM queries in Figure 4.2 are usually called *skeleton queries*, because they involve whole columns (or rows) of the table only. More generally, *multi-dimensional range queries* (or range queries for short) aggregate values in continuous multi-dimensional ranges of the table. For example, in Figure 4.2, the summation of Alice and Bob's salary adjustments in 2002 is a range query, but that of Alice's salary adjustment in 2002 and Bob's in 2003 is not. Range

	Alice Bob Mary Jim	SUM(Adj)
2002	1000 500 -2000	-500
2003	1500 -500 1000	2000
SUM(Adj)	1000 2000 -2500 1000	1500

Fig. 4.2. An Example of a Two-dimensional Data Cube.

queries involving partial columns or rows correspond to the *slicing* or *dicing* operations of data cubes.

We adopt an intuitive notation for representing multi-dimensional ranges. For example, the range $[(2002, Alice), (2002, Jim)]$ includes Alice, Bob and Mary's salary adjustments in 2002. Similarly $[(2002, Alice), (2003, Bob)]$ includes Alice and Bob's salary adjustments in 2002 and 2003. Suppose the company invites an analyst Mallory to analyze the data, but worries that Mallory may misuses the sensitive information about each individual. Therefore, Mallory is not allowed to ask for any values of the measure *Adj* but is allowed to access any aggregations of those values. Moreover, Mallory can see the value of the dimensions *Year* and *Name* and she knows the value in each empty cell.

Suppose Mallory asks a multi-dimensional range sum query (whose query set is the range) $[(2002, Alice), (2003, Alice)]$. Alice's salary adjustment in 2002 is disclosed by the answer to this query, even though Mallory is not supposed to know about this value. This kind of inferences is easy to prevent by restricting queries involving a single non-empty cell. However, an alternative way for Mallory to learn the same value is first asking the two range sum queries, $[(2002, Alice), (2002, Mary)]$ and $[(2002, Alice), (2002, Bob)]$ and then calculating the difference to their answers. It is clearly more difficult to detect such kind of *tracker*, or more generally, *linear system attacks* [16, 29]. Detecting these attacks caused by combined queries will require the system to audit the entire history of queries asked by each user. Moreover, any control mechanism can be easily subverted if users collude.

Instead of using relational terms, it is more convenient for us to model a data cube as a set system on integer vectors, where each integer vector stands for a data cube cell and each set stands for a range query (a query will refer to both the query specification and the query set). For simplicity, in this chapter we only consider one attribute for each dimension. We use k closed integer intervals $[1, d_i]$ $(1 \leq i \leq k)$ for the dimension attributes by assuming a one-to-one mapping between the integers and the domain values of that attribute. We call each integer vector of the form $(x_1, x_2, \ldots, x_k)(x_i \in [1, d_i])$ a *tuple*. The Cartesian product $\prod_{i=1}^{k}[1, d_i]$ represents all possible tuples that may appear in any core cuboid. In another word, any core cuboid is a subset of this Cartesian product. We use the same notation $[t_1, t_2]$, where t_1 and t_2 are two tuples, to specify range queries as before. We assume SUM queries and omit the aggregation function. The following example illustrates these concepts.

Example 4.1. We rephrase the previous example in above notations. The two dimensions are $[1, 2]$ and $[1, 4]$. The Cartesian product $[1, 2] \times [1, 4]$ includes eight possible tuples of which only six appear in the core cuboid $\{(1, 1), (1, 2), (1, 3), (2, 2), (2, 3), (2, 4)\}$. In Figure 4.3 we model the data cube shown in Figure 4.2 as a set system.

	1	2	3	4	
1	(1,1)	(1,2)	(1,3)		[(1,1),(1,4)]
2		(2,2)	(2,3)	(2,4)	[(2,1),(2,4)]
	[(1,1),(2,1)]	[(1,2),(2,2)]	[(1,3),(2,3)]	[(1,4),(2,4)]	[(1,1),(2,4)]

Fig. 4.3. A Data Cube Modeled as A Set System

We use the incidence matrix of a set system (recall that if $\mathcal{S}$ and $\mathcal{M}(\mathcal{S})$ are the set system and its incidence matrix, then $\mathcal{M}(\mathcal{S})[i, j] = 1$ if the jth element is a member of the ith set and $\mathcal{M}(\mathcal{S})[i, j] = 0$ otherwise) to characterize the queries represented by the set system. Example 4.2 shows an example of incidence matrices.

Example 4.2. In Figure 4.3, the incidence matrix $\mathcal{M}(\mathcal{S}_1)$ of the group $\mathcal{S}_1 = \{[(1, 1), (1, 1)]\}$ consists of a single row $[1, 0, 0, 0, 0, 0]$. The incidence matrix $\mathcal{M}(\mathcal{S}_2)$ of $\mathcal{S}_2 = \{[(1, 1), (1, 3)], [(1, 2), (1, 3)]\}$ is:

$$\begin{pmatrix} 1\,1\,1\,0\,0\,0 \\ 0\,1\,1\,0\,0\,0 \end{pmatrix}$$

We use the *derivability* relation $\preceq$ to denote the fact that all answers to a collection of queries may be represented as linear combinations of those to another collection of queries on the same core cuboid. Let $\mathcal{M}(\mathcal{S}_1)$ and $\mathcal{M}(\mathcal{S}_\in)$ be the incidence matrix of $\mathcal{S}_1$ and $\mathcal{S}_2$, respectively. Then we say that $\mathcal{S}_1$ is derivable from $\mathcal{S}_2$, denoted as $\mathcal{S}_1 \preceq \mathcal{S}_2$, if $\mathcal{M}(\mathcal{S}_1) = M \cdot \mathcal{M}(\mathcal{S}_2)$ for some $M \in \mathbb{R}^{|\mathcal{S}_1| \times |\mathcal{S}_2|}$. An inference is easy to model with the derivability relation. We say a tuple t is *compromised* by a collection of queries $\mathcal{S}$ if $\{\{t\}\}$ (or t for simplicity) is derivable from $\mathcal{S}$, denoted as $t \preceq \mathcal{S}$. We say that $\mathcal{S}$ is safe if no tuple in the core cuboid is compromised by answered queries.

Example 4.3. Following Example 4.2, we have that $\mathcal{S}_1 \preceq \mathcal{S}_2$, because $\mathcal{M}(\mathcal{S}_1) = [1, -1] \cdot \mathcal{M}(\mathcal{S}_2)$. Hence $\mathcal{S}_2$ is unsafe because it compromises the tuple $(1, 1)$.

We sometimes do not include measures in our model because the specific value of the measure is not relevant for some inferences. For example, the inferences we discussed earlier in this section does not depend on specific values of the measure *Adj*, as shown in Figure 4.1. This is generally true in the case where only SUM is considered, and measures are unbounded reals. In such a case, the only way for users to learn sensitive values is through the derivability relation. In other cases we may have to include the measure because their values may determine whether an inference is possible or not.

4.3 Arbitrary Range Queries

This section studies inferences caused by arbitrary range queries. We discuss two kind of attacks, namely, *trivial attacks* and *tracker attacks* with range queries.

Trivial Attacks with Range Queries

We begin with no restriction placed on the range queries a user may ask. In such a case, inferences are trivial because users can simply ask a range query with singleton query set whose only member is the targeted tuple. This is exactly the *small query set attack* in statistical databases as discussed in Chapter 3. In order to compromise a tuple t, users simply asks the query $[t, t]$. An alternative way is to ask a query $[t_1, t_2]$, where t_1, t_2 are two distinct tuples satisfying that t is the only member in $[t_1, t_2]$. t_1 and t_2 can be chosen such that $t_1[i] \leq t[i] \leq t_2[i]$ holds for ordered dimensions, and $t_1[i] = t[i] = t_2[i]$ for dimensions without order. The condition $| [t_1, t_2] | = 1$ can be determined by asking the query $[t_1, t_2]$ with COUNT.

Definition 4.4 (Trivial Attack). *A trivial attack happens when an answered range query has a singleton query set.*

The trivial attack can be prevented by executing the query and examining the cardinality of the results before releasing them to users. The query $[t, t]$ can be simply denied, because even if $| [t, t] | = 0$, answering such a query still discloses the fact that no tuple satisfies the specified condition, known as a *negative* inference [25]. It may be appealing to scrutinize the COUNT queries such that users can not find two tuples t_1 and t_2 satisfying the condition $| [t_1, t_2] | = 1$ through COUNT queries. Unfortunately, inferences caused by COUNT queries are especially difficult to control, because users have the extra knowledge that each cell contributes to the result of a COUNT query by either zero (a empty cell) or one. We have discussed about the intractability result on auditing COUNT queries [45] in the previous chapter.

Restrictions on the cardinality of query sets have been proven to be ineffective in statistical databases. The complement of a restricted query to the query about all tuples comprise a simple way to subvert such restrictions. In Chapter 3 we have discussed how to use other trackers to subvert restrictions on the cardinality of query sets. The basic idea of tracker is to pad the restricted query sets with more tuples such that they become legitimate, and then remove the padding with subsequent queries. Trackers can be combined to gradually obtain sensitive values even under stringent restrictions on the cardinality of query sets. Finding a tracker composed of merely multidimensional range queries turns out to be more difficult than with arbitrary queries, but nevertheless possible.

Definition 4.5 (Tracker Attack With Range Queries). *Suppose only the range queries containing no less than n_t tuples are answerable (we shall not consider the restriction on the complement of queries, which can be similarly handled). Given a targeted range query $[t_1, t_2]$ whose cardinality is smaller than n_t and hence is not allowed, a tracker attack happens when there exists a collection of answerable range queries S satisfying $[t_1, t_2] \preceq S$.*

Procedure *Range_Tracker* shown in Figure 4.4 builds a tracker to derive the restricted range query $[t_1, t_2]$ using totally $k + 2$ range queries (k is the number of dimensions). Intuitively, we can view $[t_1, t_2]$ as a k-dimensional *box* (its projection on some of the dimensions may have a size one) obtained by the intersection of totally $2k$ *planes*. Those planes divide the core cuboid C into 3^k disjointed blocks including $[t_1, t_2]$ itself. The procedure starts by searching through the $3^k - 1$ blocks around $[t_1, t_2]$ for $[t_a, t_b]$ that contains no less than n_t tuples. If the procedure can find $[t_a, t_b]$ then it returns the following $k + 1$ range queries besides $[t_a, t_b]$; $[t_c, t_d]$ is the smallest range query that contains both $[t_a, t_b]$ and $[t_1, t_2]$; and the $[u_i, v_i]$s are the largest range queries that are contained by $[t_c, t_d]$, contain $[t_a, t_b]$, but do not contain $[t_1, t_2]$.

Proposition 4.6 justifies the correctness of the Procedure *Range_Tracker* and gives a sufficient condition for finding a tracker. The result shows that unless the threshold n_t is very large, finding a tracker with range queries is always possible. However, choosing a large n_t may render the system useless because many drilling-down queries having small cardinalities will be denied. Moreover, although not discussed here, it is not difficult to combine multiple trackers to defeat a large n_t, as has been extensively studied in statistical databases (see Chapter 3 for a brief review). The tracker found by Procedure *Range_Tracker* uses only $k+2$ range queries to derive the restricted query. The queries can be formed in constant time. The running time of the procedure is dominated by search for $[t_a, t_b]$, which can be implemented by asking at most $3^k - 1$ range COUNT queries.

Proposition 4.6. *If the Procedure Range_Tracker produces a non-empty result S, then it satisfies the following:*

1. $[t_1, t_2] \preceq S$.
2. *All range queries in S are answerable with respect to n_t.*
3. *S can always be obtained if $n_t \leq \frac{|C|}{3^k}$.*

Proof:

Procedure *Range_Tracker*

Input: A core cuboid C with k dimensions $[1, d_i]$ $(1 \leq i \leq k)$, a threshold n_t, and
the targeted range query $[t_1, t_2]$ satisfying $\mid [t_1, t_2] \mid < n_t$.

Output: a collection of $k + 2$ queries S if successful, ϕ otherwise.

Method:

1 **Let** $[t_a, t_b]$ be a range query satisfying:

$\mid [t_a, t_b] \mid \geq n_t$, and for $1 \leq i \leq k$ one of the follows holds
$$t_a[i] = 1 \text{ and } t_b[i] = t_1[i] - 1,$$
$$t_a[i] = t_1[i] \text{ and } t_b[i] = t_2[i], \text{ or}$$
$$t_a[i] = t_2[i] + 1 \text{ and } t_b[i] = d_i.$$

2 **Then**

Let $[t_c, t_d]$ be a range query satisfying that
$t_c[i] = min\{t_a[i], t_1[i]\}$ and $t_c[i] = max\{t_b[i], t_2[i]\}$ for $1 \leq i \leq k$.

For $1 \leq i \leq k$

Let $[u_i, v_i]$ be a range query satisfying that
$u_i[i] = t_1[i], v_i[i] = t_2[i]$ and
$u_i[j] = t_c[j], v_i[j] = t_d[j]$ for $j \neq i$.

Let $S = \{[u_i, v_i] : 1 \leq i \leq k\} \cup [t_a, t_b] \cup [t_c, t_d].$

3 **Else**

Let $S = \phi$.

4 **Return** S.

Fig. 4.4. An Procedure For Constructing A Tracker Using Range Queries

1. $[t_1, t_2]$ can be derived from S with the a series of set operations:

$$[t_1, t_2] = [t_c, t_d] - \bigcup_{i=1}^{k} ([u_i, v_i] - [t_a, t_b]) - [t_a, t_b].$$

It then follows that $[t_1, t_2] \preceq S$, because $\mathcal{M}([t_1, t_2]) = M \cdot \mathcal{M}(S)$, where
$M = [-1, -1, \ldots, -1, k - 1, 1] \in \mathbb{R}^{1 \times (k+2)}$.

2. First, $\mid [t_a, t_b] \mid \geq n_t$ holds by the second step of Procedure *Range_Tracker*.
Second, we have $\mid [u_i, v_i] \mid \geq \mid [t_a, t_b] \mid \geq n_t$ because $[t_a, t_b] \subseteq [u_i, v_i]$ holds
for $1 \leq i \leq k$. Similarly, we have $\mid [t_c, t_d] \mid \geq n_t$. Hence all the range queries
in S can be answered with respect to n_t.

3. The procedure *Range_Tracker* is successful if it can find the range query
$[t_a, t_b]$ satisfying $\mid [t_a, t_b] \mid \geq n_t$. The $4k$ values $1, t_1[i], t_2[i], d[i]$ $(1 \leq i \leq k)$
divide the core cuboid C into totally 3^k disjointed blocks with $[t_1, t_2]$ in
the middle (some of the ranges may be empty). One out of the 3^k ranges
must contain $\frac{|C|}{3^k}$ or more tuples. Because $\mid [t_1, t_2] \mid < n_t \leq \frac{|C|}{3^k}$, $[t_a, t_b]$ can
always be found.

$\square$

Example 4.7. Figure 4.5 illustrates a tracker using two dimensional range
queries. Suppose that $\mid [t_1, t_2] \mid < n_t$ holds for some $n_t \leq \frac{|C|}{9}$. Then one of

the eight blocks around $[t_1, t_2]$ must contain no less than n_t tuples. Suppose $| [t_a, t_b] | \geq n_t$. Then we can derive $[t_1, t_2]$ as $[t_1, t_2] = [t_c, t_d] - ([u_1, v_1] - [t_a, t_b]) - ([u_2, v_2] - [t_a, t_b]) - [t_a, t_b]$. Clearly, all queries at the right hand side of this equation have a cardinality greater or equal to n_t, and hence will be answered.

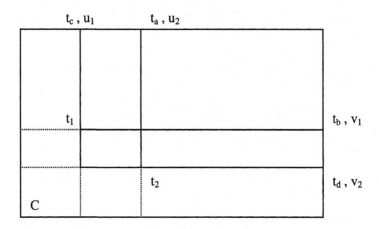

Fig. 4.5. An Example of Trackers Using Two Dimensional Range Queries.

Tracker attack, as well as the more general *linear system attack* [29], exploits the derivability relation between collections of queries to achieve inferences. These attacks can be detected by techniques that explore the same derivability relation. For example, Chapter 3 discusses the Audit Expert, which audits the entire history of queries asked by each user and constantly checks for any possible inferences [16]. Audit Expert can certainly detect inferences caused by range queries. However, such an approach suffers from several inherent drawbacks. First, an adversary can easily achieve his objective by combining a few selected queries out of the large amount of answered queries, whereas the inference control system must check all possible combinations of the answered queries. The situation becomes worse if the attacker deliberately asks many irrelevant queries. Second, whether a query will be allowed by Audit Expert depends on previously answered queries. A badly chosen order of queries may render the total number of answerable queries very small [9]. In OLAP systems, users may not be entirely clear about what queries to ask, and they typically base the next query on the result to previous queries. This implies that the actual availability may be quite poor under the auditing control.

4.4 Restricted Range Queries

The previous section demonstrates that it is relatively easy to cause inferences when no restriction is enforced on the type of range queries that a user may ask. In this section, we shall investigate cases where users are restricted to a special class of range queries. We show that inferences remain to be possible, although considerably more difficult, in those cases.

4.4.1 Even Range Query Attack

First we consider answering only *even* range queries. The intuition is that any union or difference of two even range queries yields another even range query. Hence, inference would be more difficult with even range queries since a single tuple comprises an *odd* range query. For example, the inference in Example 4.3 will no longer be possible because the query $[(1, 1), (1, 3)]$ is an odd range query and will be denied. Under this restriction, it is no longer straightforward to compromise a tuple in the core cuboid. Nevertheless, Example 4.8 shows that more sophisticated inferences remain to be possible using even range queries.

Example 4.8. In Figure 4.3, we can compromise the tuple $(1, 1)$ in a slightly more complicated way using only even range queries. First, consider $S = \{[(1, 1), (1, 2)], [(1, 2), (2, 2)], \{(1, 1), (2, 2)\}\}$. We have $\mathcal{M}((1, 1)) = [\frac{1}{2}, -\frac{1}{2}, \frac{1}{2}] \cdot \mathcal{M}(S)$. Now the question is how do we get the answer to $\{(1, 1), (2, 2)\}$ since it is not a range query. We need more queries for this purpose. Let $S' = \{[(1, 1), (2, 4)], [(1, 2), (1, 3)], [(2, 3), (2, 4)]\}$. Clearly all queries in S' are even range queries. Moreover we have that $\mathcal{M}(\{(1, 1), (2, 2)\}) = [1, -1, -1] \cdot \mathcal{M}(S')$.

Definition 4.9 (Even Range Query Attack). *An even range query attack compromises a collection of even range queries S that compromises the targeted tuple.*

The key observation in Example 4.8 is that the three queries in S form an *odd cycle* (here we consider each tuple as a vertex in a graph and each set of two tuples as an edge). As discussed in Chapter 3, with such an odd cycle we can always compromise any tuple in the cycle. Basically we begin from the targeted tuple and traverse the cycle. At each step we could *remove* a tuple shared by the two adjacent edges. When we reach the last edge we complete the inference with the targeted tuple being added twice and all other tuples in the cycle being removed.

However, unlike in Chapter 3 where we restrict all queries to be pairs of tuples, even range queries form a hypergraph instead of a graph. The even range query attack works only if all the edges in the cycle are even range queries themselves, or they can be derived from even range queries as in Example 4.8. For this purpose, we need the *QDT Graph* that will be introduced later in Chapter 6. The *QDT graph* has the core cuboid as its vertex set and a special collection of pairs of tuples as its edge set. A brief procedure is given in

Figure 4.4.1 to explain how QDT graph is constructed from the core cuboid for the given even range query $[t_1, t_2]$ (more details about the QDT graph can be found in Chapter 6). Basically we *pair* adjacent vertexes (tuples) by adding edges (sets of two tuples) to the QDT graph. The Proposition 4.10 states that the procedure guarantees every edge added to the QDT graph to be derivable from some set of even range queries over $[t_1, t_2]$.

Procedure *QDT_Graph*
Input: a core cuboid C and an even range query $[t_1, t_2]$.
Output: an edge set E.
Method:
    (1) **Let** $S = [t_1, t_2]$ and $E = \phi$.
    (2) **For** $i = 1$ to k
            Let t_a, t_b be two tuples in S satisfying:
                (2.a) t_a and t_b differ in the last i dimensions,
                (2.b) there does not exists $t_c \in S$ such that
                      $t_a[j] = t_c[j]$ for all $j < i$ and $t_a[i] < t_c[i] < t_b[i]$.
            Let $E = E \cup \{\{t_a, t_b\}\}$.
            Let $S = S - \{t_a, t_b\}$.
    (3) **Return** E.

Fig. 4.6. An Procedure for Constructing a QDT Graph

Proposition 4.10. *Any edge $\{t_a, t_b\}$ returned by the Procedure* QDT_Graph *can be derived from a set of even range queries over the input $[t_1, t_2]$.*

Proof (Sketch): The Procedure *QDT_Graph* pairs vertexes in totally k rounds, with the vertexes differing in the last i dimensions being paired in the ith round. We prove by induction on i. The initial case with $i = 1$ is trivial because the added edges are even range queries. Suppose in the edges added in up to the $i - 1$ round satisfy the hypothesis. In the ith round an edge $\{t_a, t_b\}$ is added into E. Let S_a and S_b be the sets of vertexes that have the same first $k - i$ dimensions as t_a and t_b, respectively. Then we know that all vertexes in S_a and S_b are already paired up in the first $i - 1$ rounds and the edges between them therefore satisfy the hypothesis. Moreover, let S_c be the set of vertexes satisfying that for any $t_c \in S_c$, $t_a[j] = t_c[j]$ for all $j < i$ and $t_a[i] < t_c[i] < t_b[i]$ holds. The condition (2.a) of the Procedure *QDT_Graph* implies that S_c must be an even range query. Let $S_{ab} = S_a \cup S_b \cup S_c$, then S_{ab} must also be an even range query. We conclude the proof by deriving $\{t_a, t_b\}$ as the follows:

$$\mathcal{M}(\{t_a, t_b\}) = [1, -1, -1, -1] \cdot \mathcal{M}(\{S_{ab}, S_c, S_a, S_b\}) \qquad (4.1)$$

$\square$

Now that all edges in a QDT graph are guaranteed to be derivable from even range queries, we can compromise the core cuboid by searching for an odd cycle in the QDT graph. Procedure *Even_Range_Query_Attack* given in Figure 4.4.1 additively builds an QDT graph for the even range queries enclosing the targeted tuple t. It then employs a breadth-first-search (BFS) in the QDT graph starting from t in order to find an odd cycle containing t. If it finds such a cycle, it returns the set of even range queries from which all the edges in the cycle can be derived. This set of even range queries can be found using equation (4.1) in the proof of proposition 4.10. If a cycle cannot be found, then the procedure begins to build the QDT graph for another even range query. The process is repeated with the cardinality of the even range query (for which the QDT graph is built) increasing until either t is compromised or no even range query is left unprocessed.

Procedure *Even_Range_Query_Attack*
Input: a core cuboid C and a targeted tuple t.
Output: a set of even range queries S compromising t if successful, or ϕ if failed.
Method:
    (1) **Let** $S = \phi$ and $E = \phi$.
    (2) **For** $i = 1$ to $\lfloor \frac{|C|}{2} \rfloor$
        While there exists an un-processed range query $[t_a, t_b]$ satisfying
                $\mid [t_a, t_b] \mid = 2i$, and $t \in [t_a, t_b]$.
        Let $E = E \cup QDT\_Graph(t_a, t_b, C)$
        Do   BFS in $G(C, E)$ to find an odd cycle $\mathcal{E}$ containing t.
        If $\mathcal{E}$ exists
            Let S be a set of even range queries satisfying
                $\mathcal{E} \preceq S$.
            Return S.
        Else
            Let $[t_a, t_b]$ be marked as processed.
    (3) **Return** ϕ.

Fig. 4.7. An Procedure for Even Range Query Attack

The procedure *Even_Range_Query_Attack* attempts to compromise t by asking as few range queries as possible. The procedure achieves the goal with two heuristics. First, it begins to build QDT graph for smaller even range queries and then moves to larger queries only when an odd cycle can not be found. The second heuristic is that the BFS in QDT graphs finds the shortest odd cycle, which implies that less number of even range queries are required to derive the targeted tuple. Despite these efforts, the number of queries required for the compromise largely depends on the actual core cuboid and could be large. The running time of the procedure is dominated by the construction of QDT graphs. Constructing a QDT graph for one range query takes linear time in the number of queries. However, in the worst case the procedure has to build QDT graphs for all possible range queries containing the targeted tuple before a failure is reported. In comparison to the tracker attack discussed in Section 4.3, the potentially high complexity of even range query attack reflects the effectiveness of the control of even range query.

4.4.2 Indirect Even Range Query Attack

The completeness of the Procedure *Even_Range_Query_Attack* is left open in the previous section. That is, when the procedure fails, is there any other way to compromise the targeted tuple? Unfortunately, the answer is *yes*. We shall show the tuple can still be compromised in an indirect way even when a cycle cannot be found in QDT graphs of all the range queries containing the targeted tuple.

Definition 4.11. *Indirect even range query attack happens when the targeted tuple is indirectly compromised through the compromises of other tuples.*

Example 4.12. In Figure 4.3, after we compromise the tuple $(1,1)$ basically we could successively compromise all other tuples using the even range queries connecting each pair of them.

First, we need some result proved later in Chapter 6. It states that for any range query $[t_1, t_2]$, if we build QDT graphs for all the even range queries contained by $[t_1, t_2]$ and additively union the edge sets of all these QDT graphs, then the final outcome is always a connected graph.

Lemma 4.13. *Given any even range query $[t_1, t_2]$ over the core cuboid C, let S be the collection of all even range queries contained by $[t_1, t_2]$ and let*

$$E = \bigcup_{\forall [t_a, t_b] \in S} QDT\_Graph(t_a, t_b, C)$$

Then the graph $G(C, E)$ is connected.

Due to Lemma 4.13, if a targeted tuple t cannot be compromised by the Procedure *Even_Range_Query_Attack*, there may exist another tuple t_1 that can be. That is, an odd cycle exists in the QDT graph of some query containing t_1 (but not t). We can thus first compromise the tuple t_1 using the Procedure *Even_Range_Query_Attack*. We then find the shortest path $\mathcal{P}$ from the t to t_1 in the graph $G(C, E)$ described in Lemma 4.13. All tuples from t_1 to t can then be successively compromised. The set of even range queries for indirect even range query attack is computed by Procedure *Indirect_Attack* shown in Figure 4.4.2.

Several heuristics may help the Procedure *Indirect_Attack* to minimize the number of even range queries required for the attack, although the actual

Procedure *Indirect_Attack*
Input: a core cuboid C and a targeted tuple t.
Output: a set of even range queries S if successful, ϕ otherwise.
Method:

    (1) **Let** $S =$ *Even_Range_Query_Attack*(C, t).

    (2) **If** $S = \phi$

        For any unprocessed tuple $t_1 \in C - \{t\}$

            Let $S_1 =$ *Even_Range_Query_Attack*(C, t_1)

            If $S_1 \neq \phi$

                Let $\mathcal{P}$ be the shortest path between t and t_1

                Let S_2 be the set of even range queries satisfying $\mathcal{P} \preceq S_2$.

                Let $S = S_1 \cup S_2$.

                Return S.

            Else

                Let t_1 be marked as processed.

    (3) **Return** ϕ.

Fig. 4.8. An Procedure for Indirect Even Range Query Attack

number could be large in some cases. First, the intermediate tuple t_1 may be chosen in such a way that compromising t_1 requires as few queries as possible. Second, the tuple t_1 should be close to t such that the path $\mathcal{P}$ is short. Those two goals must be balanced to reduce the overall number of required queries. Finally, redundant construction of QDT graphs should be avoided. While processing a new tuple t_{new}, the QDT graph of any even range query that contains both t_{new} and at least one processed tuple must have already been constructed and should not be considered again. The completeness of the procedure *Indirect_Attack* is guaranteed by the following result proved in Chapter 6. Given a core cuboid, if no odd cycle exists after all possible QDT graphs have been constructed and their edge sets merged, then the core cuboid is safe from even range query attacks. Hence, if the procedure *Indirect_Attack* returns an empty set for a targeted tuple t, then we know that there is no other way to compromise t with even range queries. Moreover, no other tuple can be compromised by even range query attack, either.

4.4.3 Skeleton Query Attack

When users are restricted to skeleton queries with trivial attacks suppressed, compromises are not always possible. For example, it can be verified that the core cuboid in Figure 4.3 is safe under such restrictions. In Chapter 5 we shall derive sufficient conditions for the data cube to be safe from compromises under the restrictions. However, in some cases an attack with skeleton queries is still attainable.

Definition 4.14. *A skeleton query attack compromises a targeted tuple with skeleton queries whose query sets include more than one tuple.*

Example 4.15. The core cuboid shown in Figure 4.9 is subject to skeleton query attack. The skeleton query attack is possible by the following equation:

$$\mathcal{M}(\{(1,1)\}) = [1, 1, -1, -1] \cdot \mathcal{M}(\{[(1,1),(1,4)],[(2,1),(2,4)],[(1,2),(4,2)],[(1,$$
$$3),(4,3)]\})$$

That is, we subtract the second and third column from the summation of the first and second row. The final result yields the tuple $(1,1)$. Observe that all the skeleton queries in this example have a query set including more than one tuple, as required by Definition 4.14.

	1	2	3	4
1	(1,1)	(1,2)	(1,3)	
2		(2,2)	(2,3)	
3	(3,1)			(3,4)
4	(4,1)			(4,4)

Fig. 4.9. A Core Cuboid Subject to Skeleton Query Attack.

In general, skeleton query attacks can be found using the similar techniques used in linear system attack discussed in Chapter 3. That is, we first transform the incidence matrix of a collection of queries into its reduced row echelon form (RREF). Then the queries compromise the targeted tuple iff a row vector in the RREF contains only one non-zero element corresponding to the targeted tuple. However, compared to building a QDT graph in previous section, which has a linear time complexity, the elementary row operations used to obtain RREF for m queries and n tuples runs in $O(m^2n)$ time. Hence, the skeleton query attack is more difficult, which reflects the effectiveness of restricting users to skeleton queries. Nevertheless, compromising will still be much easier than countering the compromise, because an adversary can focus on queries relevant to the attack, whereas the system must check all answered queries.

The Procedure *Skeleton_Query_Attack* shown in Figure 4.4.3 employs a simple heuristic to reduce the size of matrices to be transformed. It starts from the targeted tuple and check all the skeleton queries containing this tuple. If no compromise is possible, it checks more tuples that overlap the checked queries with at least one tuple. This is based on the simple fact that if a collection of queries compromise a tuple, then any query in the collection must share at least one tuple with some other query in the collection, and at least one query must involve the compromised tuple.

Procedure *Skeleton_Query_Attack*
Input: a core cuboid C and a targeted tuple t.
Output: a set of skeleton queries S if successful, ϕ otherwise.
Method:

(1) **Let** $S = \phi$ and $T = \{t\}$.
(2) **While** T is not empty
      Let T be the set of unprocessed skeleton queries
         involving at least one tuple in T.
      Let $S = S \cup T$.
      Let $M = \mathcal{M}(S)$.
      If the RREF of M contains a unit row vector corresponding to t
      Return S.
      Else
        Let all tuples in T be marked as processed.
        Let T be the unprocessed tuples involved by a query in S.
(3) **Return** ϕ.

Fig. 4.10. An Procedure for Skeleton Query Attack

4.5 Conclusion

This chapter has shown that the privacy breaches caused by common OLAP queries can be a serious threat. We showed that it is easy to compromise a targeted tuple even under stringent restrictions on what queries a user may ask. We showed that it is fairly easy to make an inference when arbitrary range queries are allowed. We then showed that restricting users to range queries involving even number of values makes compromises more difficult but nonetheless possible. Finally, we showed that even when users are only allowed to ask skeleton queries, inferences are still present. These findings motivate us to further investigate the issue of inference control in data cubes for the purpose of protecting sensitive data.

5

Cardinality-based Inference Control

5.1 Introduction

As described in previous chapters, inference problem may lead to inappropriate disclosures of sensitive data and consequently cause privacy breaches in OLAP systems. Although the restricted form of OLAP queries makes inferences more difficult, it does not completely remove the threat. Most inferences remain possible using OLAP queries, and exploiting these inferences is usually fairly easy. Although inference control has been investigated for more than thirty years with abundant results, most of the methods are computationally infeasible if directly applied to OLAP systems. This is due to two facts. First, the interactive nature of OLAP systems requires instant responses to most queries. Such a stringent requirement on performance prevents many off-line inference control methods, which have been successful in applications like releasing census data, from being applied to OLAP systems. Second, OLAP queries usually aggregate a large amount of data. Many existing inference control algorithms have run times proportional to the size of the query sets, and their performance decrease quickly when applied to queries with large query sets. Furthermore, these algorithms are enforced after queries arrive, which makes it difficult to shift the computational complexity to off-line processing. Every second spent on checking queries for inferences contributes to the delay in answering the queries.

Chin has pointed out that one way to make inference control practical is to give statistically meaningful queries a high priority during answering queries [13]. In traditional database applications, such as statistical databases, it is however quite difficult to predict what queries are the most valuable to users since ad-hoc queries are quite common in those applications. On the other hand, queries based on structures inherent to the data usually convey more useful knowledge to OLAP users. This implies an opportunity in developing more efficient inference control methods for OLAP systems by exploring the unique structure of OLAP data, such as data cubes. As a popular model of OLAP queries, the data cube operator generalizes many common OLAP operations such as group-by, cross-tab and sub-totals (a brief review of the data cube operator is given in Chapter 2. This chapter considers inference control of skeleton queries in data cubes, and shows that efficient inference control methods can be developed by exploring special characteristics of the skeleton queries.

Before we study the problem in a formal framework, we first show some examples in order to establish intuitions. Table 5.1 shows a data cube represented by four cross tabulations. Each cross tabulation corresponds to a quarter of the year. The two dimensions are month and employee. Each internal cell of a cross tabulation contains the monthly commission of an employee. Assume that individual commissions are sensitive and should be kept secret from users, and hence have been replaced with the symbol "?", indicating an unknown value. An empty internal cell indicates a value known to the users through outbound channels. For example, it is known that the employee is on leave and does not earn a commission (or a zero commission) in that month. Each external cell of a cross tabulation contains either the subtotal commission of the four employees in a month, or the subtotal commission of an employee in a quarter.

Table 5.1. An Example Data Cube

Quarter	Month / Employee	Alice	Bob	Jim	Mary	Sub Total
1	January	?	?	?	?	5500
	February	?	?	?	?	5500
	March	?	?	?	?	5500
	Sub Total	3000	3000	4500	6000	
2	April	?	?	?	?	6100
	May	?		?	?	6100
	June	?	?	?	?	4100
	Sub Total	4500	3300	4500	4000	
3	July	?	?	?	?	6100
	August	?	?	?	?	6100
	September				?	2000
	Sub Total	3500	2200	2500	6000	
4	October	?	?	?		7100
	November		?	?		4100
	December	?			?	4100
*	Bonus	?			?	6000
	Sub Total	7000	4300	3000	7000	

Suppose a malicious user Mallory aims to learn the unknown values represented by "?" in Table 5.1. Mallory can obtain knowledge about the table through two different channels: queries and the external knowledge (that is, the knowledge obtained through outbound channels). First, claiming for analysis purposes, she can ask legitimate skeleton queries about the subtotals in Table 5.1. Second, she has the external knowledge about the positions of empty cells in the table as she works in the same company and knows which employee is on leave in which month. Now the inference problem occurs if Mallory can determine any of the unknown values represented by "?" from these two kind of knowledge. The following observations are relevant in this respect:

1. In the first and second quarter, no hidden value can be determined by Mallory, because infinitely many choices exist for any of them with all the subtotals satisfied. To illustrate, consider the first quarter. Suppose Mallory can determine a unique value x_1 for Alice's commission in January. Then this value should not change with the choices of other values. Now let S be a set of values satisfying the subtotals, in which Alice's commission in February is x_2, and Bob's commission in January and February are y_1 and y_2 respectively, as shown in the upper cross tabulation in table 5.2. Now we can derive a different set of values S' from S by replacing x_1 with $x_1 - 100$, x_2 with $x_2 + 100$, y_1 with $y_1 + 100$ and y_2 with $y_2 - 100$, as shown in the lower tabulation in table 5.2. S' also satisfies all the subtotals in quarter one, which implies that Alice's commission in January cannot be determined by Mallory.

2. For the third quarter, Mary's commission in September can be determined by Mallory as 2000, equal to the subtotal in September, because Mallory knows from external knowledge that Mary is the only employee who works and draws a commission in that month.

3. For the fourth quarter, no hidden value can be determined in the similar way as in the third quarter, because all the subtotals in the fourth quarter are calculated from at least two hidden values. However, the following inference is possible. As shown in Table 5.3, let x_1 be Alice's commission in October; let y_1 and y_2 be Bob's commission in October and November respectively; and let z_1 and z_2 be Jim's commission in October and November respectively. Mallory asks four legitimate queries:

   a) $x_1 + y_1 + z_1 = 7100$ (The subtotal commission in October)
   b) $y_2 + z_2 = 4100$ (The subtotal commission in November)
   c) $y_1 + y_2 = 4300$ (Bob's total commission in this quarter)
   d) $z_1 + z_2 = 3000$ (Jim's total commission in this quarter)

   By adding both sides of the first two equations (a) and (b), and then subtracting from the result the last two equations (c) and (d), Mallory gets $x_1 = 3900$, which is Alice's commission in October.

To generalize the above example, unknown variables and their aggregations can be used to represent commissions and subtotals of commissions, respectively. Empty cells are used to model the values that users already learn from external knowledge (whatever these values may be). A data cube is compromised if the value of any unknown variables can be uniquely determined from

Table 5.2. Example of a Data Cube Safe from Inference

Quarter	Month / Employee	Alice	Bob	Jim	Mary	Sub Total
1	January	x_1	y_1	?	?	5500
	February	x_2	y_2	?	?	5500
	March	?	?	?	?	5500
	Sub Total	3000	3000	4500	6000	

Quarter	Month / Employee	Alice	Bob	Jim	Mary	Sub Total
1	January	$x_1 - 100$	$y_1 + 100$	?	?	5500
	February	$x_2 + 100$	$y_2 - 100$	?	?	5500
	March	?	?	?	?	5500
	Sub Total	3000	3000	4500	6000	

Table 5.3. Example of a Data Cube with Inference

Quarter	Month / Employee	Alice	Bob	Jim	Mary	Sub Total
4	October	x_1	y_1	z_1		7100
	November		y_2	z_2		4100
	December	?			?	4100
*	Bonus	?			?	6000
	Sub Total	7000	4300	3000	7000	

the aggregations and the empty cells. One important observation is possible from these examples. That is, inferences may depend on the number of empty cells, whence more empty cells (that is, more external knowledge the user possesses) makes it more likely for inference to become possible. On the other hand, inference may be impossible if there is no or few empty cells.

To justify these conjectures and to efficiently determine if any given data cube is compromised, we derive sufficient conditions based on the number of empty cells for the data cube to be free of inferences. More specifically, we show that any data cube is safe from inferences if the number of empty cells is below a given bound. The bound is tight because a counterexample to any tighter bound can always be found. We then apply the sufficient conditions on the basis of a three-tier inference control model. Besides data and queries, the model introduces a new tier, which represents a collection of safe data cubes constructed on a partition of the underlying data. The sufficient conditions help to compute the safe data cubes over a partition of the data, which are then used to provide users with inference-free queries. The overhead of inference control in terms of response time is mitigated by such an approach, because partitioning the data yields smaller input to inference control algorithms, pre-computing the aggregation tier reduces on-line delay, and using cardinality-based sufficient conditions for computation guarantees linear-time complexity.

The rest of the chapter is organized as follows. Section 5.2 formalizes sum-only data cubes and the inference. Section 5.3 proves cardinality-based sufficient conditions for data cubes free of inferences. Section 5.4 proposes a three tier inference control model. Section 5.5 integrates the sufficient conditions of safe data cubes into an inference control algorithm on the basis of the three-tier model. Section 5.6 concludes the chapter.

5.2 Preliminaries

This section describes a formal framework for further studies of the inference problem in SUM-only data cubes. First, Section 5.2.1 models the components of a *data cube*. Second, Section 5.2.2 defines *aggregation matrix* and *compromisability*. Finally, Section 5.2.3 justifies the choices made in the design of the framework.

5.2.1 Data Cube

As introduced in Chapter 2, a data cube is composed of a *core cuboid* and a collection of *aggregation cuobids*. Corresponding to the examples discussed in Section 5.1, the core cuboid captures the notion of sensitive values and empty cells (that is, external knowledge), whereas the aggregation cuboids correspond to the subtotals. Instead of using the relational terms, we choose to rephrase the data cube in a more concise model based on sets of integer vectors.

Definition 5.1 formalizes the concepts related to the core cuboid. We use closed integer intervals for *dimensions*. The Cartesian product of k dimensions form the *full core cuboid*. We call each vector in the full core cuboid a *tuple*. Hence the full core cuboid is simply the collection of all possible tuples that can be formed by the k dimensions. A *core cuboid* needs not to include all possible tuples, but has to satisfy the property that any integer from any dimension must appear in at least one tuple in the core cuboid. This property ensures that any given core cuboid corresponds to a unique full core cuboid (as well as the k dimensions), and we can thus determine the full core cuboid simply by looking at the core cuboid. The tuples not appearing in a core cuboid are said to be *missing*. By fixing a value for one of the k dimension, we can select tuples from a core cuboid to form a *slice* on that dimension. A slice is *full* if no tuple is missing from it. Clearly a slice can be full even if the core cuboid is not full.

Definition 5.1 (Core Cuboids).

1. *Given k ($k > 1$) integers $d_1, d_2, \ldots, d_k$ satisfying $d_i > 1$ for all $1 \leq i \leq k$, the ith **dimension**, denoted by D_i, is the closed integer interval $[1, d_i]$.*
2. *The k-dimensional **full core cuboid**, denoted as C_{full}, is the Cartesian product $\Pi_{i=1}^{k} D_i$. Each vector $t \in C_{full}$ is referred to as a **tuple**.*
3. *A k-dimensional **core cuboid** is any $C_{core} \subseteq C_{full}$ satisfying $\forall i \in [1, k] \ \forall x \in D_i, \exists t \in C_{core} \ t[i] = x$. Notice that we use notation $t[i]$ for the ith element of vector t from now on.*

4. t *is* **missing** *if* $t \in C_{full} \setminus C_{core}$.
5. *The jth ($j \in D_i$)* **slice** *of C_{core} on the ith dimension, denoted by $P_i(C_{core}, j)$, is the set $\{t : t \in C_{core}, t[i] = j\}$. $P_i(C_{core}, j)$ is* **full** *if $P_i(C_{core}, j) = P_i(C_{full}, j)$.*

Table 5.4 gives an example to the notions in Definition 5.1. The example describes a two dimensional core cuboid, with both dimensions as $[1, 4]$ (we use normal font for the first dimension and italic for the second for clarity purpose). The upper left tabulation shows the full core cuboid $[1, 4] \times [1, 4]$. The upper right tabulation shows a core cuboid with nine tuples. As required by Definition 5.1, any integer from any dimension appears in at least one of the nine tuples. Without this restriction, one could have argued that the first dimension is $[1, 5]$ instead of $[1, 4]$, and hence the full core cuboid contains $5 \times 4 = 20$ tuples instead of 16. That is, the full core cuboid is no longer unique. This situation must be avoided in order to use the cardinalities of missing tuples. The left lower cross tabulation shows the seven missing tuples. The right lower cross tabulation shows the first slice on the first dimension. The core cuboid in Table 5.4 is analogous to the fourth cross tabulation in Table 5.1 in the following sense. The employee names and months in Table 5.1 are abstracted as integers from one to four. The hidden values represented in "?" in Table 5.1 become integer vectors, and the empty cells correspond to missing tuples. The commissions in October are now called the first slice on the first dimension.

Definition 5.2 formalizes the concepts related to aggregation cuboids. The *-value* is a special value unequal to any integers. *-values appearing in a vector are called *-elements*. Adding the *-value into any dimension yields an *augmented dimension*. The Cartesian product of the k augmented dimensions includes all the vectors whose elements are either integers (from the dimensions), or *-elements. A vector with no *-element is simply a tuple, and a vector with j many *-elements are called a j-* *aggregation vector*. The collection of all the j-* aggregation vectors having *-elements at the same positions is called a j-* *aggregation cuboid*. Any aggregation vector can be used to *match* tuples in the core cuboid, with a *-element matching any integers and an integer matching only itself. The matched tuples form the *aggregation set* of the aggregation vector. A *data cube* is a pair of the core cuboid and the collection of all aggregation cuboids.

Definition 5.2 (Aggregation Cuboids and Data Cubes).

1. *A* ***-value**, *denoted as* $*$, *is a special value unequal to any positive integer. A *-value appearing in a vector is called a* ***-element**.
2. *Given the ith dimension D_i, the ith* **augmented dimension**, *denoted as D_i^*, is $[1, d_i] \cup \{*\}$.*
3. *A j-** **aggregation cuboid** *is the maximal subset of the Cartesian product $\Pi_{i=1}^{k} D_i^*$ satisfying,*
   a) $\forall i \in [1, k] \; \forall t, t' \in C_{aggr}, t[i] = *$ iff $t'[i] = *$; and

The Full Core Cuboid C_{full}

	1	2	3	4
1	(1,1)	(1,2)	(1,3)	(1,4)
2	(2,1)	(2,2)	(2,3)	(2,4)
3	(3,1)	(3,2)	(3,3)	(3,4)
4	(4,1)	(4,2)	(4,3)	(4,4)

A Core Cubiod C_{core}

	1	2	3	4
1	(1,1)	(1,2)	(1,3)	
2		(2,2)	(2,3)	
3	(3,1)			(3,4)
4	(4,1)			(4,4)

Missing Tuples $C_{full} \setminus C_{core}$

	1	2	3	4
1				(1,4)
2	(2,1)			(2,4)
3		(3,2)	(3,3)	
4		(4,2)	(4,3)	

1st Slice on 1st Dimension $P_1(C_{core}, 1)$

	1	2	3	4
1	(1,1)	(1,2)	(1,3)	
2				
3				
4				

Table 5.4. Example of a Core Cuboid with $k = 2$ and $d_1 = d_2 = 4$.

b) $\forall t \in C_{aggr}, |\,\{i : t[i] = *\}\,| = j$.
Each vector $t \in C_{aggr}$ *is called a* j-* **aggregation vector**.

4. *Given* C_{core}, *the* **aggregation set** *of any aggregation vector* t_{aggr}, *denoted as* $Qset(t_{aggr})$, *is the set of tuples:* $\{t : t \in C_{core}, \forall i \in [1, k],\ t_{aggr}[i] \neq * \Rightarrow t[i] = t_{aggr}[i]\}$. *The aggregation set of a set of aggregation vectors* C, *denoted as* $Qset(C)$, *is the set of tuples:* $\cup_{t_{aggr} \in C} Qset(t)$.

5. *A* k-*dimensional* **data cube** *is a pair* $< C_{core}, S_{all} >$, *where* C_{core} *is any core cuboid with dimensions* $D_1, D_2, \ldots, D_k$ *and* S_{all} *is the set of all aggregation cuboids with dimensions* $D_1, D_2, \ldots, D_k$.

Table 5.5 gives an example to the concepts in Definition 5.2. The two augmented dimensions are both $\{1, 2, 3, 4, *\}$. As shown in the left cross tabulation in Table 5.5, the Cartesian product of the two augmented dimensions yields 25 vectors. There are two 1-* aggregation cuboids: $\{(1,*),(2,*),(3,*),(4,*)\}$ and $\{*,1),(*,2),(*,3),(*,4)\}$, and one 2-* aggregation cuboids $(*,*)$. The right cross tabulation in Table 5.5 shows a 2-dimensional data cube. Notice that the two augmented dimensions are included for the purpose of clarity, and they are not a part of the data cube. As an example of aggregation set, the tuples composing the aggregation set of $(1,*)$ are underlined. The 1-* aggregation vectors in Table 5.5 abstract the subtotals in the fourth cross tabulation in Table 5.1, and the 2-* aggregation vector corresponds to the total commission in the fourth quarter.

Cartesian Product $\{1,2,3,4,*\} \times \{1,2,3,4,*\}$

	1	2	3	4	*
1	(1,1)	(1,2)	(1,3)	(1,4)	(1,*)
2	(2,1)	(2,2)	(2,3)	(2,4)	(2,*)
3	(3,1)	(3,2)	(3,3)	(3,4)	(3,*)
4	(4,1)	(4,2)	(4,3)	(4,4)	(4,*)
*	(*,1)	(*,2)	(*,3)	(*,4)	(*,*)

A Data Cube

	1	2	3	4	*
1	(1,1)	(1,2)	(1,3)		(1,*)
2		(2,2)	(2,3)		(2,*)
3	(3,1)			(3,4)	(3,*)
4	(4,1)			(4,4)	(4,*)
*	(*,1)	(*,2)	(*,3)	(*,4)	(*,*)

Table 5.5. Illustration of Aggregation Cuboids and Data Cube.

5.2.2 Compromisability

We first define *aggregation matrix*, and then formalize *compromisability*. In order to characterize a data cube, it suffices to know which tuple is in the aggregation set of which aggregation vector. Aggregation matrix captures this membership relation in a concise manner.

In order to fix notation, we use the following convention in further discussions about sets of vectors. Whenever applicable, we assume the members of a set are sorted according to the orders stated below:

1. Tuples in a core cuboid (or its subset) and aggregation vectors in an aggregation cuboid (or its subset) are in dictionary order (by saying so,

we are treating vectors as strings with the leftmost element the most significant). For example, the core cuboid C_{core} in Table 5.4 is sorted as $\{(1,1),(1,2),(1,3),(2,2),(2,3),(3,1),(3,4),(4,1),(4,4)\}$.

2. Aggregation cuboids in S_{all} or its subsets are sorted first in ascending order according to the number of *-elements in their aggregation vectors, and then in descending order on the index of the *-elements. For example, S_{all} shown in Table 5.5 is sorted as $\{\{(1,*),(2,*),(3,*),(4,*)\},\{(*,1),(*,2),(*,3),(*,4)\},\{(*,*)\}\}$.

3. We use notation $C[i]$ for the ith member of the sorted set C.

Definition 5.3 formalizes *aggregation matrix*. Suppose the full core cuboid includes n tuples, and we are given m aggregation vectors, then the aggregation matrix of those aggregation vectors is an m by n matrix M. Each element of the aggregation matrix M is either one or zero, and $M[i,j] = 1$ if and only if the jth tuple in the full core cuboid is included in the aggregation set of the ith aggregation vector. Intuitively, a column of M stands for a tuple, a row for an aggregation vector, and an element 1 for a matching between them. An element 0 could mean two things: either the tuple is missing or it is in the core cuboid but does not match the aggregation vector. The aggregation matrix is unique if the above convention of ordering is followed.

Definition 5.3 (Aggregation Matrix).

1. *In a given data cube* $< C_{core}, S_{all} >$, *suppose* $\mid C_{full} \mid = n$ *and let* C_{aggr} *be any set of m aggregation vectors. The* **aggregation matrix** *of* C_{aggr} *is the $(m \times n)$ matrix* $M_{C_{core}, C_{aggr}}$:

$$M_{C_{core}, C_{aggr}}[i,j] = \begin{cases} 1, & \text{if } C_{full}[j] \in Qset(C_{aggr}[i]); \\ 0, & \text{otherwise.} \end{cases}$$

2. *Given a set of sets of aggregation vectors S (for example, S_{all}), $M_{C_{core},S}$ is the row block matrix with the ith row block as the aggregation matrix of the ith set in S. Specially, we use S_1 for the set of all 1-* aggregation cuboids and M_1 for its aggregation matrix, referred to as the* **1-* aggregation matrix**.

Table 5.6 illustrates the concept of aggregation matrix. The cross tabulation shows the same data cube as in Table 5.5, with the tuples and aggregation vectors indexed through subscripts according to our order convention. For clarity purpose, normal font are used for the indexes of tuples while italic font for those of aggregation vectors. The 1-* aggregation matrix M_1 is shown in the lower part of Table 5.6. The rows and columns of the matrix are both indexed accordingly. As an example, the first row of M_1 contains three 1 elements, because the first aggregation vector $(1,*)$ has three tuples $(1,1)$, $(1,2)$ and $(1,3)$ in its aggregation set. The fourth column of M_1 is a zero column because the fourth tuple $(1,4)$ in the full core cuboid is missing from the core cuboid.

A Data Cube With Tuples and 1-* Aggregation Vectors Indexed

	1	2	3	4	*
1	$(1,1)_1$	$(1,2)_2$	$(1,3)_3$		$(1,*)_1$
2		$(2,2)_6$	$(2,3)_7$		$(2,*)_2$
3	$(3,1)_9$			$(3,4)_{12}$	$(3,*)_3$
4	$(4,1)_{13}$			$(4,4)_{16}$	$(4,*)_4$
*	$(*,1)_5$	$(*,2)_6$	$(*,3)_7$	$(*,4)_8$	$(*,*)$

The Aggregation Matrix M_1 With Indexes

$$
\begin{pmatrix}
 & 1\ 2\ 3\ 4\ 5\ 6\ 7\ 8\ 9\ 10\ 11\ 12\ 13\ 14\ 15\ 16 \\
\hline
1 & 1\ 1\ 1\ 0\ 0\ 0\ 0\ 0\ 0\ 0\ 0\ 0\ 0\ 0\ 0\ 0 \\
2 & 0\ 0\ 0\ 0\ 0\ 1\ 1\ 0\ 0\ 0\ 0\ 0\ 0\ 0\ 0\ 0 \\
3 & 0\ 0\ 0\ 0\ 0\ 0\ 0\ 0\ 1\ 0\ 0\ 1\ 0\ 0\ 0\ 0 \\
4 & 0\ 0\ 0\ 0\ 0\ 0\ 0\ 0\ 0\ 0\ 0\ 1\ 0\ 0\ 0\ 1 \\
5 & 1\ 0\ 0\ 0\ 0\ 0\ 0\ 1\ 0\ 0\ 0\ 1\ 0\ 0\ 0\ 0 \\
6 & 0\ 1\ 0\ 0\ 0\ 1\ 0\ 0\ 0\ 0\ 0\ 0\ 0\ 0\ 0\ 0 \\
7 & 0\ 0\ 1\ 0\ 0\ 0\ 1\ 0\ 0\ 0\ 0\ 0\ 0\ 0\ 0\ 0 \\
8 & 0\ 0\ 0\ 0\ 0\ 0\ 0\ 0\ 0\ 0\ 0\ 1\ 0\ 0\ 0\ 1
\end{pmatrix}
$$

Table 5.6. An Example of Aggregation Matrix

Before formalizing the compromisability, we first give the underlying intuitions. With the rows of an aggregation matrix M corresponding to aggregation vectors, the elementary row operations on M captures possible inferences users can make with the aggregation vectors. For example, in the discussion of Table 5.1 in Section 5.1, the addition of two subtotals can be represented by adding two corresponding rows in the aggregation matrix. The compromise of a tuple can then be captured by a sequence of elementary row operations that leads to a *unit row vector* (that is, a row vector having a single 1 elements and all other elements as 0). This unit row vector represents an aggregation of a single tuple, which is compromised. A matrix can be transformed by a sequence of elementary row operations to include at least one unit row vector, if and only if the reduced row echelon form (RREF) of the matrix has at least one unit row vector.

Definition 5.4 formalizes the *compromisability* based on the above intuition. The compromisability is decidable for any given set of aggregation vectors, because the RREF of any matrix is unique and can be obtained through a finite number of elementary row operations. Notice that here we are using the detection method of Audit Expert (a brief review of the Audit Expert is given in Chapter 3) as our definition of inferences. It is straightforward to translate this definition to a more intuitive one (for example, among all possible solutions to a linear system, one of the unknown values remains the same, or at least one of the sensitive values can be uniquely determined).

Trivial compromises occur when any of the given aggregation vectors already compromises the core cuboid (that is, it aggregates a single tuple). In the absence of trivial compromises, one has to manipulate more than one aggregation vector to compromise any tuple. This is called *non-trivial compromises*. Notice that these definitions correspond to the one-dimensional inference and the multi-dimensional inference discussed in Chapter 1, if the only type of range queries allowed are the skeleton queries; these definitions are different, otherwise.

Definition 5.4 (Compromisability).

1. *In a given data cube* $< C_{core}, S_{all} >$, *let* C_{aggr} *be any set of aggregation vectors,* C_{aggr} **compromises** C_{core} *if there exists at least one unit row vector in the reduced row echelon form (RREF) of* $M_{C_{core},C_{aggr}}$.

2. *Suppose* C_{aggr} *compromises* C_{core}. *We say* C_{aggr} **trivially compromises** C_{core} *if there exists at least one unit row vector in* $M_{C_{core},C_{aggr}}$, *and* C_{aggr} **non-trivially compromises** C_{core}, *otherwise. We say that the* i^{th} *tuple is compromised, if the RREF of* $M_{C_{core},C_{aggr}}$ *contains a unit row vector whose* i^{th} *element is 1.*

Table 5.7 gives an example of compromisability. The matrix in Table 5.7 is the RREF of the aggregation matrix M_1 in Table 5.6. The first row of M_1 is a unit row vector. Hence, in Table 5.6, the set of 1-* aggregation cuboids S_1 compromises the core cuboid C_{core}. Because M_1 contains one unit row vector e_1 and the first element of that vector is 1, the first tuple in C_{core} is compromised. Moreover, this is a non-trivial compromise because the original aggregation matrix M_1 does not contain any unit row vector.

$$
\begin{pmatrix}
 & 1 & 2 & 3 & 4 & 5 & 6 & 7 & 8 & 9 & 10 & 11 & 12 & 13 & 14 & 15 & 16 \\
1 & 1 & 0 & 0 & 0 & 0 & 0 & 0 & 0 & 0 & 0 & 0 & 0 & 0 & 0 & 0 & 0 \\
2 & 0 & 1 & 0 & 0 & 0 & 0 & -1 & 0 & 0 & 0 & 0 & 0 & 0 & 0 & 0 & 0 \\
3 & 0 & 0 & 1 & 0 & 0 & 0 & 1 & 0 & 0 & 0 & 0 & 0 & 0 & 0 & 0 & 0 \\
4 & 0 & 0 & 0 & 0 & 0 & 1 & 1 & 0 & 0 & 0 & 0 & 0 & 0 & 0 & 0 & 0 \\
5 & 0 & 0 & 0 & 0 & 0 & 0 & 0 & 0 & 1 & 0 & 0 & 0 & 0 & 0 & 0 & -1 \\
6 & 0 & 0 & 0 & 0 & 0 & 0 & 0 & 0 & 0 & 0 & 0 & 1 & 0 & 0 & 0 & 1 \\
7 & 0 & 0 & 0 & 0 & 0 & 0 & 0 & 0 & 0 & 0 & 0 & 0 & 1 & 0 & 0 & 1 \\
8 & 0 & 0 & 0 & 0 & 0 & 0 & 0 & 0 & 0 & 0 & 0 & 0 & 0 & 0 & 0 & 0 \\
\end{pmatrix}
$$

Table 5.7. The Reduced Row Echelon Form of M_1 in Table 5.6

5.2.3 Formalization Rationale

It is a common approach in the literature to model dimensions using integer intervals. The domain of a dimension is related to a set of integers by a one-to-

	1 (Alice)	2 (Bob)	3 (Jim)	4 (Mary)	5 (Sub Total)
1 (Oct)	x_1	x_2	x_3		7100
2 (Nov)		x_4	x_5		4100
3 (Dec)	x_6			x_7	4100
4 (Bonus)	x_8			x_9	6000
5 (Sub Total)	7000	4300	3000	7000	-

$$
\begin{pmatrix}
1\,1\,1\,0\,0\,0\,0\,0\,0\,0\,0\,0\,0\,0\,0\,0\,0\,0 \\
0\,0\,0\,0\,0\,1\,1\,0\,0\,0\,0\,0\,0\,0\,0\,0\,0\,0 \\
0\,0\,0\,0\,0\,0\,0\,0\,1\,0\,0\,1\,0\,0\,0\,0\,0\,0 \\
0\,0\,0\,0\,0\,0\,0\,0\,0\,0\,0\,0\,1\,0\,0\,1 \\
1\,0\,0\,0\,0\,0\,0\,1\,0\,0\,0\,1\,0\,0\,0 \\
0\,1\,0\,0\,0\,1\,0\,0\,0\,0\,0\,0\,0\,0\,0 \\
0\,0\,1\,0\,0\,0\,1\,0\,0\,0\,0\,0\,0\,0\,0 \\
0\,0\,0\,0\,0\,0\,0\,0\,0\,0\,1\,0\,0\,0\,1
\end{pmatrix}
\times
\begin{pmatrix}
x_1 \\ x_2 \\ x_3 \\ 0 \\ 0 \\ x_4 \\ x_5 \\ 0 \\ x_6 \\ 0 \\ 0 \\ x_7 \\ x_8 \\ 0 \\ 0 \\ x_9
\end{pmatrix}
=
\begin{pmatrix}
7100 \\ 4100 \\ 4100 \\ 6000 \\ 7000 \\ 4300 \\ 3000 \\ 7000
\end{pmatrix}
$$

Table 5.8. A Linear System Corresponding to The Inference in Table 5.3

one mapping. For example, dimensions month and employee in Table 5.3 are mapped to integer intervals [1, 4] in Table 5.4. Such an abstraction ignores the specific values and allows us to focus on the structure of the data cube. Although dimensions may have continuous domains and infinitely many values, any given instance of data cubes must involve only finite number of values. As stated in Definition 5.1, we map a value to an integer only if it appears in one or more tuples in the core cuboid, and those that do not appear will be ignored. Hence, it is sufficient to use an arbitrarily large but fixed integer interval for each dimension as in Definition 5.1. Notice that some inference problems depend on the specific values in each tuple, such as those discussed in [49, 52, 47]. We do not address those problems in this chapter, and they will be discussed in Chapter 7.

The core cuboid, aggregation cuboids, and data cube in Definition 5.1 are similar to the original model (a brief review of the data cube model is given in Chapter 2). For example, Table 5.4 models the data cube in Table 5.3. However, some differences are worth noting. We model data cubes as sets of vectors rather than as a relational operator. This enables us to more conveniently refer to any specific tuple or aggregation without complex relational queries. The choice thus simplifies notations. We define the core cuboid and the aggregation cuboid separately, whereas they are not explicitly distinguished in the original model. The reason is that we assume in this chapter that only tuples in core cuboid may have sensitive values, but those in aggregation cuboids do not. This may not be valid for some applications where users may be prohibited from accessing aggregated values as well. Chapter 7 will address this issue.

The missing tuples formalized in Definition 5.1 correspond to the empty cells discussed in previous chapters. They are used to model the external knowledge of users (that is, the knowledge obtained through channels other than queries). One example of external knowledge is the unpopulated cells (that is, combinations of dimension values that do not correspond to an actual record in the base relation) in a sparse data cube. Users sometimes know which cells of the data cube are populated and which are not. This is so if the dimension values of each tuple is made public since they are not sensitive. One may argue that these values should be kept secret, and then inferences become impossible. However, even if all the dimension values are hidden, users may still infer the positions of unpopulated cells through queries containing COUNT. Detecting inferences caused by COUNT queries has been shown as intractable [45]. Hence, we make the safer assumption that the positions of unpopulated cells are public knowledge.

On the other hand, our definition of missing tuples actually captures a broader concept of external knowledge than unpopulated cells in a data cube. In practice, users may learn the value of sensitive attributes through many channels. We use missing tuples to characterize such known values, regardless of the specific channels in which they are learned. From the viewpoint of both malicious users and inference control, values become irrelevant once they are learned through external knowledge, and hence can be removed from the core cuboid. The specific values being learned are also irrelevant. For example, Table 5.9 shows two variations of the data cube shown in Table 5.3. The upper cross tabulation assumes that users know employee Mary to have a zero (but valid) commission for October. The lower cross tabulation assumes that users Mary's commission is 1000. For both data cubes, the same model given in Table 5.4 can be used with no modification.

Our definition of aggregation matrix and compromisability is based on Chin's famous result of Audit Expert [16]. In Audit Expert, a set of sum queries over sensitive values is modeled as a linear system of equations, and then it follows that determining compromisability of the sensitive values is equivalent to determining the existence of unit row vectors in the RREF of the coefficient matrix of the linear system. In our study, we use this result to define the compromisability without explicitly referring to this equivalence. We distinguish trivial compromises from non-trivial ones because they exhibit different cardinality-based characterizations as we shall show in the following sections. In the literature of inference control in statistical databases, trivial and non-trivial compromises are sometimes referred to as *small query set*

Quarter	Month / Employee	Alice	Bob	Jim	Mary	Sub Total
4	October	?	?	?	0	7100
	November		?	?		4100
	December	?			?	4100
*	Bonus	?			?	6000
	Sub Total	7000	4300	3000	7000	

Quarter	Month / Employee	Alice	Bob	Jim	Mary	Sub Total
4	October	?	?	?	1000	8100
	November		?	?		4100
	December	?			?	4100
*	Bonus	?			?	6000
	Sub Total	7000	4300	3000	8000	

Table 5.9. Two Variations of Table 5.3

attack (or *single query attack*) [25], and *linear system attack* (or *multiple query attack*) [29], respectively.

5.3 Cardinality-based Sufficient Conditions

In this section we derive sufficient conditions for data cubes to be free of inferences. Those conditions relate the cardinality of missing tuples to the compromisability of data cubes. We discuss trivial compromises in Section 5.3.1 and non-trivial compromises in Section 5.3.2. As discussed before, the key difference between the two cases is whether or not compromises can be achieved with a single aggregation.

5.3.1 Trivial Compromisability

We have two results for trivial compromises as stated in Theorem 5.5. The first says that full core cuboids cannot be trivially compromised. This is straightforward since in a full core cuboid all aggregation sets are larger than one. First consider the 1-* aggregation vectors. The aggregation set of any 1-* aggregation vector is equal to the size of the dimension having *-value, which is assumed as larger than one. Moreover, the aggregation set of any aggregation vector with more than one *-elements has a cardinality no less than some 1-* aggregation vectors. Hence any aggregation set contains more than one tuple. For example, in Table 5.5, the aggregation set of all the 1-* aggregation vectors contain at least two tuples, and the only 2-* aggregation vector contains all the nine tuples in the core cuboid.

The second claim of Theorem 5.5 states that any core cuboid containing fewer tuples than the given upper bound is always trivially compromised.

Intuitively, not enough tuples exist in the core cuboid in order for all the aggregation sets to include more than one tuple. Notice that if the core cuboid includes no tuple at all, then no aggregation set includes one tuple but this extreme case does not conform to Definition 5.1, because we require all dimension values to be present in at least one tuple.

Theorem 5.5. *In a given k dimensional data cube $< C_{core}, S_{all} >$ with dimensions $D_1, D_2, \ldots, D_k$, we have:*

1. C_{full} *cannot be trivially compromised by any aggregation cuboid $C \in S_{all}$.*
2. *If $| C_{core} | < 2^{k-1} \cdot MAX(d_1, d_2, \ldots, d_k)$ is true, then C_{core} is trivially compromised by S_1.*

Proof:

1. By Definition 5.4 we need to show that for any $t \in C$, we have $| Qset(t) | > 1$. Without loss of generality, let t be the j-* aggregation vector $(*, *, \ldots, *, x_{j+1}, x_{j+2}, \ldots, x_k)$. By Definition 5.2, we have $Qset(t) = \{t' : t' \in C_{full}, t'[j+1] = x_{j+1}, t'[j+2] = x_{j+2}, \ldots, t'[k] = x_k\}$. Because $C_{full} = \Pi_{i=1}^{k}[1, d_i]$ we have $| Qset(t) | = \prod_{i=1}^{j} d_i$. Because $d_i > 1$ for all $1 \le i \le k$, we have $| Qset(t) | > 1$.

2. Suppose C_{core} is not trivially compromised. We show that $| C_{core} | \ge 2^{k-1} \cdot max(d_1, d_2, \ldots, d_k)$. Without loss of generality, assume $d_k \ge D_i$ for all $1 \le i \le k$. By Definition 5.1, there are totally d_k slices of C_{core} on the kth dimension. Without loss of generality it suffices to show that $| P_k(C_{core}, 1) | \ge 2^{k-1}$. We do so by mathematical induction on $i \le k$ as given below.

   a) The Inductive Hypothesis:
      There exists $C_i \subseteq P_k(C_{core}, 1)$ for $i = 1, 2, \ldots, k$ satisfying $| C_i | = 2^{i-1}$, and for any $t_1, t_2 \in C_i$ we have $t_1[j] = t_2[j]$ for all $j \ge i$.

   b) The Base Case:
      By Definition 5.1, there exists $t \in C_{core}$ satisfying $t[k] = 1$. Let C_1 be $\{t\}$. We have $C_1 \subseteq P_k(C_{core}, 1)$ and $| C_1 | = 1$, validating the base case of our inductive hypothesis.

   c) The Inductive Case:
      Suppose for all $1 \le i < k$ there exists $C_i \subseteq P_k(C_{core}, 1)$ satisfying $| C_i | = 2^{i-1}$, and for any $t_1, t_2 \in C_i$, $t_1[j] = t_2[j]$ for all $j \ge i$. We show that there exists $C_{i+1} \subseteq P_k(C_{core}, 1)$ such that $| C_{i+1} | = 2^i$, and for any $t_1, t_2 \in C_{i+1}$, $t_1[j] = t_2[j]$ for all $j \ge i+1$.
      For any $t_1 \in C_i$, let $t_1'[i] = *$ and $t_1'[j] = t[j]$ for all $j \ne i$. Because $t_1 \in Qset(t_1')$ we have $| Qset(t_1') | \ge 1$. Since C_{core} is not trivially compromised by S_1, according to Definition 5.4, we have $| Qset(t_1') | > 1$. Hence, there exists $t_1'' \in Qset(t_1') \subseteq C_{core}$ such that $t_1''[i] \ne t_1[i]$ and $t_1''[j] = t_1[j]$ for all $j \ne i$; which implies $t_1'' \notin C_i$.
      Similarly for any $t_2 \in C_i$ satisfying $t_1 \ne t_2$, there exists $t_2'' \in C_{core}$ such that $t_2''[i] \ne t_2[i]$ and $t_2''[j] = t_2[j]$ for all $j \ne i$. Now we show that

$t_2'' \neq t_1''$. Because $t_1[j] = t_2[j]$ for all $j \geq i$, there must be $l < i$ such that $t_1[l] \neq t_2[l]$. Because $t_1''[j] = t_1[j]$ and $t_2''[j] = t_2[j]$ for all $j < i$, we have that $t_1''[l] \neq t_2''[l]$. That is, $t_1'' \neq t_2''$.

Hence there exists $C_i' \subset C_{core}$ satisfying $\mid C_i' \mid = \mid C_i \mid$, and for any $t \in C_i$, there exists one and only one $t' \in C_i'$ such that $t[i] \neq t'[i]$ and $t[j] = t'[j]$ for all $j \neq i$. Let C_{i+1} be $C_i \cup C_i'$. Then $\mid C_{i+1} \mid = 2^i$.

This proves the inductive case of our induction, from which the claim $\mid P_k(C_{core}, 1) \mid \geq 2^{k-1}$ follows.

$\square$

For data cubes whose cardinalities are between the two limits stated in Theorem 5.5, the trivial compromisability cannot be determined solely based on the cardinality of the core cuboid. Two data cubes whose core cuboids have the same cardinality but different missing tuples can have different trivial compromisability. For example, the core cuboid C_{core} in Table 5.5 is not trivially compromised. Without changing the cardinality of C_{core}, we delete the tuple $(2, 2)$ and add a new tuple $(1, 4)$ to obtain a new core cuboid C_{core}'. C_{core}' is trivially compromised although $\mid C_{core}' \mid = \mid C_{core} \mid$, because in C_{core}' the aggregation sets of $(2, *)$ and $(*, 2)$ contain exactly one tuple.

The trivial compromisability of data cubes can also be determined by computing the cardinalities of all the rows in the aggregation matrix. With an $m \times n$ aggregation matrix this can be done in $O(mn)$. For example, for the aggregation matrix M_1 given in Table 5.6, counting the 1-elements in each row shows that C_{core} is not trivially compromised by S_1. The complexity can be further reduced considering that $M_1[i, j] = 1$ only if $M_{C_{full}, S_1}[i, j] = 1$. For example, to calculate the aggregation set $Qset(t)$ for the aggregation vector $t = (1, *)$, we only need to consider the four elements $M_1[1, 1]$, $M_1[1, 2]$, $M_1[1, 3]$ and $M_1[1, 4]$, as we know that $M_1[1, j] = 0$ for all $j > 4$.

5.3.2 Non-trivial Compromisability

The results for non-trivial compromises require the observations stated in Lemma 5.6. Intuitively, the first claim of Lemma 5.6 indicates that aggregation vectors in the same aggregation cuboid always have disjoint aggregation sets (that is, any tuple is aggregated by at most one aggregation vector), and hence they do not help each other in non-trivial compromises. The second claim of Lemma 5.6 holds because aggregation vectors having more than one *-value can be derived from some 1-* aggregation vectors. For example, in Table 5.5 the aggregation set of the 2-* aggregation vector $(*, *)$ is equal to the aggregation set of one 1-* aggregation cuboid. Because of the second claim, it is sufficient to consider S_1 instead of S_{all} to determine the compromisability of data cubes. The last condition in Lemma 5.6 says that it is impossible to determine the non-trivial compromisability of a data cube by only looking at its k dimensions (without knowing its missing tuples) . This implies that any large enough data cube is vulnerable to non-trivial compromises. Here a data cube is large enough if $d_i \geq 4$ for all $1 \leq i \leq k$. For example, when $k = 2$ and $d_1 = d_2 = 2$, no data cube will be non-trivially compromisable.

Lemma 5.6. *1. In any given data cube $< C_{core}, S_{all} >$, C_{core} can not be non-trivially compromised by any single cuboid $C \in S_{all}$.*

2. In any given data cube $< C_{core}, S_{all} >$, if C_{core} cannot be compromised by S_1, then it cannot be compromised by S_{all}.

3. For any integers k and $d_1, d_2, \ldots, d_k$ satisfying $d_i \geq 4$ for $1 \leq i \leq k$, there exists a k-dimensional data cube $< C_{core}, S_{all} >$ with the k dimensions $D_1, D_2, \ldots, D_k$, such that C_{core} is non-trivially compromised by S_1.

Proof:

1. Let $C \in S_{all}$ be any aggregation cuboid. For any $t \in C_{core}$ there exists one and only one $t_{aggr} \in C$ such that $t \in Qset(t_{aggr})$. Hence, in the aggregation matrix M each non-zero column is a unit column vector, implying that M could be transformed into its RREF by permuting its columns. Furthermore, each row of M must contain at least two 1's because no trivial compromise is assumed. Hence no unit row vector is in the RREF of M. That is, C_{core} cannot be non-trivially compromised by C.

2. Without loss of generality, let t_{aggr} be any j-* $(j > 1)$ aggregation vector satisfying that $t_{aggr}[i] = *$ for any $1 \leq i \leq j$. Let C be the set of 1-* aggregation vectors defined as: $\{t : t[1] = *, t[i] \neq * \forall i \in [2, j], t[i] = t_{aggr}[i] \forall i \in [j + 1, k]\}$. We have that $Qset(t_{aggr}) = Qset(C)$. Hence in the aggregation matrix $M_{C_{core}, S_{all}}$, the row corresponding to t_{aggr} can be represented as the linear combination of the rows corresponding to C. The rest of the proof follows from linear algebra.

3. First we justify the case $k = 2$, then we extend the result to $k > 2$. For the proof of $k = 2$, without loss of generality, we use mathematical induction on d_1, for an arbitrary, but fixed value of $d_2 \geq 4$.

   a) The Inductive Hypothesis
      For any $d_1, d_2 \geq 4$, we can build a two dimensional data cube $< C_{core}, S_{all} >$ with dimensions D_1, D_2, such that C_{core} is non-trivially compromised by S_1.

   b) The Base Case:
      When $d_1 = d_2 = 4$, the data cube shown in Table 5.5 validates the base case of our inductive hypothesis.

   c) The Inductive Case:
      Assuming that there exists non-trivially compromisable two dimensional data cube $< C_{core}, S_{all} >$ with dimensions $[1, d_1]$ and $[1, d_2]$, we show how to obtain a non-trivially compromisable two dimensional data cube with dimensions $[1, d_1 + 1]$ and $[1, d_2]$.
      Without loss of generality suppose that the tuple $(1, 1)$ is non-trivially compromised by S_1. Then, there exists a row vector a such that $a \cdot M_1 = e_1$.
      First define a set of tuples C as:

- for any $t \in C$, $t[1] = d_1 + 1$
- for any $i \in [1, d_2]$, $(d_1+1, i) \in C$ if and only if $(d_1, i) \in P_1(C_{core}, d_1)$

We define $C'_{core} = C_{core} \cup C$, and $< C'_{core}, S'_{all} >$ as a new data cube with dimensions $[1, d_1 + 1]$ and $[1, d_2]$. We have $P_1(C'_{core}, d_1 + 1) = C$. Let M'_1 be the 1-* aggregation matrix of the new data cube. We have $M'_1 = (M_1 \mid M_c)$. The non-zero columns in M_c correspond to the tuples in C. According to the definition of C we further have $M_1 = (M''_1 \mid M_c)$, where the non-zero columns of M_c correspond to the tuples in $P_1(C_{core}, d_1)$. Thus, $M'_1 = (M''_1 \mid M_c \mid M_c)$. Because $a \cdot M_1 = (a \cdot M''_1 \mid a \cdot M_c) = e_1$, we have that $a \cdot M'_1 = (a \cdot M''_1 \mid a \cdot M_c \mid a \cdot M_c) = (e_1|0)$. Hence, the tuple $[1,1]$ in C'_{core} is non-trivially compromised, validating the inductive case of our inductive hypothesis.

We briefly describe how to extend this result for $k = 2$ to $k > 2$. We do so by regarding part of the k dimensional data cube as a special two dimensional data cube. Specifically, given k dimensional data cube $< C_{core}, S_{all} >$, let $C'_{core} = \{t : t \in C_{core}, t[j] = 1 \forall 3 \leq j \leq k\}$ and C be the collection of all 1-* aggregation vectors satisfying $\forall t \in C \forall j \in [3, k], t[j] = 1$. We have $Qset(C) = C'_{core}$. Hence M_1 can be represented as:

$$\left(\frac{M'_1 | 0}{M''_1} \right)$$

Where M'_1 is a $\mid C \mid$ by $\mid C'_{core} \mid$ sub-matrix and 0 is the $\mid C \mid$ by $\mid C_{core} \setminus C'_{core} \mid$ zero matrix. M'_1 can be treated as the 1-* aggregation matrix of a special two dimensional data cube. We can build C'_{core} in such a way that this two dimensional data cube is non-trivially compromised. Hence the RREF of M'_1 contains at least one unit row vector, which implies the RREF of M_1 does so, too.

□

We have two results for non-trivial compromises as stated in Theorem 5.7. The first says that full core cuboids cannot be non-trivially compromised. The first claim of Theorem 5.7 together with the first claim of Theorem 5.5 proves that any data cube with a full core cuboid is non-compromisable. In the proof of the first claim in Theorem 5.7, we construct a set of 2^k column vectors to contain any given column vector in the aggregation matrix. This set of 2^k vectors satisfies the property that any of its 2^k members can be represented as the linear combination of the other $2^k - 1$ members. The elementary row transformation used to obtain RREF of a matrix does not change the linear dependency of the column vectors. Hence the linear dependency among the 2^k column vectors also holds in the RREF of the aggregation matrix. Consequently, the 2^k tuples corresponding to those columns cannot be non-trivially compromised.

The second and third claims of Theorem 5.7 give a tight lower bound on the cardinality of any core cuboid with missing tuples, such that it remains free of non-trivial compromises. The lower bound $2d_l + 2d_m - 9$ is a function of the two least dimension cardinalities. Roughly speaking, the justification of the lower bound is based on the following fact. The least number of missing tuples necessary for any non-trivial compromise increases monotonically with the number of aggregation cuboids involved in the compromise. This number reaches its lower bound when exactly two aggregation cuboids are used for non-trivial compromises. This is exactly the case given by the second claim of Theorem 5.7. The second claim shows that it is impossible to derive non-trivial compromisability criteria solely based on the cardinality of core cuboids, when the cardinality is not greater than the given lower bound. Thus the lower bound given by the third claim is the best possible.

Theorem 5.7 (Non-trivial Compromisability).

1. In any given data cube $< C_{core}, S_{all} >$, C_{full} cannot be non-trivially compromised by S_{all}.

2. For any integers k and $d_1, d_2, \ldots, d_k$ satisfying $d_i \geq 4$ for all $1 \leq i \leq k$, let d_l and d_m be the least two among $d_i s$. Then there exists a k-dimensional data cube $< C_{core}, S_{all} >$ with k dimensions $D_1, D_2, \ldots, D_k$, such that $| C_{full} \setminus C_{core} | = 2d_m + 2d_n - 9$ and C_{core} is non-trivially compromised by S_1.

3. Given a data cube $< C_{core}, S_{all} >$ with dimensions $D_1, D_2, \ldots, D_k$, suppose D_l and D_m $(1 \leq l, m \leq k)$ are the two with the least cardinalities. If $| C_{full} \setminus C_{core} | < 2 | D_l | + 2 | D_m | - 9$ holds, then C_{core} cannot be non-trivially compromised.

Proof:

1. Due to the second claim of Lemma 5.6 we only need to shown that C_{full} cannot be non-trivially compromised by S_1. Without loss of generality, we show that $t_0 = (1, 1, \ldots, 1)$ cannot be non-trivially compromised by S_1. In order to do so, we define $C'_{full} = \{t : \forall i \in [1, k], t[i] = 1 \vee t[i] = 2\}$. We then have $C'_{full} \subseteq C_{full}$ and $| C'_{full} | = 2^k$. Let M'_1 be a matrix comprising of the 2^k columns of M_1 that corresponds to C'_{full}. In the rest of the proof we formally show that each of those 2^k column vectors can be represented as the linear combination of the rest $2^k - 1$ column vectors. It then follows from linear algebra that the RREF of M_1 does not contain e_1. Hence t_0 cannot be non-trivially compromised by S_1.

   First we define the *sign assignment vector* as an 2^k dimensional column vector t_{sign} as follows:

   - $t_{sign}[1] = 1$
   - $t_{sign}[2^i + j] = -t_{sign}[j]$ for all $0 \leq i \leq k - 1$ and $1 \leq j \leq 2^i$

   Claim: $M'_1 \cdot t_{sign} = 0$, where 0 is the 2^k dimensional zero column vector.
   Justification:

Let t_{aggr} be the ith 1-* aggregation vector and suppose $t_{aggr}[l] = *$ for some $1 \leq l \leq k$.

Let r be the ith row of M'_1.

If $t_{aggr}[j] \leq 2$ for all $j \neq l$.

Then $\mid Qset(t_{aggr}) \cap C'_{full} \mid = 2$, and suppose $Qset(t_{aggr}) = \{t_1, t_2\}$ where $t_1 = C'_{full}[j_1]$ and $t_2 = C'_{full}[j_2]$, $t_1[l] = 1$, $t_2[l] = 2$ and $t_1[j] = t_2[j] = t_{aggr}[j]$ for all $j \neq l$

Hence, j_1, j_2 satisfy
$r[j_1] = r[j_2] = 1$ and $r[j] = 0$ for any $j \neq j_1 \wedge j \neq j_2$.
The j_1^{th} and j_2^{th} columns of M'_1 correspond to t_1 and t_2, respectively.

Since C'_{full} is in dictionary order, we have $j_2 = j_1 + 2^{l-1}$.

Hence, we have $r \cdot t_{sign} = 0$.

Otherwise, $\mid Qset(t_{aggr}) \cap C'_{full} \mid = 0$.

Hence, $r = 0$ and $0 \cdot t_{sign} = 0$.

Hence, as stated earlier, the justification of our claim concludes the main proof.

2. Without loss of generality, assume $m = 1$ and $n = 2$. Analogous to the proof for the third condition of Lemma 5.6, it suffices to consider only the case $k = 2$. For an arbitrary but fixed value of d_2, we show by induction on d_1 that the data cube as constructed in the proof for the third condition of Lemma 5.6 satisfies $\mid C_{full} \setminus C_{core} \mid = 2d_1 + 2d_2 - 9$.

   a) The Inductive Hypothesis:
      C_{core} as constructed in the proof of Lemma 5.6 satisfies:
      - $\mid C_{full} \setminus C_{core} \mid = 2d_1 + 2d_2 - 9$.
      - $\mid P_1(C_{full}, d_1) \setminus P_1(C_{core}, d_1) \mid = 2$.

   b) The Base Case:
      In Table 5.5, the core cuboid C_{core} satisfies $\mid C_{full} \setminus C_{core} \mid = 2d_1 + 2d_2 - 9$. We also have $\mid P_1(C_{full}, 4) - P_1(C_c, 4) \mid = 2$. This validates the base case of our inductive hypothesis.

   c) The Inductive Case:
      Suppose we have two-dimensional data cube $< C_{core}, S_{all} >$ with dimensions D_1 and D_2 satisfying $\mid C_{full} - C_{core} \mid = 2d_1 + 2d_2 - 9$ and $\mid P_1(C_{full}, d_1) - P_1(C_c, d_1) \mid = 2$. Use $< C'_{core}, S'_{all} >$ and C'_{full} for the data cube and full core cuboid with dimensions $[1, d_1 + 1]$ and D_2, respectively. By the definition of C in the proof of Lemma 5.6 $\mid C \mid = \mid P_1(C_{core}, d_1) \mid$, and as a consequence $\mid C'_{full} \setminus C'_{core} \mid = \mid C_{full} \setminus C_{core} \mid + 2 = 2(d_1 + 1) + 2d_2 - 9$. Since $P_1(C'_{core}, d_1 + 1) = C$, we have $\mid P_1(C'_{full}, d_1 + 1) - P_1(C'_{core}, d_1 + 1) \mid = 2$. This validates the inductive case of our inductive argument and consequently concludes our proof.

Lower Bound: Similarly we assume $m = 1$ and $n = 2$. We show that if C_{core} is non-trivially compromised then we have $\mid C_{full} \setminus C_{core} \mid \geq 2d_1 + 2d_2 - 9$. First we make following assumptions.

1. Tuple $t = (1, 1, \ldots, 1) \in C_{core}$ is non-trivially compromised by S_1.
2. No tuple in C_{core} is trivially compromised by S_1.
3. There exists a minimal subset S of S_1, such that for any $C \in S$, t cannot be non-trivially compromised by $S \setminus C$.
4. For any $t' \in C_{full} \setminus C_{core}$, t cannot be non-trivially compromised by S_1 in data cube $< C_{core} \cup \{t'\}, S_{all} >$. That is, $\mid C_{full} \setminus C_{core} \mid$ reaches its lower bound.

Assumption 2 holds by Definition 5.4. Assumption 3 holds as by the first claim of Lemma 5.6, S must contain at least two 1-* aggregation cuboids. Assumption 4 holds because by Theorem 5.7, $\mid C_{full} \setminus C_{core} \mid$ has a lower bound if C_{core} is non-trivially compromisable.

Claim: Let $C \in S$ and $t[i] = *$ for any $t \in C$. We have $\mid P_i(C_{full}, 1) \setminus P_i(C_{core}, 1) \mid \geq 1$, and $\mid P_i(C_{full}, j) \setminus P_i(C_{core}, j) \mid \geq 2$ for any $2 \leq j \leq d_i]$.
Justification: The proof is by contradiction. Without loss of generality, we only justify the claim for $i = k$ and $j = 2$. That is, given $C \in S$ satisfying $t[k] = *$ for any $t \in C$ we prove that $\mid P_i(C_{full}, 1) \setminus P_i(C_{core}, 1) \mid \geq 1$ and $\mid P_i(C_{full}, 2) \setminus P_i(C_{core}, 2) \mid \geq 2$.

First we transform $M_{C_{core}, S}$ into a singly bordered block diagonal form (SBBDF) [68] with row permutations, denoted by $M_{m \times n}$. The ith diagonal block of M corresponds to $P_k(C_{core}, i)$ and $\{t : t \in S \setminus C \wedge t[k] = i\}$, and the border of M corresponds to C. For example, Table 5.10 illustrates the SBBDF of $M_{S_1, C_{core}}$ in Table 5.6. We call the columns of M containing the ith diagonal block as the ith *slice of* M, also we use notation $M[-, i]$ for the ith column of M and $M[i, -]$ for the ith row.

SBBDF of $M_{S_1, C_{core}}$ Shown in Table 5.6 With 0-Elements Omitted

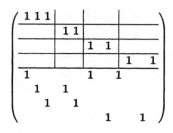

Table 5.10. An Example of SBBDF

Due to Assumption 1, there exists a m-dimensional row vector a satisfying $a \cdot M = e_1$. Use r_i for $M[i, -]$ then we get:

$$e_1 = \sum_{i=1}^{m} a[i] \cdot r_i$$

Suppose each diagonal block of M has size $m' \times n'$. Use r_i^j, for $1 \le j \le d_k$ to represent the sub-row vector of r_i intersected by the jth slice of M. We have $\mid r_i^j \mid = n'$. We also use e_1' and $0'$ to represent the n' dimensional unit row vector and n' dimensional zero row vector, respectively. Then the following are true:

$$e_1' = \sum_{i=1}^{m'} a[i]r_i^1 + \sum_{i=m-m'+1}^{m} a[i]r_i^1 \tag{5.1}$$

$$0' = \sum_{i=m'+1}^{2m'} a[i]r_i^2 + \sum_{i=m-m'+1}^{m} a[i]r_i^2 \tag{5.2}$$

First we suppose $\mid P_k(C_{full}, 2) \setminus P_k(C_{core}, 2) \mid = 0$, that is, the second slice of M contains no zero column. We then derive a contradiction to our assumptions.

Because $\mid P_k(C_{full}, 2) \setminus P_k(C_{core}, 2) \mid = 0$, the first slice of M contains no less zero columns than the second slice of M. Intuitively if the latter can be transformed into a zero row vector by some elementary row transformation, then applying the same transformation on the former leads to a zero vector, too. This is formally represented as:

$$0' = \sum_{i=1}^{m'} a[m' + i]r_i^1 + \sum_{i=m-m'+1}^{m} a[i]r_i^1 \tag{5.3}$$

Subtracting both sides of Equation 5.3 from Equation 5.1 gives:

$$e_1' = \sum_{i=1}^{m'} (a[i] - a[m' + i])r_i^1$$

That implies C_{core} is non-trivially compromised by $S \setminus \{C_k\}$, contradicting Assumption 3. Thus $\mid P_k(C_{full}, 2) \setminus P_k(C_{core}, 2) \mid > 0$.

Next assume $\mid P_k(C_{full}, 2) \setminus P_k(C_{core}, 2) \mid = 1$ and derive a contradiction to our assumptions.

Row vector r_i^3 satisfies the following condition:

$$0' = \sum_{i=2m'+1}^{3m'} a[i]r_i^3 + \sum_{i=m-m'+1}^{m} a[i]r_i^3 \tag{5.4}$$

Let $t' \in P_k(C_{full}, 2) \setminus P_k(C_{core}, 2)$. Notice that Equation 5.1 and Equation 5.2 still hold. Suppose t' corresponds to $M[-, y]$, which is a zero column. Now assume that we add t' to $P_k(C_{core}, 2)$. Consequently we have that $M[-, y] \neq 0$. Due to Assumption 4, the left side of Equation 5.2 must now become e'_1. That is, $a \cdot M[-, y] = 1$. There will also be an extra 1-element $M[x, y]$ in the border of M.

Now let t'' be the tuple corresponding to $M[-, y + n']$ in the third slice of M. Suppose $t'' \in P_k(C_{core}, 3)$ and consequently $M[-, y + n'] \neq 0$. We have that $M[-, y + n'] = M[-, y]$ and consequently $a \cdot M[-, y + n'] = 1$. Now removing t' from $P_k(C_{core}, 2)$, and we show by contradiction that $t'' \in P_k(C_{core}, 3)$ cannot be true. Intuitively, because t' is the only missing tuple in the second slice of M, the third slice of M contains no less zero vectors than the second slice of M does, except t''. Because $a \cdot M[-, y + n'] = 1$, the elements of the vector a, which transforms the second slice of M to a zero vector as shown by Equation 5.2, can also transform the third slice of M to a unit vector. This is formally represented as:

$$e'' = \sum_{i=2m'+1}^{3m'} a[i - m']r_i^3 + \sum_{i=m-m'+1}^{m} a[i]r_i^3 \tag{5.5}$$

Subtracting both sides of Equation 5.4 from those of Equation 5.5 we get:

$$e'' = \sum_{i=2m'+1}^{3m'} (a[i - m'] - a[i])r_i^3$$

This implies that C_{core} is compromised by $S \setminus \{C_i\}$. Hence, Assumption 3 is false. Consequently, $t'' \notin C_{core}$.

A similar proof exists for the ith slice of C_c for any $4 \leq i \leq d_k$. However, $M[x, -] \neq 0$ because otherwise we can let a_x be zero and then decrease $| C_{full} \setminus C_{core} |$, contradicting Assumption 4. Hence $M[x, -]$ is a unit vector with the 1-element in the first slice of M. However, this further contradicts assumption 2. That is, no trivial compromise is assumed. Hence we have that $| P_k(C_{full}, 2) \setminus P_k(C_{core}, 2) | = 1$ is false.

Now consider $| P_k(C_{full}, 1) \setminus P_k(C_{core}, 1) |$. Suppose all the assumptions hold and $| P_k(C_{full}, 1) \setminus P_k(C_{core}, 1) | = 0$. Let $t_1, t_2 \in P_k(C_{full}, 2) \setminus P_k(C_{core}, 2)$. Now define $C'_{core} = C_{core} \setminus \{t\} \cup \{t_1\}$, and use M' for $M_{C'_{core}, S}$. From $a \cdot M = e_1$ and assumption 4 we get that $a \cdot M' = e_i$, and $M[-, i]$ corresponds to t_1. This implies that t_1 is non-trivially compromised in $< C'_{core}, S_{all} >$, with $| P_k(C_{full}, 1) \setminus P_k(C'_{core}, 1) | = 1$, which contradicts what we have already proved. Hence, we get $| P_k(C_{full}, 1) \setminus P_k(C_{core}, 1) | \geq 1$. This concludes the justification of our claim.

The justified claim implies that the number of missing tuples in C_{core} increases monotonically with the following:

- The number of aggregation cuboids in S.
- d_i, if there exists $C \in S$ satisfying $t[i] = *$ for any $t \in C$.

Hence $| C_{full} \setminus C_{core} |$ reaches its lower bound when $| S | = 2$, which is equal to $2D_1 + 2D_2 - 9$, as shown in the first part of the current proof - concluding the proof of Theorem 5.7.   □

The results stated in Corollary 5.8 follow from Theorem 5.7 and Lemma 5.6 but have value of their own. The first claim of Corollary 5.8 says that if the ith 1-* aggregation cuboid is essential for any non-trivially compromises, then every slice of the core cuboid on the ith dimension must contain at least one missing tuple. As an example, in the core cuboid shown in Table 5.5, every slice on the two dimensions contains either one or two missing tuples. The second claim of Corollary 5.8 says that any core cuboid that have full slices on $k-1$ of the k dimensions must be safe from non-trivial compromises.

Corollary 5.8 (Non-trivial Compromisability With Full Slices).
In any data cube $< C_{core}, S_{all} >$ with dimensions $D_1, D_2, \ldots, D_k$:

1. *Let $C \in S \subseteq S_1$ and suppose $t[i] = *$ for any $t \in C$, where $i \in [1, k]$ is fixed. If S non-trivially compromises C_{core} but $S \setminus \{C\}$ does not, then $\mid P_i(C_{full}, j) \setminus P_i(C_{core}, j) \mid \geq 1$ for any $1 \leq j \leq d_i$.*
2. *If there exists $S \subset [1, k]$ satisfying $\mid S \mid = k-1$ and for any $i \in S$, there exists $j \in D_i$ such that $\mid P_i(C_{full}, j) \setminus P_i(C_{core}, j) \mid = 0$, then C_{core} cannot be non-trivially compromised by S_{all}.*

Proof: The first claim follows directly from the proof of Theorem 5.7. The second claim then follows from the first claim of Corollary 5.8 taken together with the first claim of Lemma 5.6.   □

As an example of Corollary 5.8, we have stated in Section 5.1 that the second quarter data shown in Table 5.1 is non-compromisable. This is so because the core cuboid, as shown in Table 5.11, contains full slices on any of the two dimensions. Hence it cannot be non-trivially compromised. Moreover, its trivial non-compromisability is straightforward.

	1	2	3	4	*
1	(1,1)	(1,2)	(1,3)	(1,4)	(1,*)
2	(2,1)		(2,3)	(2,4)	(2,*)
3	(3,1)	(3,2)	(3,3)	(3,4)	(3,*)
4	(4,1)	(4,2)	(4,3)	(4,4)	(4,*)
*	(*,1)	(*,2)	(*,3)	(*,4)	(*,*)

Table 5.11. Example of a Data Cube with Full Slices On Every Dimension

5.4 A Three-Tier Inference Control Model

Traditional view of inference control has two tiers, that is, the data set and the queries. The data set is usually modeled as a set of tuples, similar to the core cuboid defined in Section 5.2. A query is evaluated on a subset of the data set, called the *query set* of the query. The query then aggregates (for example, sums) the values of those tuples in the query set. Inference becomes a concern when the values being aggregated are sensitive. Under such a two-tier view, a typical restriction-based inference control mechanism checks a given set of queries for unwanted inferences and answers only those queries that do not compromise the sensitive values.

Inference control based on the two-tier view has some inherent drawbacks. First, allowing ad-hoc queries unnecessarily complicates inference control. Because any subset of a given data set may potentially be the query set of a query, totally 2^n queries with different query sets are possible on a data set containing n tuples. Second, inferences can be obtained with a single query as well as by manipulating multiple queries, as illustrated by the third and fourth quarter data in Table 5.1, respectively. Hence totally 2^{2^n} different sets of queries can be formed on the data set. Such a large number of possibilities partially contributes to the high complexity of most existing inference control mechanisms. In practice, most ad-hoc queries are either meaningless to users or redundant because their results can be derived from other previously answered queries. For example, for SUM queries, at most n queries with different query sets can be formed on a data set of size n before the result of any new query can be derived from the old ones, because the rank of an aggregation matrix with n columns cannot exceed n.

Inference control mechanisms developed under the two-tier view usually have high *on-line* computational complexity. Here on-line computations refer to the computation conducted after queries have been posed to the system, and conversely the *off-line* computation occurs before queries are posed. In the two-tier view of inference control, it is difficult for restriction-based inference control mechanisms to predict how incoming queries will aggregate data. Hence the major part of computational efforts required by inference control mechanisms cannot be started until queries are received. Consequently, the time needed by inference control adds to system response time. This is unacceptable considering the stringent performance requirement of OLAP systems and the high complexity of most inference control mechanisms.

Finally, the dimension hierarchy inherent to most multi-dimensional data sets are ignored by the two-tier view of inference control. This prevents inference control mechanisms from benefiting from those hierarchies. In Table 5.1, the dimension hierarchy composing of month, quarter and year naturally divides the data set into four blocks, shown as the four cross-tabulations. In OLAP systems, most meaningful queries are formed on the basis of those partitions. As an example, a query that sums Alice's commission in January and Bob's commission in August may convey little useful information to OLAP users. Without taking dimension hierarchies into account, inference control mechanisms have to make whole data set their input, even when the query involves only a block in the partition of the data set.

To address the listed issues, we propose a three-tier inference control model consisting of three tiers with three relations in between, as shown in Figure 5.1. The *data tier D* is a set of *tuples*. Both *aggregation tier A* and *query tier Q* are sets of *queries*. We do not consider the details of tuples and queries here, but instead we consider them as elements of sets. The relation R_{QD} is defined as the composition of R_{QA} and R_{AD}. We assume that a suitable definition of *compromisability* has been given. In addition, we enforce three properties on the model as follows.

1. **Three Tiers:**
   a) Data Tier D.
   b) Aggregation Tier A.
   c) Query Tier Q.
2. **Relations Between Tiers:**
   a) $R_{AD} \subseteq A \times D$.
   b) $R_{QA} \subseteq Q \times A$.
   c) $R_{QD} = R_{AD} \circ R_{QA}$.
3. **Properties:**
   a) $|A|$ is polynomial in $|D|$.
   b) D and A can be partitioned into $D_1, D_2, \ldots, D_m$ and $A_1, A_2, \ldots, A_m$, satisfying that $(a, d) \in R_{AD}$ only if $d \in D_i$ and $a \in A_i$ for some $1 \le i \le m$.
   c) A does not compromise D.

Fig. 5.1. Three-Tier Model for Controlling Inferences

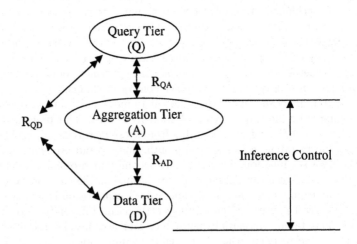

Proposition 5.9 explains how the three-tier model controls inferences. Intuitively, the aggregation set A provides a set of intermediate aggregations that are guaranteed to be safe from compromises. Queries in Q are then answered by deriving results from these intermediate aggregations. The query results will not compromise any tuple in D because they do not convey any information beyond those contained in the aggregation tier A.

Proposition 5.9. *The three-tier model guarantees that Q does not compromise D.*

Proof: For any given set of queries $Q' \subseteq Q$, we have that $R_{QD}(Q') = R_{AD}(R_{QA}(Q'))$ because $R_{QD} = R_{AD} \circ R_{QA}$. Hence Q' does not compromises D if the aggregations given by $R_{QA}(Q')$ do not compromises D. We have that $R_{QA}(Q') \subseteq A$ holds by definition. The third property of the model then guarantees that $R_{QA}(Q')$ does not compromise D.   □

In contrast to traditional two-tier view of inference control, the three-tier model improves the performance of inference control mechanisms in several ways. First, the size of the input to inference control mechanisms is dramatically reduced. Different from the two-tier view, the three-tier view makes aggregation tier A the input of inference control mechanisms. The third property of the three-tier model requires an aggregation tier A to have a size comparable to that of the data tier D. Choosing such an aggregation tier A is possible, because as we have explained, the number of non-redundant aggregations is bounded by the size of the data tier D.

Second, the three-tier model facilitates using a divide-and-conquer approach to further reduce the size of inputs to inference control mechanisms by *localizing* the inference control problem. Due to the second property of the model, for any $1 \leq i \leq m$ we have that $R_{AD}(A_i) \subseteq D_i$ and $R_{AD}(D_i) \subseteq A_i$. Hence for any given set of queries $Q' \subseteq Q$ satisfying $R_{QA}(Q') \subseteq A_i$ for some $1 \leq i \leq m$, the compromisability depends on A_i and D_i only. Intuitively, if a set of queries can be answered using some blocks of the aggregation tier A, then the inference control problem can be localized to these blocks of A and their R_{AD}-related blocks in the data tier D. In practice, partitioning D and A to satisfy the second property is possible because most multi-dimensional data sets have inherent dimension hierarchies.

Finally, the three-tier model shifts the major computational effort required by inference control to off-line processing, thereby reduces on-line performance cost. Composing aggregation tier A by defining R_{AD} to satisfy the three properties of the model is the most computationally expensive task. This task can be processed off-line, before answering any queries. The on-line processing consists of decomposing any given set of queries $Q' \subseteq Q$ by computing $R_{QA}(Q')$. Because most OLAP systems employ pre-computed aggregations for answering queries, this query decomposition mechanism is usually already in place or can be easily implemented. Hence, by decoupling off-line and on-line phases of inference control and pushing computational complexity to the off-line phase, the three-tier model can reduce the delay caused by inference control in answering queries.

Defining R_{QD} as the composition of R_{AD} and R_{QA} may reduce the total number of answerable queries. This restriction reflects the unavoidable trade-off between availability and security. However, the design of aggregation tier A should enable it to convey as much useful information as possible, while not endangering the sensitive information stored in the data tier D. The usefulness of queries usually depends on application settings. For example, in OLAP applications, data cube style aggregations, as modeled in Section 5.2, are the most popular queries users may pose to the system.

5.5 Cardinality-based Inference Control for Data Cubes

In this section we describe inference control algorithms that integrate the cardinality-based compromisability criteria developed in Section 5.3. We then show its correctness and computational complexity, implementation issues, and possible improvements.

5.5.1 Inference Control Algorithm

Our inference control algorithm is based on the three-tier inference control model discussed in Section 5.4. According to the model, inference control is between the data tier and aggregation tier. Hence we shall focus on those two tiers. We briefly address the query tier in Section 5.5.3. Given a data cube $< C_{core}, S_{all} >$, the core cuboid C_{core} constitutes the data tier. A collection of aggregation vectors S_A, to be defined shortly, constitutes the aggregation tier. A tuple $t \in C_{core}$ is R_{AD}-related to an aggregation vector $t_{aggr} \in S_A$ if and only if $t \in Qset(t_{aggr})$.

The definition of S_A is based on the following partition on C_{core}. For $i = 1, 2, \ldots, k$, we divide the ith dimension $[1, d_i]$ into integer intervals $[1, d_i^1], [d_i^1 + 1, d_i^2], \ldots, [d_i^{m_i - 1} + 1, d_i]$, where m_i is fixed for each i. Then we partition C_{core} into $\prod_{l=1}^{k} m_i$ blocks using those intervals. The partition of C_{core} satisfies the property that any two tuples $t, t' \in C_{core}$ are in the same block if and only if their i^{th} elements are in the same block of the ith dimension for all $i = 1, 2, \ldots, k$. In the partition of C_{core}, we regard each block, denoted as C_{core}^s, as the core cuboid of a *sub-data cube* $< C_{core}^s, S_{all}^s >$ (from now on we use symbols with superscripts for sub-data cubes and their components). S_A is the collection of 1-* aggregation vectors with non-empty aggregation sets in all the safe sub-data cubes. Notice that when integrating the aggregation vectors defined in sub-data cubes into S_A, the aggregation set of each aggregation vector remains the same as it is originally defined in the sub-data cube. For example, the data cube in Table 5.1 is partitioned into four sub-data cubes, each represented by a cross-tabulation. The subtotals shown in the table correspond to the 1-* aggregation vectors defined in sub-data cubes, and therefore constitute the members of S_A.

The inference control algorithm $Ctrl\_Inf\_Cube$ shown in Figure 5.2 constructs the aggregation set tier S_A by partitioning the core cuboid C_{core}. The main routine of $Ctrl\_Inf\_Cube$ accepts as input a given data cube $< C_{core}, S_{all} >$ and its k dimensions $D_1, D_2, \ldots, D_k$. For $i = 1, 2, \ldots, k$, a set of $m_i - 1$ integers between 1 and d_i partition the ith dimension $[1, D_i]$ into m_i blocks, and consequently partition C_{core} into $\prod_{i=1}^{k} m_i$ blocks. Each block of C_{core} is then normalized to be a core cuboid C_{core}^s as stated in Definition 5.1, by converting its k dimensions to integer intervals starting from 1. The core cuboid C_{core}^s is then passed to the subroutine $Ctrl\_Inf\_Sub$. The subroutine $Ctrl\_Inf\_Sub$ applies the cardinality-based sufficient conditions given in Section 5.3 to the sub-data cube $< C_{core}^s, S_{all}^s >$, in order to determine its compromisability. The 1-* aggregation vectors with non-empty aggregation sets in those non-compromisable sub-data cubes are returned to the main routine, and collectively constitute the aggregation tier.

As an example, suppose we use a core cuboid similar to Table 5.1 as the input of the algorithm $Ctrl\_Inf\_Cube$, with each quarter as a block. The subroutine $Ctrl\_Inf\_Sub$ conducts five tests consecutively for each such block. Because the first block corresponds to a full core cuboid, the second test succeeds. Hence the subroutine returns all the 1-* aggregation vectors as its output. The second block has full slices on both dimensions, and hence the fifth test for full slices succeeds with all the 1-* aggregation vectors returned. The third block is determined by the third test as trivially compromised, so nothing is returned for this block. Finally the fourth block fails all the five tests and nothing is returned, indicating possible inferences existing in the block.

5.5.2 Correctness and Time Complexity

Now we prove the correctness of algorithm $Ctrl\_Inf\_Cube$. More specifically, we show that the aggregation tier constructed by the algorithm satisfies the first and second properties of the model discussed in Section 5.4. The last property holds trivially. The first property, namely, $| S_A |$ being a polynomial in $| C_{core} |$ is justified in Proposition 5.10.

Proposition 5.10. S_A constructed in the algorithm Ctrl_Inf_Cube satisfies: $| S_A |= O(| C_{core} |)$.

Proof: Let $n =| C_{core} |$. The 1-* aggregation matrix M_1^s of any sub-data cube $< C_{core}^s, S_{all}^s >$ has $n^s =| C_{core}^s |$ non-zero columns. Hence, M_1^s has $(n^s \cdot k)$ many 1-elements, implying at most $(n^s \cdot k)$ non-zero rows in M_1^s. Therefore, the set of 1-* aggregation vectors with non-empty aggregation sets has a cardinality no bigger than $(n^s \cdot k)$, that is, $| S_A^s |\leq n^s \cdot k$. We thus have $| S_A |\leq k \cdot \sum n^s = O(n)$, assuming k is constant compared to n. $\qquad \square$

Fig. 5.2. The algorithm of inference control in data cube

Algorithm *Ctrl_Inf_Cube*
Input: data cube $< C_{core}, S_{all} >$ with dimensions $D_1, D_2, \ldots, D_k$, and integers
$1 < d_i^1 < d_i^2 \ldots < d_i^{m_i-1} < d_i$ for $1 \le i \le k$, where m_i is fixed for each i
and let $d_i^0 = 0$, $d_i^{m_i} = d_i$
Output: a set of aggregation vectors S_A
Method:

    1. Let $S_A = \phi$;

    2. **For each** k dimensional vector v in vector space $\prod_{i=1}^{k}[1, m_i]$

        Let $C_{tmp} = \{t : t \in C_{core}, \forall i \in [1, k] \; t[i] \in [d_i^{v[i]-1} + 1, d_i^{v[i]}]\}$;

        Let $C_{core}^s = \{t : \exists \, t' \in C_{tmp}, \forall i \in [1, k] \; t[i] = t'[i] - d_i^{v[i]-1}\}$;

        Let $S_A^s = CtrlInfSub(\, C_{core}^s \,)$;

        Let $S_A = S_A \cup S_A^s$;

    3. **Return** S_A.

Subroutine *Ctrl_Inf_Sub*
Input: k dimensional core cuboid C_{core}^s
Output: a set of 1-* aggregation vectors if S_1^s does not compromise C_{core}^s, and
      ϕ otherwise
Method:

    1. **If** $\mid C_{core}^s \mid < 2^{k-1} \cdot max(d_1^s, d_2^s, \ldots, d_k^s)$
        Return ϕ;

    2. **If** $\mid C_{core}^s \mid = \mid C_{full}^s \mid$
        Return $\cup_{C \in S_1^s} C$;

    3. **If** C_{core}^s is trivially compromised by S_1^s
        Return ϕ;

    4. **If** $\mid C_{full}^s - C_{core}^s \mid < 2d_l^s + 2d_m^s - 9$ (d_l^s, d_m^s are smallest among d_i^s's)
        Return $\cup_{C \in S_1^s} C$;

    5. **If**   there exists $D \subset [1, k]$ satisfying
        $\mid D \mid = k - 1$ and for any $i \in D$, there exists $j \in [1, d_i^s]$ such that
        $\mid P_i(C_{full}^s, j) \setminus P_i(C_{core}^s, j) \mid = 0$
        Return $\cup_{C \in S_1^s} C$;

    6. **Return** ϕ.

The second property of the model, namely, the ability to partition S_A and C_{core} is satisfied by the partitions constructed in the algorithm *Ctrl_Inf_Cube*. Let t_{aggr}^s be any aggregation vector in sub-data cube $< C_{core}^s, S_{all}^s >$. We have $Qset(t_{aggr}^s) \subseteq C_{core}^s$. Because as stated earlier, in the data cube $< C_{core}, S_{all} >$, $Q(t_{aggr}^s)$ remains the same as it is defined in $< C_{core}^s, S_{all}^s >$. Hence it is also a subset of C_{core}^s. Consequently, a tuple $t \in C_{core}$ is in $Qset(t_{aggr}^s)$ only if $t \in C_{core}^s$. That is, t and t_{aggr}^s are R_{AD} related only if they are in the same sub-data cube $< C_{core}^s, S_{all}^s$.

Proposition 5.11. *The computational complexity of algorithm* Ctrl_Inf_Cube *is* $O(\mid C_{core} \mid)$.

Proof: Let $n = | \ C_{core} \ |$. The main routine *Ctrl_Inf_Cube* partitions C_{core} by evaluating the k elements of each tuple and assigning the tuple to the appropriate block of the partition. This operation has a runtime of $O(nk) = O(n)$. The subroutine *Ctrl_Inf_Sub* is called for each of the $\prod_{i=1}^{k} m_i$ blocks of the partition. For any block with cardinality n^s, we show the complexity of the subroutine to be $O(n^s)$.

First consider the matrix M_1' that contains all non-zero rows and zero columns in M_1^s. From the proof of Proposition 5.10, M_1' has n^s columns, $O(n^s)$ rows and $(n^s \cdot k)$ many 1-elements. Hence M_1' can be populated in $O(n^s)$ time (we only need to populate the 1-elements).

Once M_1' is established, we show that the cardinality-based tests in the subroutine *Ctrl_Inf_Sub* can be done in $O(n^s)$ time. The first, second and fourth tests can be done in constant time because they only need the cardinalities $| \ C_{core}^s \ | = n^s$ and $| \ C_{full}^s \ | = \prod_{i=1}^{k} d_i^s$. The third test for trivial compromisability can be done by counting the 1-elements of M_1' in each row. The complexity is $O(n^s)$ because the total number of 1-* elements is $(n^s \cdot k)$. The last test for full slices requires counting the number of columns of M_1' in each slice along all k dimensions. Hence, the complexity is $k \cdot n^s = O(n^s)$. $\square$

The computational complexity of the algorithm, as stated in Proposition 5.11, is $O(n)$, where n is the cardinality of the core cuboid C_{core}. In contrast, determining compromisability by transforming an m by n aggregation matrix to its RREF has a complexity of $O(m^2 n)$ (and the maximum subset of non-compromisable aggregation vectors cannot be found in polynomial time). Moreover, the complexity of our algorithm is handled by off-line processing, according to the three-tier inference control model.

5.5.3 Implementation Issues

This section discusses various implementation issues. We first discuss how the proposed techniques can be integrated into OLAP systems. We then discuss how recording tuples may help to improve the usability. Finally, we address the update operations and aggregations other than SUM.

5.5.3.1 Integrating Inference Control into OLAP

Using pre-computed aggregations to reduce the response time in answering queries is a common approach in OLAP. OLAP queries are split into sub-queries whose results are computed from materialized aggregations. Our algorithm also uses pre-computed aggregations, only for a different purpose, that is inference control. It is a natural choice to integrate the inference control algorithm with caching mechanisms that already exist in OLAP applications. However, inference control may require modifications to such mechanisms. For example, after splitting a query into sub-queries, one may find that some sub-queries do not correspond to any aggregation in the aggregation tier. A caching mechanism may choose to answer them by computing them from the raw data. However, answering such sub-queries may lead to inferences because the disclosed information goes beyond the aggregation tier. In such a case the query should either be denied or modified in order for them to be answerable from the aggregation tier. For example, in Table 5.1, suppose that a query asks for the total commission of each employee in the first two quarters. This query can be split into two sub-queries corresponding to the subtotals in the first two quarters. The query is safe to answer, because all the required subtotals are in the aggregation tier. Next, suppose another query asks for the total commission of each employee in the first four months. Splitting this query leads to unanswerable sub-queries, because only the data of April is selected by the query. Answering this query discloses all individual commissions in April if the subtotals in the first quarter are previously answered.

The partition on the data tier and the aggregation tier has an important impact on the *usability* of OLAP systems with inference control enforced. Partitioning should be based on dimension hierarchies, so that most useful queries correspond to whole blocks in the partitions. The choice of dimension granularity of the partitioning is also important. Most practical data sets have deep dimension hierarchies composing of many different granularities for each dimension, with the coarser ones at the top of the hierarchy and finer ones at the bottom. Choosing coarser dimensions as the basis for partitioning leads to fewer and larger blocks. Larger blocks cause less answerable queries. In the above example the query for commissions in the first four months cannot be answered because the granularity used in the query (month) is finer than the dimension used to partition the data (quarter). This can be avoided if blocks are formed by months. However, such partitioning does not provide inference control at all. Because of such subtleties, it may be attractive to use a query-driven or dynamic partition. However, varying partitions at run-time causes more online performance overhead and hence is less feasible.

5.5.3.2 Re-ordering Tuples in Unordered Dimensions

In practice, many data cubes have unordered dimensions. That is, the order of values in the domain of those dimensions have no apparent semantics associated with it. For example, in Table 5.1 the dimension employee has no natural ordering. In the core cuboid of a data cube tuples can usually be re-ordered such that their orders in ordered dimensions are not affected. For example, in Table 5.1 assuming the dimension employee is unordered, tuples can be horizontally re-ordered along employee dimension.

Cardinality-based compromisability of data cubes depends on the *density* of each block of the core cuboid. As shown in Section 5.3, full blocks or dense blocks with cardinalities above the upper bound given in Theorem 5.7 cannot be non-trivially compromised. Without losing any useful information, the tuples in a core cuboid can be re-ordered such that partitioning the core cuboid leads to more full blocks and dense blocks. One consequence of this re-ordering is that aggregation tier will contain more safe aggregations leading to better *usability* of the system.

Techniques already exist in increasing the number of dense blocks in data cubes by re-ordering tuples along un-ordered dimensions. For example, the row shuffling algorithm presented in [5] re-orders tuples in the core cuboid, so that the tuples containing similar values are moved closer to each other. We can implement the row shuffling algorithm as a step prior to the algorithm *Ctrl_Inf_Cube*, by applying it to the full core cuboid of data cubes. In [5] the similarity between two tuples is defined as their p-norm distance. To apply the row shuffling algorithm, this similarity definition needs to be revised, such that two tuples are similar if they are both missing, or none of them are. That is, the similarity is based on whether a cell is empty (known by the adversary) or not, instead of on the value in the cell. The reason lies in that the cardinality-based inference control only depends on the number of empty cells and is independent of the specific value in each cell. The algorithm yields outputs desirable to inference control, because tuples in the core cuboid are clustered to form more dense blocks that are likely non-compromisable. Consequently, more answerable aggregations will be included in S_A. Other clustering techniques may also be used for this purpose as long as they do not lose the information contained in the ordering of tuples.

5.5.3.3 Update Operations

Although update operations are less common in OLAP systems than they are in traditional databases, the data in data warehouses need to be modified over time. Typical update operations include inserting or deleting tuples, and modifying the values contained in tuples. Those updates need to be done efficiently to reduce their impact on availability of the system. Three-tier inference control facilitates pre-defined aggregations, which may also need to be updated as underlying data change. However, because we employ off-line processing to compute the aggregations, the update of the aggregations can be handled off-line, causing little online performance overhead.

In the special settings of this chapter, that is SUM-only queries on un-bounded real, the cardinality-based inference control is independent of the sensitive values (inferences do depend on the sensitive values in other settings). Hence, modifying sensitive values usually has no effect on compromisability and can be ignored by inference control mechanisms. For example, changing the commissions in Table 5.1 does not affect the compromisability of the data cube. On the other hand, modifying the non-sensitive values contained in a tuple may affect the compromisability, because the modified tuple may belong to a different block than the original tuple in the partition of the core cuboid. We treat the modification of non-sensitive values contained in a tuple as two separate operations, deletion of the original tuples and insertion of new tuples containing the modified values.

Figure 5.3 and Figure 5.4 show the algorithms for the deletion and insertion of a tuple, respectively. These two update operations are handled similarly, therefore we discuss deletion only. The subroutine *Ctrl_Inf_Delete* in Figure 5.3 updates S_A upon the deletion of a tuple. It first finds the sub-data cube that contains the tuple to be deleted. If the sub-data cube is already compromised before the deletion, then it must remain so after the deletion. Hence in such a case the subroutine *Ctrl_Inf_Delete* returns immediately. If the sub-data cube is not compromised before the deletion, the subroutine *Ctrl_Inf_Sub_Delete* is called to determine the compromisability of the sub-data cube after the deletion of the tuple. The subroutine *Ctrl_Inf_Sub_Delete* reduces a dimension cardinality by one if the corresponding value is contained in the deleted tuple only. The cardinality-based compromisability criteria are then applied to the sub-data cube similarly as in *Ctrl_Inf_Sub*. There is no need to check if the core cuboid is full after deleting a tuple from it. The complexity of the subroutine *Ctrl_Inf_Sub_Delete* is bound by $O(\mid C^s_{core} \mid)$. The complexity can be reduced if we keep the cardinality results computed in the subroutine *Ctrl _Inf_Sub* and *Ctrl_Inf_Sub_Delete*, such as $\mid C^s_{core} \mid$ and $\mid P_i(C^s_{core}, j) \mid$. Although more space is needed to do so, the subroutine *Ctrl_Inf_Sub_Delete* runs in constant time if those results do not need to be re-computed.

5.5.3.4 Aggregation Operators Other Than Sum

Although sum queries compose an important portion of OLAP queries, other aggregation operators such as count, average, max and min are also used in practice. In some applications counts also need to be protected from compromises. Count queries can be treated as sum queries on binary values, when considering the value of each tuple as one, and the value of each missing tuple as zero. It has been shown in [45] that compromisability of queries on binary values has a much higher complexity than the case of real numbers. Hence efficiently controlling inference of counting queries is still an open problem. Because we do not restrict counting queries, inference control of the queries that contain averages becomes equivalent to that of sums. Other aggregation operators exhibiting similar algebraic property with sum may also be handled by our algorithm. Holistic aggregation operators such as median invalidates the partitioning approach adopted by the three-tier model, because they can not be calculated with partial results obtained in each block of the partition. We shall discuss these issues in more details in following chapters.

5.6 Conclusions

This chapter has studied controlling inferences based on the cardinality of empty cells, that is the number of cells known to the adversary. The intuition is that with more prior knowledge an adversary is more likely to succeed in

Fig. 5.3. Deletion of A Tuple

Subroutine *Ctrl_Inf_Delete*
Input: tuple $t \in C_{core}$ to be deleted
Output: a set of aggregation vectors S_A
Method:

    1. Find the sub-data cube C^s_{core} containing t;
    2. **If** $S^s_A \neq \phi$
        Let $S_A = S_A \setminus S^s_A$;
        Let $S^s_A = Ctrl\_Inf\_Sub\_Delete(C^s_{core}, t)$;
        Let $S_A = S_A \cup S^s_A$;
    3. **Let** $C_{core} = C_{core} \setminus \{t\}$;
    4. **Return** S_A.

Subroutine *Ctrl_Inf_Sub_Delete*
Input: tuple t and sub-data cube C^s_{core}
Output: a set of aggregation vectors if S^s_1 does not compromise $C^s_{core} \setminus \{t\}$, and
      ϕ otherwise
Method:

    1. **For each** $i \in [1, k]$
        If $\mid P_i(C^s_{core}, t[i]) \mid = 1$
            $d^s_i = d^s_i - 1$;
    2. **If** $\mid C^s_{core} \mid -1 < 2^{k-1} \cdot max(d^s_1, d^s_2, \ldots, d^s_k)$
        Return ϕ;
    3. **If** $C^s_{core} \setminus \{t\}$ is trivially compromised by S^s_1
        Return ϕ;
    4. **If** $\mid C^s_{full} - C^s_{core} \mid < 2d^s_l + 2d^s_m - 8$ (d^s_l, d^s_m are smallest among d^s_i's)
        Return $\cup_{C \in S^s_1} C$;
    5. **If** there exists $D \subset [1, k]$ satisfying
        $\mid D \mid = k - 1$ and for any $i \in D$, there exists $j \in [1, d^s_i]$ such that
        $\mid P_i(C^s_{full}, j) \setminus P_i(C^s_{core}, j) \mid = 0$
        Return $\cup_{C \in S^s_1} C$;
    6. **Return** ϕ.

---

compromising the data cube, and vice versa. This connection is straightforward for trivial inferences caused by a single aggregation, since the aggregation causes an inference if and only if its aggregation set is singleton. However, such connection is less obvious when no single aggregation may cause an inference but an inference can be achieved by combining multiple aggregations. Nonetheless, our study revealed that such a connection does exist in the latter case. As the first result, we have shown that a full data cube (that is, with no empty cells) can never be compromised using skeleton queries. However, assuming no cells are previously known to the adversary may not be realistic in practice. Hence, to relax this rigid result, we have shown that there is a tight bound on the number of empty cells in order for the data cube to remain

Fig. 5.4. Insertion of A Tuple

Subroutine *Ctrl_Inf_Insert*
Input: tuple $t \in C_{core}$ to be inserted
Output: a set of aggregation vectors S_A
Method:

    1. **If** t should be inserted into the sub-data cube C^s_{core} and $S^s_A = \phi$
        Let $S_A = S_A \setminus S^s_A$;
        Let $S^s_A = Ctrl\_Inf\_Sub\_Insert(\ C^s_{core},\ t\ )$;
        Let $S_A = S_A \cup S^s_A$;
    3. **Let** $C_{core} = C_{core} \cup \{t\}$;
    4. **Return** S_A.

Subroutine *Ctrl_Inf_Sub_Insert*
Input: tuple t and sub-data cube C^s_{core}
Output: a set of aggregation vectors if S^s_1 does not compromise $C^s_{core} \cup \{t\}$, and
      ϕ otherwise
Method:

    1. **For** each $i \in [1, k]$
        If $t[i] \notin [1, d^s_i]$
           $d^s_i = d^s_i + 1$;
    2. **If** $|\ C^s_{core}\ | + 1 < 2^{k-1} \cdot max(d^s_1, d^s_2, \ldots, d^s_k)$
        Return ϕ;
    3. **If** $C^s_{core} \cup \{t\}$ is trivially compromised by S^s_1
        Return ϕ;
    4. **If** $|\ C^s_{full} - C^s_{core}\ | < 2d^s_l + 2d^s_m - 8$ (d^s_l, d^s_m are smallest among d^s_i's)
        Return $\cup_{C \in S^s_1} C$;
    5. **If**   there exists $D \subset [1, k]$ satisfying
        $|\ D\ | = k - 1$ and for any $i \in D$, there exists $j \in [1, d^s_i]$
        such that $|\ P_i(C^s_{full}, j) \cup P_i(C^s_{core}, j)\ | = 0$
        Return $\cup_{C \in S^s_1} C$;
    6. **Return** ϕ.

---

free of inferences. The bound is a function of the cardinality of the two small-est dimensions. This reflects the fact that an inference can be achieved with least number of empty cells if it only involves the two aggregation cuboids formed along these two dimensions. The bound is tight in the sense that any data cube with more than the specified number of empty cells is subject to inferences, and the existence of such inferences can no longer be decided solely based on the cardinality of empty cells. That is, two data cubes may have the same cardinality of empty cells and yet differ in the existence of inferences.

We have observed that most existing studies take a two-tier view of in-ference control, that is data and query. Although this two-tier view may be a natural choice in traditional database systems, we have shown that it may cause high complexity and poor adaptability of inference control methods.

Moreover, it is not suitable for OLAP in that it ignores the rich dimension hierarchies inherent to most OLAP systems. Therefore, we have proposed a three-tier model for simplifying the task of inference control in OLAP. The model introduces an additional tier, namely, the aggregation tier. The aggregation tier acts as a bridge between queries and data. The aggregation tier is designed to meet several requirements. These include a size comparable to the data, being partitionable and free of inferences. Inferences can be efficiently eliminated from the aggregation tier due to such properties. No inference is possible as long as the results to queries are computed using the aggregation tier. Based on the model, we have devised inference control algorithms by integrating the cardinality-based sufficient conditions. We have also discussed various implementation issues of the proposed algorithms. We have shown that the proposed methods can be implemented in OLAP systems by employing existing techniques. We have shown that by reordering values in the unordered dimensions a data cube can be transformed to one with denser blocks, and hence the usability of an OLAP system can be improved due to more answerable blocks. We have studied how to deal with update operations in OLAP systems.

6

Parity-based Inference Control for Range Queries

6.1 Introduction

In the previous chapter, we have studied cardinality-based inference control method. However, two limitations of the proposed method motivate us to investigate other alternatives. First, the method can only deal with skeleton queries, which correspond to complete rows or columns in a cuboid. The method is not applicable to non-skeleton queries that aggregate partial rows or columns. Second, the cardinality-based conditions are sufficient but not necessary, which mean that we cannot tell whether a data cube can be compromised by inferences once the number of its empty cells is greater than the upper bound. These cause the proposed methods to have only limited power in controlling inferences.

In this chapter, we aim to remove the above limitations. We study multi-dimensional range (MDR) queries, which is known as an important class of decision support query in OLAP (On-line Analytical Processing) systems [41]. Inference control for skeleton queries is a special case of that for MDR queries since skeleton queries in a data cube can be regarded as a special collection of MDR queries. As shown in Chapter 4, although MDR queries are intended for analysts to generalize data and to discover statistical trends and patterns, they may actually be used to infer protected sensitive values and leading to the breach of privacy.

A critical observation in this chapter is that restricting users to even MDR queries, that is MDR queries aggregating even number of values, can make inferences significantly more difficult. The reason is that even number is closed under addition and subtraction, and an inference targets at exactly one value (one is an odd number). Inferences combine SUM queries by employing the set union or set difference operations, which correspond to addition and subtraction operation, respectively. Therefore, it is not straightforward to derive a single value by combining even MDR queries. We assume the restriction can be enforced by access control mechanisms existing in OLAP systems.

However, Chapter 4 has shown that inferences remain possible under the restriction of even MDR queries, although they require combining queries in a more sophisticated way. To detect and remove such inferences, existing inference control methods proposed for general-purpose databases can certainly be applied. For example, we can apply the Audit Expert to check whether requested queries cause inferences (Chapter 3 gives a brief review of Audit Expert). However, we shall see that applying existing inference control methods to the special case of even MDR queries yields no better result in terms of complexity and usability. As pointed out by Chin, *one obvious approach to bring the complexity to a practical level is to include restrictions on user's queries, such that only statistically meaningful queries can be specified*. We strive to find more efficient inference control methods under the restriction of even MDR queries.

The contributions of this chapter are as follows. First, we propose the concept of *parity-based* inference control. Based on the above-mentioned intuition, we start by restricting users to even MDR queries that sum even number of sensitive values. This restriction renders inferences more difficult and places us in a better position in defending against inferences. Second, we show that the collection of all even MDR queries is free of inferences, if and only if a special collection of sum-two queries (that is, the summation of exactly two values) is so. Finding such a collection of sum-two queries takes time $O(mn)$, and determining whether it causes inferences takes time $O(m+n)$, for m MDR queries over n values. This result thus leads to an inference control method with the computational complexity $O(mn)$, which is an improvement to the best known result of $O(m^2 n)$ of Audit Expert.

Third, we show that in addition to answering even MDR queries, no MDR query involving odd number of values can be answered without causing inferences. However, for any such *odd* MDR query, we can always find a small number of even MDR queries whose union differs from the odd MDR query by exactly one value. The odd MDR query can thus be approximately answered using these even MDR queries. We study how to detect inferences for Non-MDR queries in linear time in the number of values involved by the queries. We also study the case where the collection of all even MDR queries does cause inferences. We show how to find large inference-free subsets of the collection. Finally, we show that the proposed methods can be integrated on the basis of a three-tier inference control model proposed in the previous chapter.

The rest of the chapter is organized as follows. Section 6.2 gives motivating examples and defines our notations. Section 6.3 shows that directly applying existing inference control methods to MDR queries may not be desirable. Section 6.4 studies the parity-based inference control method. Section 6.5 discusses how to integrate the results in a three-tier inference control model. Section 6.6 concludes the chapter.

6.2 Preliminaries

We give a running example in Section 6.2.1 to motivate further studies. We then describe our notations in Section 6.2.2.

6.2.1 Motivating Examples

Table 6.1 depicts a fictitious core cuboid that represents salary adjustments of four employees in two consecutive years. Assume the salary adjustments are sensitive and should be kept secret. In the example, the empty cells denote the fact that the employee's salary is not adjusted in the year, which is known to adversaries. More generally, the empty cell models the values previously known through outbound channels. Suppose a third-party analyst Mallory is invited to analyze the above data set. Considering that Mallory may later misuse the information about individuals and consequently causes privacy issues, she is not supposed to know each employee's salary adjustment. Access control mechanisms will thus deny any queries about an employee's salary adjustment in a year.

	Alice	Bob	Mary	Jim
2002	1000	500	-2000	
2003		1500	-500	1000

Table 6.1. An Example of Sensitive Data Set and Inferences

However, Mallory's analyzing tasks may require her to know the summation of a range of values with similar characteristics, such as each employee's total salary adjustments in the two years (each column in Table 6.1) or the total salary adjustments in a year (each row). Intuitively, those values are inside a *box*, which can be represented by any of its longest *diagonals*. For example, [(*Alice*, 2002), (*Alice*, 2003)] stands for the first column of the table and [(*Alice*, 2002), (*Bob*, 2003)] for the first two columns. A query asking for the summation of values in a range is called a *multi-dimensional range* SUM query (or simply MDR query).

Although access control will prevent Mallory from directly asking for a salary adjustment, Mallory can easily get around the restriction by asking MDR queries. For example, the MDR query [(*Alice*, 2002), (*Alice*, 2003)] gives Alice's adjustment in 2002, because the query sums a single value. As another example, the difference between the answers to [(*Bob*, 2002), (*Mary*, 2002)] and [(*Alice*, 2002), (*Mary*, 2002)] yields the same result. Mallory can combine any answered MDR queries for an inference, whereas inference control must prevent any such possibility.

The key observation from above examples is that at least one of the queries asks for the summation of odd number of values. Considering the fact that even number is closed under addition and subtraction, it would be more difficult to infer one (which is an odd number) value if only *even* MDR queries are allowed. For example in Table 6.1, inferences may no longer be straightforward if only even MDR queries are to be asked. We shall call the restriction as *parity-based inference control* henceforth.

Nonetheless, more sophisticated inferences are still possible using only even MDR queries. Table 6.2 depicts five even MDR queries and their answers. The first query sums all six values and the remaining four queries each sum two values. Mallory then adds the answers to the last four queries (2500) and subtracts from the result the answer to the first query (1500). Dividing the result of the subtraction (1000) by two gives Bob's adjustment in 2002 (500).

Ranges	Answer
$[(Alice, 2002), (Jim, 2003)]$	1500
$[(Alice, 2002), (Bob, 2002)]$	1500
$[(Bob, 2002), (Mary, 2002)]$	−1500
$[(Bob, 2002), (Bob, 2003)]$	2000
$[(Mary, 2003), (Jim, 2003)]$	500

Table 6.2. An Example of Even MDR Queries.

The rest of the chapter answers following questions naturally motivated by the above example:

1. How can we efficiently determine whether the collection of all even MDR queries causes inferences?
2. In addition to even MDR queries, what else can be answered without causing inferences?
3. If the collection of even MDR queries does cause inferences, how can we find its large subsets that are inference-free?

6.2.2 Definitions

We use $\mathbb{I}, \mathbb{R}, \mathbb{I}^k, \mathbb{R}^k, \mathbb{R}^{m \times n}$ to denote the set of integers, reals, k-dimensional integer vectors, k-dimensional real vectors and m by n real matrices, respectively. For any $u, v, t \in \mathbb{R}^k$, we write $u \leq v$ and $t \in [u, v]$ to mean that $u[i] \leq v[i]$ and $min\{u[i], v[i]\} \leq t[i] \leq max\{u[i], v[i]\}$ hold for all $1 \leq i \leq k$, respectively. We use t for the singleton set $\{t\}$ whenever clear from the context.

Definition 6.1 formalizes *domain, data set* and *tuple*. The domain is the Cartesian product of closed integer intervals. A core cuboid is any subset of the domain. A tuple is any vector in the domain, and a tuple *missing* from the core cuboid is any vector in the complement of the core cuboid with respect to the domain. In our study, the missing tuples represent values that adversaries have learned through outbound channels.

Definition 6.1 (Core Cuboid). *For any* $d \in \mathbb{I}^k$, *use* $\mathcal{F}(d)$ *to denote the Cartesian product* $\Pi_{i=1}^k [1, d[i]]$. *We say* $F = \mathcal{F}(d)$ *is the* **domain,** *any* $C \subseteq F$ *a* **data set,** *any* $t \in F$ *a* **tuple,** *and any* $t \in F \setminus C$ *a tuple* **missing** *from* C.

Example 6.2. Table 6.3 gives an example of the core cuboid containing six tuples. The subscripts will be used to denote the correspondence between tuples and columns of the incidence matrix.

The Core Cuboid C			
1	2	3	4
1 $(1,1)_1$ $(1,2)_2$ $(1,3)_3$			
2 $\quad\quad\quad$ $(2,2)_4$ $(2,3)_5$ $(2,4)_6$			

Table 6.3. An Example of Core Cuboid

Definition 6.3 formalizes *arbitrary query*, *MDR query* and *sum-two query*. An arbitrary query is any non-empty subset of the given core cuboid. Intuitively, we view an MDR query as an axis-parallel box. An MDR query $q^*(u, v)$ is thus a non-empty subset of the core cuboid that includes all and only those tuples *bounded* by the two given (missing) tuples u and v (although an MDR query may be denoted by up to k pair of tuples if the core cuboid is k dimensional, this lack of uniqueness in the notation will not affect our study). A sum-two query is simply a pair of tuples. We use $\mathcal{Q}_d$ and $\mathcal{Q}_t$ for the set of all MDR queries and all sum-two queries, respectively.

Definition 6.3 (Arbitrary Query, MDR Query, and Sum-two Query). *Given any domain F and core cuboid $C \subseteq F$,*

1. *Define functions*
   a) $q^*(.) : F \times F \to 2^C$ *as* $q^*(u, v) = \{t : t \in C, t \in [u, v]\}$.
   b) $q^2(.) : C \times C \to 2^C$ *as* $q^2(u, v) = \{u, v\}$ *if* $u \neq v$, *and* ϕ *otherwise.*
2. *Use $\mathcal{Q}_d(C)$ and $\mathcal{Q}_t(C)$ (or simply $\mathcal{Q}_d$ and $\mathcal{Q}_t$ when C is clear from context) for $\{q^*(u, v) : q^*(u, v) \neq \phi\}$ and $\{q^2(u, v) : q^2(u, v) \neq \phi\}$, respectively.*
3. *We call any non-empty subset of C an* **arbitrary query,** *any $q^*(u, v) \in \mathcal{Q}_d$ an* **MDR query** *(or simply a query), and any $q^2(u, v) \in \mathcal{Q}_t$ a* **sumtwo query.**

Example 6.4. Table 6.4 gives an example of five MDR queries.

Definition 6.5 formalizes the concept of *compromisability*. Because an arbitrary query is a set of tuples, any given collection of arbitrary queries can be characterized by the incidence matrix of the set system formed by the

A Set of MDR Queries:$\mathcal{S}$

$q^*((1,1),(2,4))$	$\{(1,1),(1,2),(1,3),(2,2),(2,3),(2,4)\}$
$q^*((1,1),(1,2))$	$\{(1,1),(1,2)\}$
$q^*((1,2),(1,3))$	$\{(1,2),(1,3)\}$
$q^*((1,2),(2,2))$	$\{(1,2),(2,2)\}$
$q^*((2,3),(2,4))$	$\{(2,3),(2,4)\}$

Table 6.4. An Example of MDR Queries

core cuboid and the collection of arbitrary queries. Given two collections of arbitrary queries $\mathcal{S}_1$, $\mathcal{S}_2$, and the incidence matrices $\mathcal{M}(\mathcal{S}_1)$, $\mathcal{M}(\mathcal{S}_2)$, we say $\mathcal{S}_1$ is *derivable* from $\mathcal{S}_2$ if the row vectors of $\mathcal{M}(\mathcal{S}_1)$ can be represented as the linear combination of those of $\mathcal{M}(\mathcal{S}_2)$. Intuitively, this means the former can be computed from the latter and hence discloses less information than the latter does. We say $\mathcal{S}_1$ *compromises* a tuple t in the core cuboid, if the singleton set of queries $\{\{t\}\}$ (notice $\{t\}$ is an arbitrary query) is derivable from $\mathcal{S}_1$, and $\mathcal{S}_1$ is *safe* if it compromises no tuple in the core cuboid. We say any two set of arbitrary queries are *equivalent* if they are mutually derivable. Example 6.6 illustrates the concepts we just defined.

Definition 6.5 (Compromisability). *Given any domain F, core cuboid $C \subseteq F$, and set of arbitrary queries $\mathcal{S}$, use $\mathcal{M}(\mathcal{S})$ for the incidence matrix of the set system formed by C and $\mathcal{S}$ (that is, $\mathcal{M}(\mathcal{S})[i,j] = 1$ if the ith arbitrary query in $\mathcal{S}$ contains the jth tuple in C, and $\mathcal{M}(\mathcal{S})[i,j] = 0$ otherwise), we say that*

1. *$\mathcal{S}_1$ is* **derivable** *from $\mathcal{S}_2$, denoted as $\mathcal{S}_1 \preceq_d \mathcal{S}_2$, if there exists $M \in \mathbb{R}^{|\mathcal{S}_1| \times |\mathcal{S}_2|}$ such that $\mathcal{M}(\mathcal{S}_1) = M \cdot \mathcal{M}(\mathcal{S}_2)$ holds, where $\mathcal{S}_1$ and $\mathcal{S}_2$ are sets of arbitrary queries.*
2. *$\mathcal{S}_1$* **compromises** *$t \in C$ if $t \preceq_d \mathcal{S}_1$ (we write t for $\{\{t\}\}$), and $\mathcal{S}_1$ is* **safe** *if it compromises no $t \in C$.*
3. *$\mathcal{S}_1$ is* **equivalent** *to $\mathcal{S}_2$, denoted as $\mathcal{S}_1 \equiv_d \mathcal{S}_2$, if $\mathcal{S}_1 \preceq_d \mathcal{S}_2$ and $\mathcal{S}_2 \preceq_d \mathcal{S}_1$*

Example 6.6. Table 6.5 gives an example of the compromisability. The equation shows that the five queries given in Table 6.4 compromise a tuple $(1,2)$ in the core cuboid given in 6.3. The left side of the equation is the incidence matrix of the query $\{(1,2)\}$, and the right side is a linear combination of the row vectors in the incidence matrix of the MDR queries $\mathcal{S}$. Notice that Table 6.5 characterizes exactly the same example given in Table 6.1 and Table 6.2.

The relation $\equiv_d$ of Definition 6.5 is an equivalence relation on the family of all sets of arbitrary queries, because it is clearly reflexive, symmetric and transitive. Hence, if any two sets of arbitrary queries are equivalent, then one is safe if and only if the other is. This observation is the basis for our discussions in Section 6.4 about reducing the compromisability of even MDR queries to that of sum-two queries.

$(1, 2) \preceq_d S$ because

$$[0, 1, 0, 0, 0, 0] = [-\tfrac{1}{2}, \tfrac{1}{2}, \tfrac{1}{2}, \tfrac{1}{2}, \tfrac{1}{2}] \cdot \begin{pmatrix} 1\,1\,1\,1\,1\,1 \\ 1\,1\,0\,0\,0\,0 \\ 0\,1\,1\,0\,0\,0 \\ 0\,1\,0\,1\,0\,0 \\ 0\,0\,0\,0\,1\,1 \end{pmatrix}$$

Table 6.5. An Example of Compromisability.

6.3 Applying Existing Methods to MDR Queries

This section studies the feasibility of applying existing restriction-based inference control methods to MDR queries. First, Section 6.3.1 considers three methods, namely, *Query set size control, overlap size control* and *Audit Expert*. Second, Section 6.3.2 studies the problem of finding maximal safe subsets of unsafe MDR queries.

6.3.1 Query Set Size Control, Overlap Size Control and Audit Expert

Query Set Size Control

As discussed in Chapter 3, *Query Set Size Control* prohibits users from asking queries whose query sets have cardinalities smaller than some pre-determined threshold n_t [33]. For arbitrary queries, query set size control can be easily subverted by asking two legitimate queries whose intersection yields a prohibited one, a mechanism known as the *tracker* in statistical databases (see Chapter 3 for a brief review of trackers). It is shown that finding a tracker for arbitrary queries is possible even when n_t is about half of the cardinality of the core cuboid. At first glance, trackers may seem to be more difficult to find when users are restricted to MDR queries. However, the range query tracker attack discussed in Chapter 4 has shown that in most cases a tracker consisted of MDR queries can be found to derive any given small MDR query. To make this chapter self-contained, we rephrase the result in Proposition 6.7 and illustrates it via a simple one-dimensional case in Example 6.8.

Proposition 6.7. *Given $d \in \mathbb{R}^k$, $F = \mathcal{F}(d)$ and $C \subseteq F$, let $n_t = \lfloor \frac{|C|}{3^k} \rfloor$. For any $q^\star(u_a, v_a) \in \mathcal{Q}_d$ satisfying $| q^\star(u_a, v_a) | < n_t$, we have that $q^\star(u_a, v_a) \preceq_d \{q^\star(u, v) : | q^\star(u, v) | \geq n_t\}$.*

Proof: Let $S = \{q^\star(u, v) : \forall i \in [1, k], (u[i] = 1, v[i] = u_a[i] - 1) \vee (u[i] = u_a[i], v[i] = v_a[i]) \vee (u_a[i] = v_a[i] + 1, v_a[i] = d[i])\}$. We have that $C = \bigcup_{\forall q \in S} q$, and $q^\star(u, v) \cap q^\star(u_a, v_a) = \phi$ holds for any $q^\star(u, v) \in S \setminus q^\star(u_a, v_a)$. Because $| S | = 3^k$, there must exist $q^\star(u_b, v_b) \in S$ such that $q^\star(u_b, v_b) \geq \frac{|C|}{n_t}$. Next we define

1. u_c, v_c satisfying that $u_c[i] = min\{u_a[i], u_b[i], v_b[i]\}$, and $v_c[i] = max\{u_b[i], v_a[i], v_b[i]\}$ for all $1 \le i \le k$.
2. For all $1 \le i \le k$, u_i satisfying that $u_i[i] = u_a[i]$, $v_i[i] = v_a[i]$, and for each fixed i, $u_i[j] = u_c[i]$ and $v_i[j] = v_c[i]$) for any $j \ne i$.

Then we have that

$$q^\star(u_a, v_a) = q^\star(u_c, v_c) \setminus \bigcup_{i=1}^{k}(q^\star(u_i, v_i) \setminus q^\star(u_b, v_b)) \setminus q^\star(u_b, v_b)$$

Let $r = (1, -1, -1, \ldots, -1, k-1) \in \mathbb{R}^{k+2}$, then we have

$$\mathcal{M}(q^\star(u_a, v_a)) = r \cdot$$

$$(\mathcal{M}(q^\star(u_c, v_c)), \mathcal{M}(q^\star(u_1, v_1)), \mathcal{M}(q^\star(u_2, v_2)), \ldots, \mathcal{M}(q^\star(u_k, v_k)), \mathcal{M}(q^\star(u_b, v_b)))^T$$

Moreover, $q^\star(u_b, v_b) \subseteq q^\star(u_c, v_c)$ and $q^\star(u_b, v_b) \subseteq q^\star(u_i, v_i)$ for all $1 \le i \le k$ hold. Hence we have that $\mid q^\star(u_c, v_c) \mid \ge n_t$ and $\mid q^\star(u_i, v_i) \mid \ge n_t$ holds for all $1 \le i \le k$.   □

Example 6.8. When $k = 1$ the core cuboid contains n integers between one and n. Given any $q^\star(u, v)$ satisfying $0 < v - u < \frac{n}{3}$, we have that either $\mid q^\star(0, u-1) \mid \ge \frac{n}{3}$ or $\mid q^\star(v+1, d) \mid \ge \frac{n}{3}$ holds. Without loss of generality, if $\mid q^\star(0, u-1) \mid \ge \frac{n}{3}$ then we have that $q^\star(u, v) = q^\star(0, v) \setminus q^\star(0, u-1)$ holds, and $\mid q^\star(0, v) \mid \ge \frac{n}{3}$ and $\mid q^\star(0, u-1) \mid \ge \frac{n}{3}$ are both true.

Overlap Size Control

As discussed in Chapter 3, the *Overlap Size Control* prevents users from asking queries whose query sets have large intersections [29]. More specifically, any answerable query must have a cardinality of at least n, and the intersection of any two queries is required to be no larger than r. In order to compromise any tuple t, one must first ask one query $q \ni t$ and subsequently $(n-1)/r$ or more queries to form the complement of t with respect to q. Therefore, no inference is possible if less than $(n-1)/r + 1$ queries are answered (the converse is not true). Proposition 6.9 shows that this bound is not improved (increased) by restricting users to MDR queries. Therefore, applying the overlap size control to MDR queries still renders most of the queries unanswerable. Example 6.10 illustrates how to compromise a tuple under this control.

Proposition 6.9. *Given any* $d \in \mathbb{R}^k$, $F = \mathcal{F}(d)$ *and* $C \subseteq F$, *for any* $q^\star(u, v)$ *satisfying* $\mid \{i : u[i] \ne v[i]\} \mid < k$ *and any* $t \in q^\star(u, v)$, *there exists an* $S \subseteq Q_d$ *such that*

$$t = q^\star(u, v) \setminus \bigcup_{q \in S} q \cap q^\star(u, v)$$

Moreover, for all $q \in S$ *we have that* $\mid q \cap q^\star(u, v) \mid = 1$.

Proof: Suppose tuples in $q^*(u, v)$ are in dictionary order and use t_i for the ith tuple. Without loss of generality suppose $t = t_1$ and $u[1] = v[1]$. For all $1 < i \leq | q^*(u, v) | -1$ let $u_i[1] = 1$, $v_i[1] = d[1]$, and for each fixed i, $u_i[j] = v_i[j] = t_i[j]$ for all $j > 1$. Let $S = \{q^*(u_i, v_i)\}$. Because $q^*(u_i, v_i) \cap q^*(u, v) = t_i$ we have

$$t = q^*(u, v) \setminus (\bigcup_{q \in S} q \cap q^*(u, v))$$

□

Example 6.10. Consider the core cuboid given in Table 6.3. To compromise $(1, 1)$, one first asks $q^*((1, 1), (1, 3))$ that contains $(1, 1)$. Then to form the complement of $(1, 1)$ with respect to $q^*((1, 1), (1, 3))$, queries $q^*((1, 2), (2, 2))$ and $q^*((1, 3), (2, 3))$ are asked. Asking one more query $q^*((2, 2), (2, 3))$ would be sufficient for the intended compromise.

Audit Expert

As discussed in Chapter 3, Audit Expert is based on a necessary and sufficient condition for safe arbitrary queries. By regarding tuples and queries as a set system, the queries are safe iff the incidence matrix of the set system contains one or more unit row vector in its reduced row echelon form (RREF). The elementary row transformation used to obtain the RREF of a m by n matrix has the complexity $O(m^2 n)$. Using this condition *on-line* (after queries arrive) may incur unacceptable delay in answering queries, because m and n can be very large in practice. Moreover, the method requires tracking the entire history of queries asked by each user. Another way to employ the condition is to first determine what queries are to be allowed off-line [9]. Although this condition applies to MDR queries, it is not efficient because it does not take into consideration the inherent redundancy among MDR queries, as illustrated by Example 6.11. We shall further discuss this issue later in Section 6.4.

Example 6.11. In Table 6.5 we can easily observe redundancy among the MDR queries. For example, $q^*((1, 1), (2, 2))$ is derivable from $q^*((1, 1), (2, 1))$ and $q^*((1, 2), (2, 2))$. Hence if $q^*((1, 1), (2, 1))$ and $q^*((1, 2), (2, 2))$ are both safe then $q^*((1, 1), (2, 2))$ must be safe. The converse is not true, that is, $q^*((1, 1), (2, 2))$ is safe but $q^*((1, 1), (2, 1)) = \{(1, 1)\}$ is not.

6.3.2 Finding Maximal Safe Subsets of Unsafe MDR Queries

When a collection of queries is not safe, it is desirable to find a maximum safe subset of the collection. Finding a maximum safe subset of unsafe arbitrary queries (the MQ problem) or sum-two queries (the RMQ problem) have both been shown as computationally infeasible, as discussed in Chapter 3. A natural question is whether restricting users to MDR queries makes the problem feasible. Unfortunately, Theorem 6.12 shows this is not the case, because finding a maximum safe subset of MDR queries, namely, the *MDQ problem* is also NP-hard. The result is based on the fact that given any set of sum-two queries, we can always find a set of MDR queries such that the maximum safe subset of the former gives the maximum safe subset of the latter in polynomial time.

Theorem 6.12. *The MDQ problem is NP-hard.*

Proof: Chin et. al show the NP hardness of the *RMQ problem* [16]. We show that every instance of the RMQ problem is polynomially reduciable to an instance of the MDQ problem.

Suppose an instance of the RMQ problem is given as

1. The core cuboid $C_0 = \{t_1, t_2, \ldots, t_n\}$.
2. The set of sum-two queries $S_0 = \{q^2(t_{i_1}, t_{j_1}), q^2(t_{i_2}, t_{j_2}), \ldots, q^2(t_{i_m}, t_{j_m})\}$, where $1 \leq i_x \leq n$ and $1 \leq j_x \leq n$ for all $1 \leq x \leq m$.

We construct an instance of the MDQ problem as

1. $d = (2, 2, \ldots, 2) \in \mathbb{R}^m$.
2. The core cuboid $C_1 = \{s_1, s_2, \ldots, s_n\}$ satisfying that $s_{i_x}[x] = s_{j_x}[x] = 1$ for all $1 \leq x \leq m$, and for each fixed x, $s_y[x] = 2$ for all $y \neq i_x$ and $y \neq j_x$.
3. The set of MDR queries $S_1 = \{q^*(u_1, v_1), q^*(u_2, v_2), \ldots, q^*(u_m, v_m)\}$, where for all $1 \leq i \leq m$, $u_i[i] = v_i[i] = 1$, and for each fixed i, $u_j[i] = 1$, $v_j[i] = 2$ for all $j \neq i$.

We have that $q^*(u_x, v_x) = \{s_{i_x}, s_{j_x}\}$ for all $1 \leq x \leq m$. Hence for any $I \subseteq [1, m]$ we have that $\{q^2(t_{i_x}, t_{j_x}) : x \in I\}$ is safe if and only if $\{q^*(u_x, v_x) : x \in I\}$ is safe. Consequently, the maximum safe subset of S_1 gives the maximum safe subset of S_0.   □

Knowing that the MDQ problem is NP-hard, one may want to place further restrictions on queries such that the complexity of inference control can be reduced. We consider restricting users to data cubes, which is a special class of MDR queries. In Definition 6.13, we rephrase the concept of data cubes using MDR queries and demonstrate those definitions in Example 6.14. Corollary 6.15 then shows that the MDQ problem remains NP-hard for such special MDR queries.

Definition 6.13 (Data Cube). *Given $d \in \mathbb{R}^k$, $F = \mathcal{F}(d)$ and $C \subseteq F$,*

1. *A skeleton query is any $q^*(u, v)$ satisfying the condition that $u[i] \neq v[i]$ implies $u[i] = 1$ and $v[i] = d[i]$ for all $1 \leq i \leq k$. A skeleton query $q^*(u, v)$ is called a j-star query $(1 \leq j \leq k)$ if $\mid \{i : i \in [1, k], u[i] \neq v[i]\} \mid = j$.*
2. *For any non-empty $J \subseteq [1, k]$, let $j = \mid J \mid$. The set Q of j-star queries satisfying that $q^*(u, v) \in Q$ iff $\{i : i \in [1, k], u[i] \neq v[i]\} = J$ is called a (j-star) cuboid.*
3. *The data cube is the union of all cuboids (or equivalently all skeleton queries).*

Example 6.14. In Table 6.3, we can view $\{q^*((1,1),(1,4)),q^*((2,1),(2,4))\}$ and $\{q^*((1,1),(2,1)),q^*((1,2),(2,2)),q^*((1,3),(2,3)),q^*((1,4),(2,4))\}$ as two 1-star cuboids. The only 2-star cuboid is a singleton set $\{q^*((1,1),(2,4))\}$. The data cube is the union of the three cuboids, which also includes all skeleton queries.

Corollary 6.15. *The problem MDQ remains NP-hard under the restriction that the given set of MDR queries must be:*

1. *A set of skeleton queries*
2. *The union of some cuboids*
3. *A data cube*

Proof: Suppose the instance of the RMQ problem is given same as in the proof of Theorem 6.12.

1. Because the set of MDR queries constructed in the proof of Theorem 6.12 are indeed skeleton queries.
2. We first construct an instance of the MDQ problem under the restriction that the set of MDR queries is the union of some cuboids. The core cuboid C_1 and the set of MDR queries S_1 are given as follows.
   a) $d = (n-1, n-1, \ldots, n-1) \in \mathbb{R}^m$.
   b) The core cuboid $C_1 = \{s_1, s_2, \ldots, s_m\}$, where for all $1 \le x \le m$, $s_{i_x}[x] = s_{j_x}[x] = 1$ and $1 < s_y[i] < s_z[i]$ for any $y < z$ and $y, z \in [1, n] \setminus \{i_x, i_y\}$.
   c) $S_t = \{q^*(u_1, v_1), q^*(u_2, v_2), \ldots, q^*(u_m, v_m)\}$, where for all $1 \le i \le m$, $u_i[i] = v_i[i] = 1$, and for each fixed i, $u_j[i] = 1, v_j[i] = n-1$ for all $j \ne i$.
   d) $S_1 = \bigcup_{i=1}^m Q_i$, where each Q_i is the cuboid containing $q^*(u_i, v_i)$.
   For any $q \in \bigcup_{i=1}^m Q_i \setminus S_t$, we have that $\mid q \mid = 1$. Hence, trivially the maximal safe subset of S_1 is a subset of S_t. For any $1 \le x \le m$ we have that $q^*(u_x, v_x) = \{s_{i_x}, s_{j_x}\}$. Therefore, for any $I \subseteq [1, m]$, $\{q^2(t_{i_x}, t_{j_x}) : x \in I\}$ is safe if and only if $\{q^*(u_x, v_x) : x \in I\}$ is safe. Consequently the maximal safe subset of S_1 gives the maximal safe subset of S_0.
3. We modify this instance of the MDQ problem to the third restriction as follows.
   a) $d = (n+1, n+1, \ldots, n+1) \in \mathbb{R}^m$.
   b) $C_1 = \{s_1, s_2, \ldots, s_n, s_{n+1}, s_{n+2}\}$, where $s_{n+1} = (n, n, \ldots, n)$ and $s_{n+2} = (n+1, n+1, \ldots, n+1)$.
   c) $S_t = \{q^*(u_1, v_1), q^*(u_2, v_2), \ldots, q^*(u_m, v_m)\}$, where for all $1 \le i \le m$, $u_i[i] = v_i[i] = 1$ and for each fixed i, $u_j[i] = 1, v_j[i] = n+1$ for all $j \ne i$.
   d) Q_i is the cuboid containing q^{u_i, v_i} for all $1 \le i \le m$.
   e) S_1 is the data cube.

Suppose S_{max1} is the maximal safe subset of S_1. Then similarly S_{max1} does not contain any $q \in \bigcup_{i=1}^{m} Q_i \setminus S_t$. Moreover, S_{max1} does not contain any j-* query for all $j < m - 1$. As we shall show shortly, S_{max1} contains the m-* query $q^*(u_*, v_*)$, where $u_* = (1, 1, \ldots, 1)$ and $v_* = (n+1, n+1, \ldots, n+1)$. Hence we have that $S_{max1} \subseteq S_t \cup \{q^*(u_*, v_*)\}$ and $q^*(u_*, v_*) \in S_{max1}$. For all $1 \leq x \leq m$, we have that $q^*(u_x, v_x) = \{s_{i_x}, s_{j_x}\}$. Hence for any $I \subseteq [1, m]$, $\{q^2(t_{i_x}, t_{j_x}) : x \in I\}$ is safe if and only if $\{q^{u_x, v_x} : x \in I\}$ is safe. Consequently finding S_{max1} gives the maximal safe subset of S_0.

It remains to show that $q^*(u_*, v_*) \in S_{max1}$. We do so by contradiction. Suppose $q^*(u_*, v_*) \notin S_{max1}$ and $S_{max1} \cup \{q^*(u_*, v_*)\}$ compromises some $t \in C_1$. Then we have that $S_{max1} \subseteq S_t$. Suppose $| S_{max1} |= l$. Then there exists $r \in \mathbb{R}^{l+1}$ such that $r \cdot \mathcal{M}(\{q^*(u_*, v_*)\} \cup S_{max1})^T = \mathcal{M}(t)$ holds. Let $r' = (r[2], r[3], \ldots, r[l])$. Then

$$r[1] \cdot \mathcal{M}(q^*(u_*, v_*))^T + r' \cdot \mathcal{M}(S_{max1})^T = \mathcal{M}(t)$$

We have that $s_{n+1}, s_{n+2} \notin \bigcup_{q \in S_{max1}} q$ because $S_{max1} \subseteq S_t$. Moreover, from

$$\mathcal{M}(q^*(u_*, v_*)) = \mathcal{M}(s_{n+1}) + \mathcal{M}(s_{n+2}) + \sum_{i=1}^{n} \mathcal{M}(s_i)$$

we have

$$r[1] \cdot \mathcal{M}(s_{n+1})^T + r[1] \cdot \mathcal{M}(s_{n+2})^T + \sum_{i=1}^{n} x_i \cdot \mathcal{M}(s_i)^T = \mathcal{M}(t)$$

holds for some $x_i \in \mathbb{R}$, $i = 1, 2, \ldots, n$.

There are two cases:

a) Suppose $t \in \{s_1, s_2, \ldots, s_n\}$, then we have that $r[1] = 0$. Consequently we have that $r' \cdot \mathcal{M}(S_{max1})^T = \mathcal{M}(t)$, which contradicts the assumption that S_{max1} is safe.

b) Suppose $t \in \{s_{n+1}, s_{n+2}\}$. Without loss of generality, assume $t = s_{n+1}$, which leads to the contradiction that $r[1] = 1$ and $r[1] = 0$. Hence, we have proved that $q^*(u_*, v_*) \in S_{max1}$.

$\square$

6.4 Parity-Based Inference Control

Previous sections have shown that restricting users to even MDR queries can alleviate the threat of inferences but cannot completely eliminate more sophisticated inferences. This section studies methods that can detect such remaining inferences. First, Section 6.4.1 shows how to determine whether the collection of even MDR queries are safe. Second, Section 6.4.3 studies what other queries can be answered without causing inferences. Finally, Section 6.4.4 then discusses how to find large safe subsets of even MDR queries.

6.4.1 Even MDR Queries

Denote the collection of all even MDR queries as $\mathcal{Q}_e$. As illustrated by Example 6.11, $\mathcal{Q}_e$ contains much redundancy, which renders inference control less efficient. On the other hand, the relation $\equiv_d$ given in Definition 6.5 allows us to transform a set of queries to another equivalent set while one is compromised if and only if the other is. Hence, we want to transform $\mathcal{Q}_e$ through $\equiv_d$, such that the result contains less redundancy and hence its inferences can be more easily controlled.

Just like we can rewrite any even number as the multiplication of certain number of 2's, we can also *decompose* $\mathcal{Q}_e$ into a collection of sum-two queries. More specifically, In order to determine whether $\mathcal{Q}_e$ cause inferences, we show that there exists a subset of sum-two queries $\mathcal{Q}_{dt} \subseteq \mathcal{Q}_t$ satisfying $\mathcal{Q}_{dt} \equiv_d \mathcal{Q}_e$. By Definition 6.5, we can then determine whether $\mathcal{Q}_e$ is safe simply by checking if $\mathcal{Q}_{dt}$ is safe.

There are two natural but untrue conjectures. First, one might expect the collection of even MDR queries is equivalent to the collection of sum-two queries, that is $\mathcal{Q}_e \equiv_d \mathcal{Q}_t$. It is straightforward that $\mathcal{Q}_e$ is derivable from $\mathcal{Q}_t$, since we can simply arrange the tuples contained in each query in $\mathcal{Q}_e$ into arbitrary pairs and the result must be a subset of $\mathcal{Q}_t$. However, the converse is not true. Consider the counter-example with the one-dimensional core cuboid $C = \{1, 2, 3\}$. We have that $q^2(1, 3) \in \mathcal{Q}_t$ is not derivable from $\mathcal{Q}_e = \{q^\star(1, 2), q^\star(2, 3)\}$ (indeed, in the incidence matrix of the set system, the three row vectors are linearly independent).

Second, considering that any even MDR query that includes exactly two tuples is also a sum-two query, one might suspect that the collection of even MDR queries is equivalent its subset formed by those that are at the same time sum-two queries. That is, $\mathcal{Q}_e \equiv_d \mathcal{Q}_e \cap \mathcal{Q}_t$. Unfortunately, this is not true. Example 6.16 gives a counter-example. In the example, the only two even MDR queries that are not at the same time sum-two queries (and hence are missing in $\mathcal{Q}_e \cap \mathcal{Q}_t$) are $q^\star((1, 2), (2, 3))$ and $q^\star((1, 1), (2, 4))$), since they include more than two tuples. Among the two queries, the first even MDR query $q^\star((1, 2), (2, 3))$ is derivable from $\mathcal{Q}_e \cap \mathcal{Q}_t$, but the second, $q^\star((1, 1), (2, 4))$), is not (this can be easily verified using the incidence matrix).

Example 6.16. Table 6.6 shows $\mathcal{Q}_e \not\equiv_d \mathcal{Q}_e \cap \mathcal{Q}_t$ because $q^\star((1, 1), (2, 4)) \in \mathcal{Q}_e$ is not derivable from $\mathcal{Q}_e \cap \mathcal{Q}_t$.

A key observation can be made based on Example 6.16. The reason that $q^\star((1, 2), (2, 3))$ is derivable from $\mathcal{Q}_e \cap \mathcal{Q}_t$ but $q^\star((1, 1), (2, 4))$) is not lies in the fact that the latter is the union of *odd components* like $q^\star((1, 1), (1, 3))$ and $q^\star((2, 2), (2, 4))$. Intuitively, we always need at least one sum-two queries that are not parallel to the axis to derive a query like $q^\star((1, 1), (2, 4))$). For example, if we start with $q^2((1, 1), (1, 2))$ and $q^2((2, 2), (2, 3))$, we end up requiring $q^2((1, 3), (2, 4))$, which is not an even MDR query; if we start with $q^2((1, 2), (2, 2))$ and $q^2((1, 3), (2, 3))$ we would need $q^2((1, 1), (2, 4))$.

The Core Cuboid C

	1	2	3	4
1	(1,1)	(1,2)	(1,3)	
2		(2,2)	(2,3)	(2,4)

$\mathcal{Q}_e$	$q^\star((1,1),(1,2)), q^\star((1,2),(1,3))$
	$q^\star((2,2),(2,3)), q^\star((2,3),(2,4))$
	$q^\star((1,2),(2,2)), q^\star((1,3),(2,3)))$
	$q^\star((1,2),(2,3)), q^\star((1,1),(2,4))$
$\mathcal{Q}_e \cap \mathcal{Q}_t$	$q^\star((1,1),(1,2)), q^\star((1,2),(1,3))$
	$q^\star((2,2),(2,3)), q^\star((2,3),(2,4))$
	$q^\star((1,2),(2,2)), q^\star((1,3),(2,3)))$

$$q^\star((1,1),(2,4)) \not\preceq_d \mathcal{Q}_e \cap \mathcal{Q}_t$$

Table 6.6. An Example Showing $\mathcal{Q}_e$ Not Equivalent to $\mathcal{Q}_e \cap \mathcal{Q}_t$.

On the other hand, if we proceed in such a manner, and add the required sum-two queries to $\mathcal{Q}_e \cap \mathcal{Q}_t$, we can achieve the goal of equivalence. More specifically, suppose that from $\mathcal{Q}_e \cap \mathcal{Q}_t$ we can derive each odd component of the targeted even MDR query up to the *last tuple*. Then we *pair* the adjacent last tuples of all odd components as including additional sum-two queries. Hence, we can derive the even query with $\mathcal{Q}_e \cap \mathcal{Q}_t$ plus these additional sum-two queries. Conversely, these additional sum-two queries can be derived from $\mathcal{Q}_e$ by reversing this process, that is to subtracting the queries in $\mathcal{Q}_e \cap \mathcal{Q}_t$ from the targeted even MDR query. We demonstrate the discussion in Example 6.17 and generalize the result in Theorem 6.18.

Example 6.17. In Example 6.16, we can let $\mathcal{Q}_{dt} = \mathcal{Q}_e \cap \mathcal{Q}_t \cup \{q^2((1,3),(2,4))\}$. Consequently, $q^\star((1,1),(2,4))$ is the union of $q^2((1,1),(1,2))$, $q^2((2,2),(2,3))$ and $q^2((1,3),(2,4))$. Conversely, $q^2((1,3),(2,4)$ is derived as $q^\star((1,1),(2,4)) \setminus (q^2((1,1),(1,2)) \cup q^2((2,2),(2,3)))$. Hence now we have $\mathcal{Q}_e \equiv_d \mathcal{Q}_{dt}$.

Theorem 6.18. *For any core cuboid* C, *there exists* $\mathcal{Q}_{dt} \subseteq \mathcal{Q}_t$ *such that* $\mathcal{Q}_e \equiv_d \mathcal{Q}_{dt}$ *holds.*

Proof: In the following discussion, we assume that $d \in \mathbb{R}^k$, $F = \mathcal{F}(d)$, $C \subseteq F$, and any $S \subseteq C$ is sorted in dictionary order. For $i = 1, 2, \ldots, |S|$, we use $S[i]$ for the ith tuple in S. For any $u, v \in F$ satisfying $u \leq v$ and $q^\star(u,v) \in \mathcal{Q}_e$, use S_{uv} to denote the set of sum-two queries added to $\mathcal{Q}_{dt}$ by calling the subroutine Sub_QDT in Figure 6.4.1.

1. In order to prove $\mathcal{Q}_e \preceq \mathcal{Q}_{dt}$, we show that for any $u \leq v$ and $q^\star(u,v) \in \mathcal{Q}_e$, $q^\star(u,v) \preceq S_{uv}$ holds. Specially, we show that $q^\star(u,v) = \bigcup_{q \in S_{uv}} q$. Because $q_1 \cap q_2 = \phi$ holds for any $q_1, q_2 \in S_{uv}$, it then follows that $\mathcal{M}(q^\star(u,v)) = r \cdot \mathcal{M}(S_{uv})^T$, where $r = (1, 1, \ldots, 1) \in \mathbb{R}^{|S_{uv}|}$. We do so by mathematical induction on $|I|$, where $I = \{i : i \in [1, k], u[i] < v[i]\}$.

a) The Inductive Hypothesis:

For $| I |= 0, 1, \ldots, k$, if $q^\star(u, v) \in Q_e$, then

$$q^\star(u, v) = \bigcup_{q \in S_{uv}} q$$

Otherwise,

$$q^\star(u, v) = (\bigcup_{q \in S_{uv}} q) \cup \{Sub\_QDT(C, u, v)\}$$

b) The Base Case:

For $| I |= 0$, we have that $u = v$, and $q^\star(u, v) = \{u\}$. Because $I = \phi$, the subroutine Sub_QDT in Figure 6.4.1 returns u at the second step, with $S_{uv} = \phi$. Hence $s(q^\star(u, v)) = \phi \cup \{u\}$, validating the base case of our inductive hypothesis.

c) The Inductive Case:

Suppose the inductive hypothesis holds for $| I |= 0, 1, \ldots, j < k$, we show that it holds for $| I |= j + 1$. Let u and v satisfy that $u < v$ and $| I |= j + 1$, where $I = \{i : i \in [1, k], u[i] < v[i]\}$.

For all $u[m] \leq i \leq v[m]$, where $m = max(I)$, the pair(u_i, v_i) defined in the subroutine Sub_QDT satisfy $| \{i : i \in [1, k], u_i[i] < v_i[i]\} | = j$. Hence, when the subroutine Sub_QDT recursively calls itself with the input (C, u_i, v_i), the inductive hypothesis holds inside the recursion. Let $J = \{i : i \in [u[m], v[m]], q^\star(u_i, v_i) \notin Q_e\}$ and $J' = [u[m], v[m]] \setminus J$. Due to the inductive hypothesis, $q^\star(u_i, v_i) = \bigcup_{q \in S_{u_i v_i}} q$ holds for all $i \in J'$. Conversely, for all $i \in J$, let $t_i = Sub\_QDT(C, u_i, v_i)$, then we have

$$q^\star(u_i, v_i) = (\bigcup_{q \in S_{u_i v_i}} q) \cup \{t_i\}$$

If $q^\star(u, v) \in Q_e$, we have that $| J |$ is even. For $i = 1, 2, \ldots, \frac{|J|}{2}$, we know that $q^2(t_{2i-1}, t_{2i}) \in S_{uv}$ is true by referring to the four step of the subroutine Sub_QDT. Hence, we have that

$$q^\star(u, v) = \bigcup_{i=u[m]}^{v[m]} q^\star(u_i, v_i) = (\bigcup_{i=u[m]}^{v[m]} (\bigcup_{q \in S_{u_i v_i}} q)) \cup (\bigcup_{i=1}^{\frac{|J|}{2}} \{q^2(t_{2i-1}, t_{2i})\})$$

$$= \bigcup_{q \in S_{uv}} q$$

Conversely, if $q^\star(u, v) \in Q_d \setminus Q_e$, we have that $| J |$ is odd. For $i = 1, 2, \ldots, \frac{|J|-1}{2}$, we have that $q^2(t_{2i-1}, t_{2i}) \in S_{uv}$. Furthermore, we have that $Sub\_QDT(C, u, v) = t_{|J|} \notin S_{uv}$. Hence the following holds:

$$q^*(u,v) = \bigcup_{i=u[m]}^{v[m]} q^*(u_i,v_i) = S_{uv} \cup \{Sub\_QDT(C,u,v)\}$$

This proves the inductive case of our inductive hypothesis.

2. In order to prove $\mathcal{Q}_{dt} \preceq \mathcal{Q}_e$, we show that for any $q \in \mathcal{Q}_{dt}$, $q \preceq \mathcal{Q}_e$ holds.
   Suppose in the subroutine Sub_QDT in Figure 6.4.1 a sum-two query
   $q^2(t_i,t_j)$ is added to $\mathcal{Q}_{dt}$, where $u[m] \leq i < j \leq v[m]$.
   We only need to show that

$$q^*(u_i,v_i) \setminus \{t_i\} = \bigcup_{q \in S_i} q$$

and similarly

$$q^*(u_j,v_j) \setminus \{t_j\} = \bigcup_{q \in S_j} q$$

where $S_i, S_j \subseteq \mathcal{Q}_e$ and u_i, v_i, u_j, v_j are defined in Figure 6.4.1. Because
then we have

$$q^2(t_i,t_j) = q^*(u_i,v_j) \setminus ((\bigcup_{l=i+1}^{j-1} q^*(u_l,v_l)) \cup (\bigcup_{q \in S_i \cup S_j} q))$$

This implies that $q^2(t_i,t_j) \preceq \mathcal{Q}_e$, because $q^*(u_i,v_j) \in \mathcal{Q}_e$ and $q^*(u_l,v_l) \in \mathcal{Q}_e$ for any $i < l < j$.
We do so by induction on $|I|$.

a) The Inductive Hypothesis:
   For any $i \in [u[m], v[m]]$, if $t_i \neq null$ then

$$q^*(u_i,v_i) \setminus \{t_i\} = \bigcup_{\forall q \in S_i} s(q)$$

   holds for some $S_i \subseteq \mathcal{Q}_e$, where $u[m]$, $v[m]$, t_i are defined in Figure 6.4.1.

b) The Base Case:
   For $|I| = 0$, we have that $u = v$, $i = u[m]$, and $t_i = u$. Hence $q^*(u,u) \setminus \{u\} = \phi$. The base case of the inductive hypothesis trivially holds with $S_i = \phi$.

c) The Inductive Case:
   Suppose the inductive hypothesis holds for all $|I| = 0,1,\ldots,j$ for some $0 \leq j < k$, we show that it holds for $j+1$. Because the subroutine Sub_QDT recursively calls itself, inside the recursion we have that $|I| = j$. Suppose the inputs to the recursive call are C, u, v and $q^*(u,v) \notin \mathcal{Q}_e$. We have that $q^*(u,v) = q^*(u,v_{l-1}) \cup q^*(u_{l+1},v) \cup q^*(u_l,v_l)$ if $l < v[m]$, or $q^*(u,v) = q^*(u,v_{l-1}) \cup q^*(u_l,v_l)$ if $l = v[m]$. Moreover, because of the inductive hypothesis, we have that

$$q^*(u_l, v_l) \setminus \{t_l\} = q^*(u_l, v_l) \setminus \{t_l\} = \bigcup_{\forall q \in S_l} s(q)$$

holds for some $S_l \subseteq Q_e$. Hence, we have

$$q^*(u, v) \setminus \{t_l\} = \bigcup_{\forall q \in S} s(q)$$

where $S = S_l \cup \{q^*(u, v_{l-1}), q^*(u_{l+1}, v)\}$ if $l < v[m]$, or $Q = Q_l \cup \{q^*(u, v_{l-1})\}$ if $l = v[m]$. Because $q^*(u, v) \notin Q_e$, we have that $| \{i : i \in [u[m], v[m]], t_i \neq null\} |$ is odd. Hence, we have $q^*(u, v_{l-1}) \in Q_e$ and $q^*(u_{l+1}, v) \in Q_e$ both hold. Consequently, $S \subseteq Q_e$ is true. Because $t_l = Sub\_QDT(C, u, v)$, this validates the inductive case of our inductive hypothesis.

□

The time complexity of building Q_{dt} using Sub_QDT is $O(mn)$, where $m = | Q_e |$ and $n = | C |$. Because $| Q_{dt} | \leq | Q_t | \leq \binom{|C|}{2}$ and $m = O(\binom{|C|}{2})$), we have $| Q_{dt} | = O(m)$. Hence, no more storage is required by Q_{dt} than by Q_e.

Definition 6.19. *For any $S \subseteq Q_{dt}$, use $G(C, S)$ for the undirected simple graph having C as the vertex set, S as the edge set and each edge $q^2(t_1, t_2)$ incident the vertices t_1 and t_2, then we call $G(C, Q_{dt})$ the QDT Graph.*

Figure 6.2 illustrates the QDT graph for our running example.

Chin has shown that a set of sum-two queries is safe if and only if the corresponding graph is a bipartite graph, that is, a graph with no cycle containing odd number of edges (as discussed in Chapter 3) [12]. The latter can easily be decided with a breadth-first search (BFS) on $G(C, Q_{dt})$, taking time $O(n+ | Q_{dt} |) = O(m + n)$. Hence the complexity of determining the compromisability of Q_e is dominated by the construction of Q_{dt}, which is $O(mn)$. Notice that from Section 6.3 we know that directly applying the condition of Audit Expert has the complexity of $O(m^2 n)$. Therefore, our solution is more efficient than Audit Expert with respect to MDR queries.

6.4.2 Characterizing the QDT Graph

Lemma 6.20 gives some properties of the QDT graph that are useful for later discussions. First, any even MDR query that is at the same time a sum-two query will appear in the QDT graph. The proof of this property is straightforward. Second, we can always find an even MDR query as the subset of any given even MDR query including more than two tuples such that the former query appears in the QDT graph. The intuition behind the proof is as follows. If any two tuples t_1, t_2 in the core cuboid are not *close enough* in the sense that the even MDR query bound by them does not appear in the QDT graph, then we can find a third tuple t_3 in this even MDR query such that t_3 is closer

Procedure QDT
Input: d, $F = \mathcal{F}(d)$, $C \subseteq F$
Output: A set of sum-two queries $\mathcal{Q}_{dt}$
Method:
    1. Let $\mathcal{Q}_{dt} = \phi$
    2. For any $q^\star(u, v) \in \mathcal{Q}_e$, where $u < v$
        Call $Sub\_QDT(C, u, v)$;
    3. Return $\mathcal{Q}_{dt}$;

Subroutine Sub_QDT
Input: The core C, tuples u and v satisfying $u \leq v$
Output: t_{odd}
Method:
    1. Let $I = \{i : i \in [1, k], u[i] < v[i]\}$ and $m = max(I)$;
    2. If $I = \phi$ //Stop when $u = v$
      Return u;
    3. For $i = u[m]$ to $v[m]$ //Divide
      let $t_i = null$;
      If $q^\star(u_i, v_i) \neq \phi$
        Let $t_i = Sub\_QDT(C, u_i, v_i)$,   //Recursion
           where $\forall j \in I \setminus \{m\}, u_i[j] = u[j] \wedge v_i[j] = v[j]$
           and $u_i[m] = v_i[m] = i$;
    4. For $i = u[m]$ to $v[m]$ //Conquer
      If $t_i \neq null$
        Let $j = min\{j : j > i, t_j \neq null \vee j > v[m]\}$;
        If $j > v[m]$
          Return t_i;
        Else
          Let $\mathcal{Q}_{dt} = \mathcal{Q}_{dt} \cup \{q^2(t_i, t_j)\}$ and $i = j$;
    5. **Return** $null$;

Fig. 6.1. Procedure QDT

to t_1 than t_2 does. We can repeat this process less than $\mid q^\star(t_1, t_2) \mid$ times, and upon termination we have a tuple that is close enough to t_1. The third claim is a natural extension of the first two.

Lemma 6.20.   *1. $\mathcal{Q}_e \cap \mathcal{Q}_t \subseteq \mathcal{Q}_{dt}$.*
  2. For any $t_1, t_2 \in C$ satisfying that $\mid q^\star(t_1, t_2) \mid > 2$, there exists $t_3 \in q^\star(t_1, t_2)$ such that $q^\star(t_1, t_3) \in \mathcal{Q}_{dt}$.
  3. $G(C, \mathcal{Q}_{dt})$ is connected.

Proof:

1. The first claim of is true because $Sub\_QDT(C, u_0, v_0)$ will be called for all u_0, v_0 satisfying $q^\star(u_0, v_0) = \{u_0, v_0\}$.

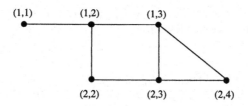

Fig. 6.2. An Example of QDT Graph

2. For the second claim, suppose $t_3 \neq t_1$, $t_3 \neq t_2$ and $\mid q^\star(t_1, t_3) \mid > 2$. Then $t_2 \notin q^\star(t_1, t_3)$ holds. For otherwise, for any $i \in [1, k]$ we have $min\{t_1[i], t_2[i]\} \leq t_3[i] \leq max\{t_1[i], t_2[i]\}$ and $min\{t_1[i], t_3[i]\} \leq t_2[i] \leq max\{t_1[i], t_3[i]\}$, and hence $t_2 = t_3$ contradicting our assumption. Consequently we have that $\mid q^\star(t_1, t_3) \mid < \mid q^\star(t_1, t_2) \mid$. Let $t_4 \in q^\star(t_1, t_3)$ satisfying $t_4 \neq t_1$ and $t_4 \neq t_3$. We can repeat the same argument by replacing t_3 with t_4 and so on, until $\mid q^\star(t_1, t) \mid = 2$ for some $t \in q^\star(t_1, t_2)$. This together with the first claim of Lemma 6.20 justifies the second claim.

3. We prove the third claim by contradiction. Suppose G_1 and G_2 are any two connected components of any $G(C, \mathcal{Q}_{dt})$, and let $t_1 \in V(G_1)$ (the vertex set of G_1), $t_2 \in V(G_2)$. By the first claim of Lemma 6.20 we have that $\mid q^\star(t_1, t_2) \mid > 2$. By the second claim there exists $t_3 \in q^\star(t_1, t_2)$ such that $q^\star(t_1, t_3) \in \mathcal{Q}_{dt}$ and hence $t_3 \in V(G_1)$. Similarly as stated above, $t_1 \notin q^\star(t_3, t_2)$ and hence $\mid q^\star(t_1, t_2) \mid > \mid q^\star(t_3, t_2) \mid$. Repeat above reasoning with t_1 replaced by t_3 and so on, until that for some t we have $\mid q^\star(t, t_2) \mid = 2$, and hence $q^\star(t, t_2) \in \mathcal{Q}_{dt}$ by the first claim. But then G_1 and G_2 are connected because $t \in V(G_1)$, contradicting our assumption.

□

Although we have shown the equivalence between $\mathcal{Q}_{dt}$ and $\mathcal{Q}_e$, $\mathcal{Q}_{dt}$ may neither be the smallest nor be the largest subset of $\mathcal{Q}_t$ that is equivalent to $\mathcal{Q}_e$. The smallest subset can be obtained by removing all the cycles containing even number of edges from $G(C, \mathcal{Q}_{dt})$. If $\mathcal{Q}_e$ is safe, we then have a spanning tree of $G(C, \mathcal{Q}_{dt})$, which corresponds to a set of linearly independent row vectors in the incidence matrix. On the other hand, we are interested in the maximal subset of $\mathcal{Q}_t$ that is equivalent to $\mathcal{Q}_e$. By Theorem 6.21, a safe $\mathcal{Q}_e$ essentially allows users to sum any two tuples from difference color classes of $G(C, \mathcal{Q}_{dt})$, and to subtract any two tuples of the same color. The maximal subset of $\mathcal{Q}_t$ equivalent to $\mathcal{Q}_e$ is thus the complete bipartite graph with the same bipartition as that of $G(C, \mathcal{Q}_{dt})$.

Theorem 6.21. *Given $\mathcal{Q}_e$ is safe, let (C_1, C_2) be the bipartition of $G(C, \mathcal{Q}_{dt})$ and $\mathcal{Q}_{dt}^\star = \{q^2(u, v) : u \in C_1, v \in C_2\}$. We have that*

1. $\mathcal{Q}_{dt}^\star \equiv_d \mathcal{Q}_{dt}$.
2. For any $S \subseteq \mathcal{Q}_t$, if $S \equiv_d \mathcal{Q}_{dt}$ then $S \subseteq \mathcal{Q}_{dt}^\star$.

3. For any $t_1, t_2 \in C_1$ (or $t_1, t_2 \in C_2$), there exists $r \in \mathbb{R}^{|\mathcal{Q}_{dt}|}$ such that $\mathcal{M}(t_1) - \mathcal{M}(t_2) = r \cdot \mathcal{M}(\mathcal{Q}_{dt})$.

Proof:

1. $\mathcal{Q}_{dt} \preceq \mathcal{Q}_{dt}^{\star}$ is trivial because $\mathcal{Q}_{dt} \subseteq \mathcal{Q}_{dt}^{\star}$. We only need to show $\mathcal{Q}_{dt}^{\star} \preceq \mathcal{Q}_{dt}$. By Lemma 6.20 $G(C, \mathcal{Q}_{dt})$ is a connected bipartite. Hence there exists a path containing odd number of edges between any $t_1 \in C_1$ and $t_0 \in C_2$. Let it be $S = \{q^2(t_1, t_2), q^2(t_2, t_3), \ldots, q^2(t_{2n}, t_{2n+1}), q^2(t_{2n+1}), t_0)\}$, where $n \geq 0$. We have that

$$\mathcal{M}(q^2(t_1, t_0)) = ((-1)^0, (-1)^1, (-1)^2, \ldots, (-1)^{2n}) \cdot \mathcal{M}(S)^T$$

Hence, $q^2(t_1, t_0) \preceq \mathcal{Q}_{dt}$ is true.

2. Because $\mathcal{Q}_{dt}^{\star}$ corresponds to the complete bipartite graph(a bipartite graph whose edge set includes all the edges that incident two vertices from different color classes) with bipartition (C_1, C_2), any proper superset S of $\mathcal{Q}_{dt}^{\star}$ is not a bipartite. Hence, S cannot be safe, and consequently $S \npreceq \mathcal{Q}_{dt}$.

3. For any $t_1, t_{11} \in S_1$, because $G(C, \mathcal{Q}_{dt})$ is connected, there must exists $t_2 \in S_2$ such that $q^2(t_1, t_2) \in \mathcal{Q}_{dt}$. Taken together with $q^2(t_2, t_{11}) \preceq \mathcal{Q}_{dt}$ we have proved the third claim.

□

6.4.3 Beyond Even MDR Queries

Now that we can decide if even MDR queries cause inferences, we want to study whether other queries can also be answered safely.

Odd MDR Queries

First we consider odd MDR queries, which form the complement of $\mathcal{Q}_e$ with respect to all MDR queries. If we give any odd MDR query $q^{\star}(u_0, v_0)$ as the input to the subroutine Sub_QDT, then we will have as result a single tuple t, since all other tuples will be pieced together as a collection of even MDR queries (also as pairs). This means we can derive that single tuple from the collection of even MDR queries plus the given odd MDR query. That is, no odd query can be answered without causing an inference.

On the other hand, Suppose the above $q^{\star}(u_0, v_0)$ is a j-dimensional box. Then it can be divided into two j dimensional boxes excluding t, together with a $(j-1)$-dimensional box containing t. We can recursively divide the $(j-1)$-dimensional box in this manner into boxes with lower dimensionality until t is isolated. Hence, $q^{\star}(u_0, v_0)$ is always the union of a few disjoint even MDR queries together with a singleton set $\{t\}$. These are formally stated in Corollary 6.22.

Corollary 6.22. *Given $d \in \mathbb{R}^k$, $F = \mathcal{F}(d)$, $C \subseteq F$ and any $q^\star(u, v) \in \mathcal{Q}_d \setminus \mathcal{Q}_e$ satisfying $\mid \{i : u[i] \neq v[i]\} \mid = j$, there exists $q^\star(u_i, v_i) \in \mathcal{Q}_e$ for all $1 \leq i \leq 2j - 1$, such that*

1. $\mid q^\star(u, v) \setminus \bigcup_{i=1}^{2j-1} q^\star(u_i, v_i) \mid = 1$
2. $q^\star(u_i, v_i) \cap q^\star(u_l, v_l) = \phi$

   both hold for $1 \leq i < l \leq 2j - 1$.

Proof: Call subroutine *Sub_QDT* in Figure 6.4.1 with the input $(q^\star(u, v), u, v)$, and let the output be t_{odd}. For $i = 1, 2, \ldots, k$ and $l = 1, 2, 3, 4$, define tuples u_{il} as:

1. $u_{il}[j] = t_{odd}[j]$ for all $j > i$ and $l = 1, 2, 3, 4$
2. $u_{i1}[i] = u[i]$
3. $u_{i2}[i] = u_{odd}[i] - 1$
4. $u_{i3}[i] = t_{odd}[i] + 1$
5. $u_{i4}[i] = v[i]$
6. $u_{i1}[j] = u_{i3}[j] = u[j]$
7. $u_{i2}[j] = u_{i4}[j] = v[j]$ for all $j < i$

We then have that

$$q^\star(u, v) = \bigcup_{i=1}^{k} (q^\star(u_{i1}, u_{i2}) \cup q^\star(u_{i3}, u_{i4})) \cup \{t_{odd}\}$$

and all the $q^\star(u_{il}, u_{il})$s are disjoint. Because $q^\star(u_{13}, u_{14}) = \phi$, we have totally $2k - 1$ disjoint even MDR queries. $\square$

Example 6.23. In Table 6.6, use $q^\star((1, 1), (2, 3))$ as the input of *Sub_QDT* will yield the output $(1, 3)$.

The odd MDR query $q^\star((1, 1), (2, 3))$ can be divided into $q^\star((1, 1), (1, 3))$ and $q^\star((2, 2), (2, 3))$. Then $q^\star((1, 1), (1, 3))$ can be divided into $q^\star((1, 1), (1, 2))$ and $\{(1, 3)\}$. Hence, $q^\star((1, 1), (2, 3)) = q^\star((1, 1), (1, 2)) \cup q^\star((2, 2), (2, 3)) \cup \{(1, 3)\}$ is true.

Corollary 6.22 has two immediate consequences. First, no odd MDR query is safe in addition to $\mathcal{Q}_e$. In another word, any set of MDR queries with $\mathcal{Q}_e$ as its proper subset will be unsafe. Second, since any odd MDR query is different from the union of a few number of even MDR queries by only one tuple, the odd query can be approximated using the collection of even MDR queries, if the error of one tuple is considered tolerable.

Arbitrary Queries

Theorem 6.21 has shown how we can interpret $\mathcal{Q}_e$ in terms of sum-two queries from Theorem 6.21. Hence we can easily decide which arbitrary queries can be answered in addition to $\mathcal{Q}_e$. Corollary 6.24 shows that any arbitrary query can be answered if and only if it contains the same number of tuples from the two color classes of the QDT graph $G(C, \mathcal{Q}_{dt})$. This can be decided in linear time in the size of the query simply by counting the tuples. The result on odd MDR queries now becomes a special case of Corollary 6.24, because no odd MDR query can satisfy this condition.

Corollary 6.24. *Given that $\mathcal{Q}_e$ is safe, $q \preceq_d \mathcal{Q}_e$ is true for any $q \subseteq C$ if and only if $\mid q \cap C_1 \mid = \mid q \cap C_2 \mid$, where (C_1, C_2) is the bipartition of $G(C, \mathcal{Q}_{dt})$.*

Proof: If $\mid c \cap C_1 \mid = \mid c \cap C_2 \mid$, then $c = \bigcup_{q \in S} q$ for some $S \subseteq \mathcal{Q}_{dt}^\star$. Hence, $c \preceq \mathcal{Q}_{dt}^\star$, and consequently $c \preceq \mathcal{Q}_e$.

We prove the only if part by contradiction. Without loss of generality, suppose $\mid c \cap C_1 \mid > \mid c \cap C_2 \mid$ and $c \preceq \mathcal{Q}_e$. Then $c = c_0 \cup c_1$, where c_0 and c_1 satisfy that $c_0 \cap c_1 = \phi$, $\mid c_0 \cap C_1 \mid = \mid c_0 \cap C_2 \mid$ and $c_1 \subseteq C_1$. Then we have that $c_0 \preceq \mathcal{Q}_e$ and hence $V(c_1) \preceq \mathcal{Q}_e$ follows. Suppose $c_1 = \{t_0, t_1, \ldots, t_n\}$ where $n \geq 1$. Then by the third claim of Theorem 6.21 we have that $\mathcal{M}(t_0) - \mathcal{M}(t_i) = r_i \cdot \mathcal{M}(\mathcal{Q}_{dt})^T$ holds for all $1 \leq i \leq n$, where each $r_i \in \mathbb{R}^{\mid \mathcal{Q}_{dt} \mid}$. By adding the two sides of all the n equation we have that

$$n \cdot \mathcal{M}(t_0) = \sum_{i=1}^{n} \mathcal{M}(t_i) + \sum_{i=1}^{n} r_i \cdot \mathcal{M}(\mathcal{Q}_{dt})^T$$

Let $\mathcal{M}(c_1) = r \cdot \mathcal{M}(\mathcal{Q}_{dt})^T$, where $r \in \mathbb{R}^{\mid \mathcal{Q}_{dt} \mid}$. Because

$$\sum_{i=1}^{n} \mathcal{M}(t_i) = \mathcal{M}(c_1) - \mathcal{M}(t_0) = r \cdot \mathcal{M}(\mathcal{Q}_{dt})^T - \mathcal{M}(t_0)$$

we have that

$$(n+1)\mathcal{M}(t_0) = \sum_{i=1}^{n} r_i \cdot \mathcal{M}(\mathcal{Q}_{dt})^T + r \cdot \mathcal{M}(\mathcal{Q}_{dt})^T$$

Hence, t_0 is compromised by $\mathcal{Q}_{dt}$, contradicting our assumption that $c \preceq \mathcal{Q}_e$. $\square$

6.4.4 Unsafe Even MDR Queries

When the collection of even MDR queries $\mathcal{Q}_e$ is not safe, we may want to find its safe subsets. Section 6.3.2 shows that finding maximum safe subsets of queries is infeasible even for queries of restricted forms, such as sum-two queries and data cubes. Hence, we turn to large but not necessarily maximum safe subsets. Recall that Section 6.4 determines the compromisability of $\mathcal{Q}_e$ by finding an equivalent collection of sum-two queries $\mathcal{Q}_{dt}$. Therefore, if we can establish the same equivalence between their subsets, we would be able to extend the results in Section 6.4 to these subsets. However, for arbitrary subsets of $\mathcal{Q}_e$ or $\mathcal{Q}_{dt}$, such equivalence may not exist at all, as illustrated by Example 6.25.

Example 6.25. For the $\mathcal{Q}_{dt}$ in Example 6.17, let $S_{dt} = \mathcal{Q}_{dt} \setminus \{q^2((1,1),(1,2))\}$. Suppose $S_{dt} \equiv_d S_e$ for some $S_e \subseteq \mathcal{Q}_e$. Because $q^2((1,3),(2,4)) \preceq_d S_e$, S_e must contain $q^\star((1,1),(1,2))$, but then $q^\star((1,1),(1,2)) \npreceq_d S_{dt}$ leads to a contradiction. Hence S_{dt} cannot be equivalent to any subset of $\mathcal{Q}_e$. Similarly, $\mathcal{Q}_e \setminus \{q^\star((1,1),(1,2))\}$ is not equivalent to any subset of $\mathcal{Q}_{dt}$.

However, we can regard any MDR query as a smaller core cuboid C', and the equivalence given by Theorem 6.18 must also hold in this new core cuboid as follows. First, we say an even MDR query is *defined on* C' if it is a subset of C'. The collection of all even MDR queries defined on C' must then be equivalent to the set of sum-two queries produced by the procedure *Sub_QDT* with those even MDR queries as the inputs. This simple result can be extended to any subset of the core cuboid because we can always regard the subset as the union of multiple disjoint MDR queries.

The extension of the result can be done in two ways depending on whether a subset of even MDR queries or that of sum-two queries is given. Given any $S \subseteq \mathcal{Q}_e$, we first find a subset C' of the core cuboid such that all the queries defined on C' are included in S. This allows us to regard C' as a new core cuboid and apply the above discussion to establish the equivalence for these queries. Similarly, given any $S \subseteq \mathcal{Q}_{dt}$, we can find a new core cuboid to establish the equivalence, too. Those are formally stated in Proposition 6.26 and illustrated in Example 6.27.

Proposition 6.26.   *1. For any $S \subseteq \mathcal{Q}_e$, let*

    a) $S_e = S \setminus \{q^\star(u,v) : \exists q^\star(u_0,v_0) \in \mathcal{Q}_e \setminus S, q^\star(u,v) \cap q^\star(u_0,v_0) \neq \phi\}$
    b) $S_{dt} = \{q^2(u,v) : \exists q^\star(u_0,v_0) \in S_e, q^2(u,v) \in \mathcal{Q}_{dt} \text{ due to } q^\star(u_0,v_0)\}$
    Then $S_e \equiv_d S_{dt}$.

  2. For any $S \subseteq \mathcal{Q}_{dt}$, let

    a) $S_e = \mathcal{Q}_e \setminus \{q^\star(u,v) : \exists(u_0,v_0), q^2(u_0,v_0) \in S \wedge q^\star(u,v) \cap q^\star(u_0,v_0) \neq \phi\}$
    b) $S_{dt} = \{q^2(u,v) : \exists q^\star(u_0,v_0) \in S_e, q^2(u,v) \in \mathcal{Q}_{dt} \text{ due to } q^\star(u_0,v_0)\}$
    Then $S_{dt} \equiv_d S_e$.

Proof: We only need to justify the first claim. For any $q^2(u_0,v_0) \in S_{dt}$, suppose $q^2(u_0,v_0) \in \mathcal{Q}_{dt}$ because of $q^\star(u_1,v_1) \in S_e$. Then $\{q^\star(u,v) : q^\star(u,v) \in \mathcal{Q}_e \wedge q^\star(u,v) \subseteq q^\star(u_1,v_1)\} \subseteq S_e$ holds. Therefore, $q^2(u_0,v_0) \preceq S_e$. Conversely, for any $q^\star(u_0,v_0) \in S_e$, we have $\{q^2(u,v) : q^2(u,v) \in \mathcal{Q}_{dt} \text{ because of } q^\star(u_0,v_0)\} \subseteq S_{dt}$. Hence, $q^\star(u_0,v_0) \preceq S_{dt}$. $\square$

Example 6.27. Following Example 6.25, given $S = \mathcal{Q}_{dt} \setminus \{q^2((1,1),(1,2))\}$, we obtain S_e as $\{q^*((1,3),(2,3)), q^*((2,2),(2,3)), q^*((2,3),(2,4))\}$ and S_{dt} as $\{q^2((1,3),(2,3)), q^2((2,2),(2,3)), q^2((2,3),(2,4))\}$. Notice S_e includes all and only the queries defined on the core cuboid $C' = \{(1,3),(2,2),(2,3),(2,4)\}$.

Proposition 6.26 guarantees the equivalence at the cost of reduced availability of queries. In some situations, we may be satisfied with a weaker result, such as $S_{dt} \succeq S_e$. That is, if the S_{dt} is safe then S_e must also be safe, although the converse is not necessarily true. The result in Proposition 6.28 is similar to Corollary 6.24 but gives only the sufficient condition. In Proposition 6.28, S_e can be found by examining each query in $\mathcal{Q}_e$ against the bipartition (C_1, C_2), taking time $O(mn)$, where $m = | \mathcal{Q}_e |$ and $n = | C |$.

Proposition 6.28. *For any $S_{dt} \subseteq \mathcal{Q}_{dt}$, let (C_1, C_2) be the bipartition of $G(C, S_{dt})$. Then $S_{dt} \succeq S_e$ holds, where $S_e \subseteq \mathcal{Q}_e$ satisfies that for any $q^*(u,v) \in S_e$, $| q^*(u,v) \cap C_1 | = | q^*(u,v) \cap C_2 | = | q^*(u,v) | /2$ holds.*

Proof: Let $S \subseteq \mathcal{Q}_t$ satisfy that $G(C, S)$ is the complete bipartite with bipartition (C_1, C_2). Clearly $S_e \preceq S \equiv S_{dt}$.

$\square$

By Proposition 6.26 and Proposition 6.28, we can find a safe subset S_e of $\mathcal{Q}_e$ if a safe subset S_{dt} of $\mathcal{Q}_{dt}$ is given. The ideal choice of S_{dt} should maximize $| S_e |$. This is equivalent to computing the *combinatorial discrepancy* of the set system formed by C and $\mathcal{Q}_e$ [6]. The alternative approach is to maximize $| S_{dt} |$, which is equivalent to finding the maximum bipartite subgraph of $G(C, \mathcal{Q}_{dt})$. Unfortunately, both solutions incur high computational complexity.

We can instead apply a simple procedure given in [32], as shown in Figure 6.3. It takes the graph $G(C, \mathcal{Q}_{dt})$ as the input and outputs a bipartite subgraph. It starts from an empty vertex set and empty edge set and processes one vertex at each step. The unprocessed vertex is colored blue if at least half of the processed vertices that it connects to are red. It is colored red, otherwise. Any edge in the original graph is included in the output bipartite subgraph if it connects two vertices in different colors. The procedure terminates with a bipartite graph $G(C, \mathcal{Q}_{ds})$ satisfying that $| \mathcal{Q}_{ds} | \geq | \mathcal{Q}_{dt} | /2$.

6.5 Discussion

We have discussed the three-tier inference control model in the previous chapter. The parity-based inference control method introduced in this chapter can be applied to OLAP systems based upon the model. This section justifies this claim. To make this chapter self-contained, we first briefly review the three-tier model.

Procedure *Bipartize_QDT*
Input: The core C, $\mathcal{Q}_{dt}$
Output: the safe subset $\mathcal{Q}_{ds}$
Method:

    1. **Let** $\mathcal{Q}_{ds} = \phi$, $S_{old} = \phi$;

    2. **For each** $t_{new} \in C \setminus S_{old}$

        Let $C_{red} = \{t : t \in S_{old}, \text{t is red, and } q^2(t, t_{new}) \in \mathcal{Q}_{dt}\}$

            and $C_{blue} = \{t : t \in S_{old}, \text{t is blue, and } q^2(t, t_{new}) \in \mathcal{Q}_{dt}\}$;

        If $\mid C_{red} \mid > \mid C_{blue} \mid$

          Color t_{new} blue;

          For each $t_{old} \in C_{red}$

              Let $\mathcal{Q}_{ds} = \mathcal{Q}_{ds} \cup \{q^2(t_{old}, t_{new})\}$;

        Else

          Color t_{new} red;

          For each $t_{old} \in C_{blue}$

              Let $\mathcal{Q}_{ds} = \mathcal{Q}_{ds} \cup \{q^2(t_{old}, t_{new})\}$;

    3. **Return** $\mathcal{Q}_{ds}$;

Fig. 6.3. A Procedure for Finding Large Safe Subsets of $\mathcal{Q}_{dt}$

The Three-Tier Inference Control Model

The objective of the three-tier inference control model is to minimize the performance penalty of inference control methods. This is achieved through introducing a new tier, *aggregation tier A*, to the traditional query-data view of inference control. The three tiers are related by three relations $R_{AD} \subseteq A \times D$, $R_{QA} \subseteq Q \times A$, and their composition $R_{QD} = R_{AD} \circ R_{QA}$. The aggregation tier A satisfies three properties. First, $\mid A \mid$ is comparable to $\mid D \mid$. Second, there exists partition $\mathcal{P}$ on A such that the composition of R_{AD} and the equivalence relation given by $\mathcal{P}$ gives a partition on D. Third, inferences are removed from the aggregation tier A.

The three-tier model owes its advantages to the three properties of the aggregation tier. First, because $\mid A \mid$ is relatively small (in most cases $\mid Q \mid >> \mid D \mid$ is true), controlling inferences caused by A is easier than that by Q because of the smaller input to inference control methods. Second, due to the second property of A, inference control can be *localized* to the R_{AD}-related blocks of A and D, which further reduces the complexity. Moreover, the consequences of any undetected external knowledge are confined to blocks, making inference control more *robust*. Finally, as the most expensive task of three-tier inference control, the construction of A can be processed off-line (i.e., before any query arrives). Answering queries using pre-computed aggregations is a built-in capability in most OLAP systems, and hence inference control can easily take advantage of this capability.

Applicability of The Parity-Based Method

Partitions of the core cuboid based on the dimension hierarchies naturally compose the data tier. Each block in the partition is regarded as a separate core cuboid upon which the safe collection of even MDR queries $\mathcal{Q}_{dt}$ (or its safe subsets if it is unsafe) composes each block of the aggregation tier. The query tier includes any arbitrary query derivable from the aggregation tier. If we characterize $\mathcal{Q}_e$ using the row vectors in $\mathcal{M}(\mathcal{Q}_e)$, then the query tier is the linear space these vectors span. The relation R_{AD} and R_{QA} are both the derivarability relation $\preceq_d$ given in Definition 6.5, and $R_{QD} = R_{AD} \circ R_{QA}$ is a subset of $\preceq_d$, because $\preceq_d$ is transitive.

Next we show that the aggregation tier satisifies the three required properties. In Section 6.4, we have shown that $\mid \mathcal{Q}_{dt} \mid = O(n^2)$, where $n =\mid C \mid$, satisfying the first property of the three tier model. Because $\mathcal{Q}_{dt}$ is separately defined on each core cuboid, the aggregation tier has a natural partition corresponding to the partition of the data tier, satisfying the second property. The last property is satisfied because we use the safe subsets of $\mathcal{Q}_{dt}$ when it is unsafe. Hence by integrating our results on the basis of the three tier model, we inherit all the advantages the model provides, such as low online performance overhead and the robustness in the face of undetected external knowledge (that is, the disclosure caused by undetected external knowledge is confined to blocks in the partition of the data tier).

In contrast to the cardinality-based inference control method discussed in the previous chapter, the parity-based method has several advantages. First, the cardinality-based conditions are only valid for skeleton queries in a data cube, whereas the parity-based method addresses general MDR queries. MDR queries cover data cubes and various data cube operations, such as slicing, dicing, roll up and drill down. Second, the cardinality-based method simply denies a data cube if it is unsafe, but in this chapter we are able to give partial answers to an unsafe collection of even MDR queries. Third, we use necessary and sufficient conditions (the equivalence relation) in this chapter to determine safe even MDR queries, whereas the cardinality-based conditions are sufficient but not necessary. Therefore, we can provide users with an answer if only it does not cause inferences.

6.6 Conclusion

In this chapter we have proposed to start by restricting users to even MDR queries. This restriction makes inferences significantly more difficult, since inference targets at odd number of values and even number is closed under addition and subtraction. However, we have shown that more sophisticated inferences are still possible using only even MDR queries. To remove these remaining inferences by directly applying existing inference control methods has been shown as inefficient, because those methods typically fail to take into consideration the inherent redundancy among even MDR queries.

We then proved the equivalence between the collection of even MDR queries and a special collection of sum-two queries, which can be obtained using a given algorithm. On the basis of this equivalence, we have shown how to determine the compromisability of even MDR queries with better performance than that of existing methods. We showed that odd MDR queries must be prohibited to prevent inferences, but they can be approximately answered using the even ones. We showed that the compromisability of arbitrary queries can be determined in linear time in the size of the query. We have also established the equivalence between subsets of even MDR queries and sum-two queries and given sufficient conditions for safe subsets of MDR queries. Finally, we have shown that these results can be integrated into OLAP systems based on the three-tier inference control model previously proposed.

7

Lattice-based Inference Control in Data Cubes

7.1 Introduction

We have discussed two different methods for controlling inferences in data cubes. Many lessons can be learned from these results as well as from the previous research on inference control in statistical databases. Most restriction-based methods adopt a *detecting-then-removing* approach. That is, the queries are checked for inferences and only those that do not cause inferences are answered. However, the detection of inferences usually demands on-line (that is, after queries are posed) computations or the bookkeeping of all answered queries. This fact leads to the high on-line performance overhead and storage requirements exhibited by many existing methods.

Even at such a high cost, the detection of inferences is usually only effective in limited cases where unrealistic assumptions are abundant. For instance, many methods assume only one or two specific type of aggregations (for example, SUM-only), and a fixed criteria for determining what information disclosure is sensitive (for example, only the disclosure of exact values causes privacy breaches). Compared to statistical databases, OLAP usually demands shorter response time even for large queries. Applying existing techniques to OLAP places us in no better situations than before.

The contribution of this chapter is two-fold. First, instead of simply regarding the core cuboid as sensitive, we devise a framework for formally specifying authorization objects in data cubes. The specification is flexible. It partitions the data cube both vertically based on dimension hierarchies and horizontally based on slices of data. The objects in the model are closures of the specified data cube cells. This approach ensures that the finer aggregations implied by the specified ones are also protected. The specification is also distributive over set union, making overlapping objects easy to handle.

Second, we propose a solution for controlling inferences caused by unprotected aggregations. Instead of detecting inferences, we first prevent the adversary from combining multiple aggregations for inferences by restricting queries. We then remove remaining inferences caused by individual aggregations. This novel approach greatly eases inference control. The result is provably secure. It not only eliminates malicious inferences, but also prevents unauthorized accesses by enclosing the result of access control in that of inference control.

The proposed method is broadly applicable. It applies to any combination of aggregation functions, external knowledge, and sensitivity criteria as long as they meet some clearly stated properties. The technique is efficient and readily implementable. The on-line performance overhead is comparable to that of basic access control, which comprises the minimal security requirement. The off-line complexity and storage requirement are both bounded. The pre-computed result can be enforced with little modification to existing OLAP systems.

The rest of the chapter is organized as follows. Section 7.2 reviews the data cube model and gives notations that are the most suitable for this chapter. Section 7.3 devises a framework for specifying authorization objects in data cubes. Section 7.4 proposes a solution for controlling inferences in data cubes. Section 7.5 discusses the implementation options and complexity. Section 7.6 concludes the chapter.

7.2 The Basic Model

Chapter 2 has discussed the data cube model proposed by Gray et. al. We shall closely follow this model. We first review the concepts through an example. Then we introduce our notations for these concepts, and state our assumptions.

Figure 7.1 depicts a fictitious *data cube*. It has two *dimensions*: *time* and *organization*. The *time* dimension has three *attributes*: *quarter*, *year*, and *all* (we regard *all* as a special attribute having one attribute value *ALL*, which depends on all other attribute values). The *organization* dimension has four attributes: *employee*, *department*, *branch*, and *all*. The attributes of each dimension are partially ordered (totally ordered in this special case) by the *dependency relation* $\preceq$ into a *dependency lattice* [40]. That is, *quarter* $\preceq$ *year* $\preceq$ *all* for the *time* dimension and *employee* $\preceq$ *department* $\preceq$ *branch* $\preceq$ *all* for the *organization* dimension. The product of the two lattices gives the dependency lattice of cuboids.

Each element of the dependency lattice is a tuple $< T, O >$, where T is an attribute of the *time* dimension and O is an attribute of the *organization* dimension. Attached to each such tuple $< T, O >$ is an empty two-dimensional array, namely, a *cuboid*. Each *cell* of the cuboid $< T, O >$ is also a tuple $< t, o >$, where t and o are *attribute values* of the attribute T and O, respectively. The dependency relation exists among cells, too. For example, the cuboid $< year, employee >$ depends on the cuboid $< quarter, employee >$, hence a cell $< Y1, Bob >$ of the former also depends on the cells $< Q1, Bob >$,

$< Q2, Bob >$, $< Q3, Bob >$, and $< Q4, Bob >$ of the latter. Similarly, the cell $< Q1, Book >$ depends on the cells $< Q1, Bob >$, $< Q1, Alice >$, $< Q1, Jim >$, and $< Q1, Mallory >$ (suppose the book department only has those four employees). Hence, all cells also form a dependency lattice.

The base table has the schema $(quarter, employee, commission)$. The base table is used to populate the data cube with values of the *measure* attribute *commission*. Each record in the base table, a triple (q, e, m), is used to populate a cell $< q, e >$ of the *core cuboid* $< quarter, employee >$, where q, e, and m are values of the attributes *quarter*, *employee*, and *commission*, respectively. Some cells of $< quarter, employee >$ remain empty (or having the $NULL$ value), if corresponding records are absent in the base table. If multiple records correspond to the same cell (the two attributes *quarter* and *employee* are not necessarily a key of the base relation), they are aggregated using the *aggregation function* SUM.

All cuboids are then populated using the same aggregation function (for simplicity purposes, only three populated cuboids are shown in Figure 7.1). For example, in the cuboid $< year, employee >$, a cell $< Y1, Bob >$ takes the value 8500, which is the total amount of the four cells it depends on, $< Q1, Bob >$, $< Q2, Bob >$, $< Q3, Bob >$, and $< Q4, Bob >$. An empty cell is deemed as zero in this aggregation (which depends on the aggregation function). As another example, the cuboid $< all, employee >$ (its cells are not shown in Figure 7.1) can be computed from either the core cuboid $< quarter, employee >$ or the cuboid $< year, employee >$, because it depends on both.

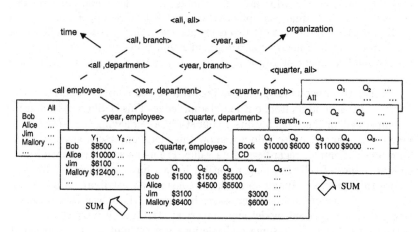

Fig. 7.1. An Example of Data Cubes

To fix notations, assume a fixed order among dimensions, among attributes of each dimension, and among values of each attribute. Analog to a relational table, which has schema and instances, a data cube can also be viewed at these two different levels. For schema, denote the ith ($1 \leq i \leq k$ for some fixed k) dimension D_i as a set of attributes $D_i = \{d_i^j : 1 \leq j \leq |D_i|\}$ (superscripts and subscripts will be omitted whenever appropriate), where $|D_i|$ denotes the cardinality of D_i. The data cube is then the collection of all cuboids, denoted by the Cartesian product of the k dimensions, $\mathcal{L} = \prod_{i=1}^{k} D_i$. Each cuboid $\mathbf{c} \in \mathcal{L}$ is a k-tuple of attributes $\mathbf{c} = < d_1, d_2, \ldots, d_k >$, with $d_i \in D_i$. This collection of k-tuples comprises the schema-level view of a data cube.

At the instance level, each attribute d_i denotes a set of attribute values. A cuboid $\mathbf{c} = < d_1, d_2, \ldots, d_k >$ is thus a collection of cells, denoted by the Cartesian product $\prod_{i=1}^{k} d_i$. Each cell $\mathbf{t} \in \mathbf{c}$ (here $\mathbf{c}$ means $\prod_{i=1}^{k} d_i$) is a k-tuple of attribute values. Use $\mathcal{A} = \bigcup_{\mathbf{c} \in \mathcal{L}} \mathbf{c}$ for the set of all cells in a data cube $\mathcal{L}$. Use $< \mathcal{L}, \preceq >$ for the dependency lattice of cuboids. Then $< \mathcal{A}, \preceq >$ is the dependency lattice of all cells. This collection of cells comprises the instance-level view of a data cube. The content of a cell, the aggregation of measure attribute values, is not explicitly denoted. Instead, we use a cell to interchangeably refer to both the cell itself and its content, when the actual meaning is clear from context.

We review some concepts related to lattices, which will appear in this chapter. In a lattice $< L, \preceq >$ (such as $< \mathcal{L}, \preceq >$ and $< \mathcal{A}, \preceq >$), any $x \in L$ and $y \in L$ are *non-comparable*, if neither $x \preceq y$ nor $y \preceq x$ hold; they are comparable, otherwise. Any $y \in L$ is an *ancestor* of $x \in L$ (and dually x is a *descendant* of y) if $y \preceq x$ holds (notice that in our graphical representation, such as in Figure 7.1, the descendants are always above the ancestors). For any $L' \subseteq L$, the *GLB* (greatest lower bound) of L' is any $x \in L$ satisfying that the condition $x \preceq y$ for any $y \in L'$ holds and no descendant of x satisfies the condition. The dual concept of GLB is *LUB* (lowest upper bound). The GLB and LUB of any (set of) two elements $x \in L$ and $y \in L$ are called their *meet* and *joint*, and denoted as $x \wedge y$ and $x \vee y$, respectively. x is a *maximal* (or *minimal*) element of any $L' \subseteq L$, if $x \preceq y$ (or $y \preceq x$) and $y \in L$ implies $y = x$.

Similar to previous chapters, we regard a cell as empty if and only if its value is known to users from outbound knowledge. This is different from using an empty cell for the $NULL$ value. In our study, a cell having the $NULL$ value may be non-empty, if users do not know this fact; conversely, any previously known cell is empty, regardless of its value. From the security point of view, specific values of cells not longer matter, if they have been learned by users before they pose any query. Second, we consider an attribute as a measure attribute (for example, the commission in Figure 7.1) only if it is sensitive, whereas in the original model any numerical attribute of interest may be a measure attribute. We assume multiple measure attributes are independent, so they can be considered separately, and hence we consider only one measure in further discussions.

7.3 Specifying Authorization Objects in Data Cubes

In Chapter 5 and Chapter 6, we have regarded the core cuboid of a data cube as the authorization object. This approach can accommodate the security requirement of many applications. However, it has two limitations. First, some of the aggregation cuboids may also be regarded as sensitive. Second, different cells in a core cuboid may have different security requirements. We thus need a more flexible way to specify authorization objects, that is which part of a data cube should be protected. This section devises a framework for this purpose.

An authorization is usually a triple: $< object, subject, (signed)action >$, indicating that the subject is allowed (or prohibited, depending on the sign of action) to execute the action on the object [43]. We only consider one type of action, *read*, since the confidentiality of data is the major security concern in OLAP systems. Other actions such as updates are relatively infrequent, and are accessible to only a few privileged operators. Subjects are users or user groups. We assume subjects do not collude, but users may do so. That is, a group of users inclined to collusion should be regarded as a single subject. We assume an open policy, where only prohibitions are specified, and permissions are implied by the absence of prohibitions.

The major difference between the authorization requirements of OLAP systems and that of relational databases lies in their authorization objects. This is decided by their different data models. In a *flat* relational model, typical objects include tables, records in a table, or fields of a record. By partitioning tables vertically into records and horizontally into fields, authorizations become finer grained. An analogous spectrum of objects needs to be defined in a multi-dimensional data cube model. However, unlike in the relational model, two independent aspects of a data cube come across in defining objects.

First, a data cube includes aggregations with different level of details, as shown in Figure 7.1. A subject's responsibilities may only entitle him/her to the aggregations above a certain level. Anything below is either sensitive or irrelevant to the subject's responsibilities, and hence should be prohibited according to the principle of least privilege (that is, only what is needed is permitted). Second, a data cube can be divided into slices by selection operations on one or more dimensions. Similarly, the least privilege principle requires a subject to be confined to some slices based on needs. Example 7.1 illustrates such requirements.

Example 7.1. Suppose an analyst Eve is invited to study the data cube in Figure 7.1, given that following two authorization requirements are satisfied. First, due to privacy concerns, Eve should not learn the value of any employee's commission, although she may access the aggregated values of departments or branches. Second, assume that any data no older than the quarter $Q5$ should not be used for the analysis. As illustrated in Figure 7.2, Eve should not access the three cuboids $< quarter, employee >$, $< year, employee >$, and $< all, employee >$. Moreover, she needs not to access cells like $< Y2, Book >$ (not shown in Figure 7.1), since the data is no older than $Q5$ (suppose $Y2$ depends on $Q5$, $Q6$, $Q7$, and $Q8$). Notice the difference between the two requirements. The former divides the *organization* dimension into two parts: *employee* and $\{department, branch, all\}$, based on the dimension hierarchy. The latter partitions the *time* dimension into *older than Q5* and *no older than Q5*, based the attribute values.

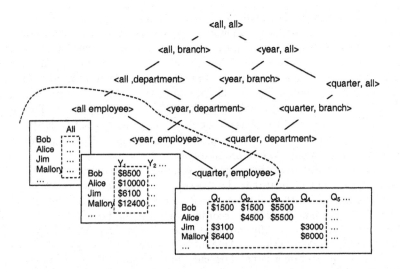

Fig. 7.2. An Example of Authorization Objects in Data Cubes

In Example 7.1, suppose an administrator specifies the first requirement with a cuboid $< all, employee >$, indicating that no aggregation finer than those in this cuboid should be accessed by Eve. Clearly, the two cuboids $< year, employee >$ and $< quarter, employee >$ are implied by this specification in the sense that from either of them the specified cuboid $< all, employee >$ can be computed. It is thus not always feasible to directly regard the specification given by administrators as an object, since one cannot protect an object while allowing ways to derive that object.

At the same time, the administrator should not be burdened with the responsibility of ensuring all implied cuboids to be included by a specification. Instead, we allow an *l-specification* (that is, level specification) S_l to be an arbitrary set of cuboids. Definition 7.2 then describes the concept of the *closure* $Below(S_l)$ of an l-specification S_l. A closure gives all and only the cuboids that are implied by the l-specification. The closure can be regarded as a *vertical partition* of the data cube.

Definition 7.2. *In any data cube $\mathcal{L}$, define a function $Below(.) : 2^{\mathcal{L}} \to 2^{\mathcal{L}}$ as $Below(S_l) = \{\mathbf{c} : \text{ there exists } \mathbf{c}_s \in S_l, \text{ such that } \mathbf{c} \preceq \mathbf{c}_s \text{ holds}\}$. We say*

- *A set of cuboids S_l is an l-**specification** (that is, level specification).*
- *$Below(S_l)$ is the **closure** of S_l.*

Example 7.3. The requirement that Eve should not learn an employee's information can now be represented by the closure $Below(< all, employee >)$.

The second requirement in Example 7.1 that data no older than the quarter $Q5$ should not be used for analysis requires a *horizontal partition* of the data cube. Generally, an *s-specification* (that is, slice specification) r is an arbitrary set of cells (usually, but not necessarily, in one cuboid). The *slice $Slice(r)$* of an s-specification r, as formalized in Definition 7.4, includes all and only the cells comparable to at least one cell in the s-specification.

Definition 7.4. *In any data cube $\mathcal{L}$ with the set of all cells $\mathcal{A}$ (that is, $\mathcal{A} = \bigcup_{\mathbf{c} \in \mathcal{L}} \mathbf{c}$), define a function $Slice(.) : 2^{\mathcal{A}} \to 2^{\mathcal{A}}$ as $Slice(r) = \{\mathbf{t} : \text{ there exists } \mathbf{t}_1 \in r \text{ such that } \mathbf{t} \preceq \mathbf{t}_1 \text{ or } \mathbf{t}_1 \preceq \mathbf{t} \text{ holds}\}$. We say*

- *Any $r \subseteq \mathcal{A}$ is an s-**specification** (that is, slice specification)*
- *$Slice(r)$ is the **slice** of r*

Example 7.5. The requirement that Eve should not learn anything no older than $Q5$ can be represented by the slice $Slice(\{< q, e >: q \in quarter, e \in employee, q \geq Q5\})$.

Authorization objects may be specified independently by several administrators over time. Hence, each subject may be regulated by more than one pair of s-specification and l-specification. Without loss of generality, suppose two pairs (r_1, S_1) and (r_2, S_2) are specified for the same subject, where r_1 and r_2 are s-specifications, and S_1 and S_2 are l-specifications. Further suppose that neither $Below(S_1) \subseteq Below(S_2)$ nor $Below(S_2) \subseteq Below(S_1)$ holds. Then the intersection of the two slices $Slice(r_1) \cap Slice(r_2)$ corresponds to a new closure $Below(S_1 \cup S_2)$. It would be prohibitive if such a new closure needs to be computed for every intersection of slices, since there are potentially exponential (in the number of slices) number of intersections.

Fortunately, the function $Below()$ is distributive over set union, as stated in Proposition 7.6. This desired property allows the intersections of slices to be ignored in controlling accesses to an object, given that the open policy is properly enforced for each slice respectively (that is, a request is permitted only if no prohibition exists). Similarly, the *boundary* cells among slices can also be ignored. For example, a cell $< ALL, Book >$ (not shown in Figure 7.1) belongs to both the slice *older than Q5* and the slice *no older than Q5* (since the value ALL depends on all other values). The request for such a cell will be denied, because a prohibition exists in the second slice, according to Example 7.5.

Proposition 7.6. *In any data cube* $\mathcal{L}$*,* $Below(S_1 \cup S_2) = Below(S_1) \cup Below(S_2)$ *holds for any* $S_1 \in \mathcal{L}$ *and* $S_2 \in \mathcal{L}$*.*

Proof: We show $Below(S_1 \cup S_2) \subseteq Below(S_1) \cup Below(S_2)$ and $Below(S_1) \cup Below(S_2) \subseteq Below(S_1 \cup S_2)$ hold. By Definition 7.2, $Below(S_1 \cup S_2) = \{\mathbf{c} : \exists \mathbf{c}_s \in S_1 \cup S_2 \; \mathbf{c} \preceq \mathbf{c}_s\}$. Hence, for any $\mathbf{c} \in Below(S_1 \cup S_2)$, either $\mathbf{c} \succeq \mathbf{c}_1 \in S_1$ or $\mathbf{c} \succeq \mathbf{c}_2 \in S_s$ (or both) holds. That is, $Below(S_1 \cup S_2) \subseteq Below(S_1) \cup Below(S_2)$ holds. Conversely, any $\mathbf{c}_1 \in Below(S_1)$ must satisfy $\mathbf{c}_1 \succeq \mathbf{c} \in S_1 \subseteq S_1 \cup S_2$, and hence $\mathbf{c}_1 \in Below(S_1 \cup S_2)$ holds. Similar case for any $\mathbf{c}_2 \in Below(S_2)$. Hence, $Below(S_1) \cup Below(S_2) \subseteq Below(S_1 \cup S_2)$ holds. This shows that $Below(S_1) \cup Below(S_2) = Below(S_1 \cup S_2)$ is true.   □

We are now ready to define authorization objects in Definition 7.7 by combining closures and slices. An example of objects is then given in Example 7.8. Given $(Object(O), subject)$, a basic access control mechanism will deny any request for accesses to a protected cell $\mathbf{t} \in Object(O)$. This comprises the *minimal security requirement*. It is, however, ineffective to protect the object due to potential inferences, as illustrated in Section 7.4.1. Moreover, we shall show in Section 7.4.2.2 that the object of the basic access control is actually enclosed by that of the inference control. Hence, we conclude this section without further addressing access control.

Definition 7.7. *In any data cube* $\mathcal{L}$ *with the set of all cells* $\mathcal{A}$*, define a function* $Object(.) : 2^{2^{\mathcal{A}} \times 2^{\mathcal{L}}} \to 2^{\mathcal{A}}$ *as* $Object(\{(r_i, S_i) : 1 \leq i \leq n\}) = \{\mathbf{t} : \mathbf{t} \in Slice(r_i) \text{ and } \mathbf{t} \in \mathbf{c} \text{ both hold, for some } 1 \leq i \leq n \text{ and } \mathbf{c} \in Below(S_i)\}$*. We say*

- *$Object(O))$ is an* **authorization object** *(or simply an object) specified by the pairs of s-specification and l-specification* $O = \{(r_i, S_i) : 1 \leq i \leq n\}$
- *A cell* $\mathbf{t} \in Object(O)$ *is* **protected**

Example 7.8. Following previous examples, the object for Eve is $Object(O)$, where $O = \{(r_1, S_1), (r_2, S_2)\}$. Then we have $r_1 = < ALL, ALL >$, $S_1 = < all, employee >$, $r_2 = \{< q, e >: q \in quarter, e \in employee, q \geq Q5\}$, and $S_2 = < all, all >$ (notice that $< ALL, ALL >$ is a cell and $< all, all >$ is a cuboid). Examples of protected cells include $< Y1, Bob >$ (in both $Slice(r_1)$ and $Below(S_1)$), $< ALL, Book >$ (in both $Slice(r_2)$ and $Below(S_2)$) and $< Y2, Alice >$ (in both $Slice(r_1) \cap Slice(r_2)$ and $Below(S_1 \cup S_2)$).

7.4 Controlling Inferences in Data Cubes

Our definition of an authorization object prevents any protected cell from being computed from *below* (that is, from its ancestors). However, in many cases a protected cell can be inferred from *above* (that is, from its descendants). Such inferences can easily infiltrate the first line of defense established by access control. This section addresses inference control in data cubes. First, in Section 7.4.1 we illustrate inferences in data cubes through examples. Then, in Section 7.4.2 and 7.4.3 we propose methods to prevent and eliminate inferences.

7.4.1 Inferences in Data Cubes

In data cubes, an *inference* occurs when sensitive values in protected cells can be computed from the values of their unprotected descendants combined with external knowledge. The inference thus depends on several factors. That is, the *source* and *target*, which denotes the set of unprotected cells causing the inference and the set of protected cells being inferred, respectively; the *aggregation function*, which is used to compute the value of each cell; the *sensitive criterion*, which decides what information is sensitive; and *external knowledge*, which has been learned through outbound channels other than queries.

Most inference control methods, including those discussed in previous sections, adopt a *detecting-then-removing* approach. This approach usually relies on the assumption of one or more specific type of aggregation functions, sensitivity criteria, and external knowledge. For example, only SUMs are allowed; only the exact values are sensitive; adversaries know nothing about the data type of sensitive attributes. Unfortunately, a practical OLAP system does not restrict its users to SUM-only, nor hides from users the data type of an attribute. Different systems may also adopt different sensitivity criteria.

Extending a detection method to remove its various assumptions is usually infeasible. For example, as discussed in Chapter 3, Chin shows that detecting inferences by *auditing* [16] is polynomial for both SUM-only and MAX-only cases, but it becomes NP-hard for the case of both SUM and MAX [13]. Even for the SUM-only case, the detection becomes infeasible, if both exact sensitive values and the small intervals enclosing such values are considered as sensitive [22, 47], or when a subject knows that the sensitive attributes are binary [45].

However, a special kind of inferences, one-dimensional inferences (or 1-d inferences for short), is usually easy to detect. As illustrated in Example 7.9, in 1-d inferences, the source, as well as the target, is the subset of a single cuboid. In such a case, the cells in the source depend on disjoint sets of cells in the target. In Example 7.9, each cell in the source $< quarter, department >$ depends on a different column (in the viewable area) of the target $< quarter, employee >$. Conversely, to infer a cell in the target, one can use exactly one cell in the source. This corresponds to the single query attack (or small query set attack) in statistical databases, as discussed in Chapter 3.

Informally, the above property implies that the detection of 1-d inferences can be *partitioned* in the sense that cells in the source do not help each other in gaining inferences (a more formal statement will be given later in Definition 7.13). Hence, 1-d inferences can be detected by evaluating each cell in the source against its ancestors in the target, using any given sensitivity criteria. There is no need to worry about adversaries in combining multiple cells in the source. This simple detection procedure will remain effective independent of the sensitivity criteria being used.

Example 7.9 (1-d Inferences). In Figure 7.3, suppose Eve is not allowed to access $< quarter, employee >$, but can access $< quarter, department >$. Further suppose Eve already knows about the empty cells, and the fact that Bob and Alice are taking the same amount of commission in $Q3$. Eve can then infer the cell $< Q3, Bob >$ and $< Q3, Alice >$ as 5500, which is half the amount 11000 of $< Q3, Book >$.

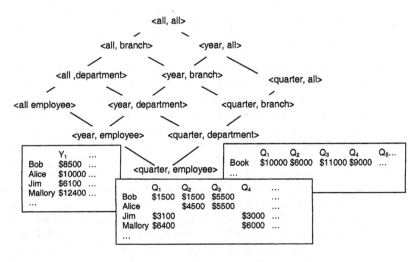

Fig. 7.3. Inferences in Data Cubes

Detection is more expensive and less effective for multi-dimensional inferences (or m-d inferences for short), where multiple cells in the source can be combined to infer a cell in the target. m-d inference is the complement of 1-d inference in the sense that the intersection of the source with any single cuboid does not cause an inference, but the source does. m-d inferences are possible when the source is composed of multiple non-comparable descendants of the target. Example 7.10 illustrates two-dimensional inferences in SUM-only data cubes (three or more dimensional inferences can be easily constructed). Example 7.11 and 7.12 then illustrate m-d inferences in MAX-only data cubes and in data cubes with SUM, MAX, and MIN. These examples show that different aggregation functions will require different detection methods, and unlike the detection of 1-d inferences, the detection of m-d inferences is not partitionable.

Example 7.10 (m-d Inferences in SUM-only Data Cubes). Suppose that the external knowledge about identical values cannot be learned, and hence the inference described in Example 7.9 can no longer by achieved by Eve. Assume Eve has accesses to the cuboid $<$ *quarter, department* $>$ as well as to $<$ *year, employee* $>$. Notice that the two cuboids are both free of 1-d inferences, because each of their cells depends on two or more cells in the target $<$ *quarter, employee* $>$ (suppose only exact values are sensitive). However, m-d inferences are possible in the following way.

- Eve first sums the two cells $< Y1, Bob >$ and $< Y1, Alice >$ in the cuboid $<$ *year, employee* $>$
- She then subtracts from the result 18500 the two cells $< Q2, Book >$ (that is, 6000) and $< Q3, Book >$ (that is, 11000) in the cuboid $<$ *quarter, department* $>$
- The protected cell $< Q1, Bob >$ is then inferred as 1500.

Example 7.11 (m-d Inferences in MAX-only Data Cubes). Suppose the external knowledge about empty cells is now prevented. Now the cuboid $<$ *quarter, employee* $>$ seems to Eve as being full of unknown values. Such a *full* SUM-only data cube is safe from m-d inferences by results of the previous chapter. However, the following m-d inference is possible with MAXs (the MAXs are not shown in Figure 7.3).

- Eve applies the MAX to $< Y1, Mallory >$ and $< Q4, Book >$ and gets 6400 and 6000 as the result, respectively.
- She can infer one of the three cells $< Q1, Mallory >$, $< Q2, Mallory >$, and $< Q3, Mallory >$ must be 6400, because $< Q4, Mallory >$ must be no greater than 6000.
- Eve concludes that $< Q2, Mallory >$ and $< Q3, Mallory >$ cannot be 6400, either.
- The protected cell $< Q1, Mallory >$ is then successfully inferred as 6400.

Example 7.12 (m-d Inferences with SUM, MAX and MIN). Finally, suppose Eve can ask SUMs, MAXs and MINs. By Example 7.11, $< Q1, Mallory >$ is 6400. Eve can then make following inferences.

- Eve applies to $< Y1, Mallory >$ MAX,MIN, and SUM, and gets 6400,6000, and 12400 as the answers (the MAXs and MINs are not shown in Figure 7.3).
- Eve infers $< Q2, Mallory >$, $< Q3, Mallory >$, and $< Q4, Mallory >$ must be 6000 and two zeroes, although she does not know exactly which is 6000.
- Eve then applies MAX,MIN, and SUM to $< Q2, Book >$, $< Q3, Book >$ and $< Q4, Book >$, whose result tells Eve the following facts, although she cannot match the values to exact cells yet.
  1. In $<$ *quarter, employee* $>$, two cells in $Q2$ are 1500 and 4500
  2. In $Q3$ the values are 5500 and 5500

3. In $Q4$ the values are 3000 and 6000
4. The rest are all zeroes

- Eve then conclude that $< Q4, Mallory >$ must be 6000, because the values in $Q3$ and $Q2$ cannot be.
- Similarly, Eve can infer $< Q4, Jim >$ as 3000

Consequently, Eve infers all the cells in cuboid $< quarter, employee >$, and hence the whole data cube, even without any external knowledge.

¿From previous chapters we know that in a few special cases, such as in the SUM-only or MAX-only data cubes in Example 7.10 and 7.11, detecting m-d inferences is possible. However, to the best of our knowledge, no known methods can effectively detect m-d inferences in the more general case. Moreover, even for those special cases, the computational complexity and storage requirement render the detection infeasible. Because unlike 1-d inferences, any cells in a source may help each other in gaining m-d inferences. To make it worse, any cells known by adversaries in the past may also help them to make an inference. Therefore, a detecting method must either keep tracking all released cells for each subject, or examine the whole data cube for just a few requested cells.

7.4.2 Preventing Multi-Dimensional Inferences

¿From the examples and discussions in Section 7.4.1, m-d inferences are clearly the main difficulty in inference control. In this section, we propose a method to prevent m-d inferences from emerging, instead of detecting and removing them. This novel approach enables our method to remain effective for different aggregation functions, sensitivity criteria, and external knowledge. It also reduces the complexity of the method to a practical level.

7.4.2.1 Assumptions

We do not assume specific aggregation functions, sensitivity criteria or external knowledge. Instead, we assume that they satisfy some algebraic properties, stated as three conditions in Definition 7.13. Although these conditions are stated in terms of sensitivity criteria, they actually encode the requirements on aggregation functions and external knowledge as well. The first condition says that if a source S includes both a cell and all its ancestors in a cuboid, then removing the cell from S does not change its sensitivity with respect to the target T. This is reasonable, because a cell can usually be computed from its ancestors, and hence it does not bring additional knowledge.

The first condition implies that we assume *distributive* aggregation functions [37] such as SUM, MAX, and MIN. For a non-distributive aggregation function, we can keep the assumption valid through a conservative approach as follows. We replace the non-distributive function with an *intermediate function*. For example, AVG is not distributive, but the pair $(SUM, COUNT)$ is distributive, and AVG can certainly be computed from $(SUM, COUNT)$. As another example, the identity function, which is clearly distributive, can act as an intermediate function for any aggregation function.

The second condition in Definition 7.13 says that inferences are caused by descendants only. This does not hold if external knowledge can relate two cells in non-comparable cuboids. In that case, we could regard one as empty (that is, known from external knowledge) if the other is unprotected. One immediate implication of the two conditions is a generalization of the observation made about Example 7.9. That is, inferences can be partitioned, if the source S can be divided into blocks that depend on disjoint sets of cells in the target T.

Definition 7.13. *In any data cube $\mathcal{L}$ with the set of all cells $\mathcal{A}$, we say*

- *Any binary function $Sensitive(.) : 2^{\mathcal{A}} \times 2^{\mathcal{A}} \rightarrow \{TRUE, FALSE\}$ is a* **sensitivity criterion,** *if the following all hold:*
  1. *$Sensitive(S, T) = Sensitive(S \setminus \{\mathbf{t}_1\}, T)$, for any cell $\mathbf{t}_1$ in a cuboid $\mathbf{c}_1$, if there exists $\mathbf{c} \prec \mathbf{c}_1$ satisfying $\{\mathbf{t} : \mathbf{t} \in \mathbf{c}, \mathbf{t} \preceq \mathbf{t}_1\} \subseteq S$.*
  2. *$Sensitive(S, T) = Sensitive(S \setminus \mathbf{c}_1, T)$, for any cuboid $\mathbf{c}_1$, if $\mathbf{c}_1$ is non-comparable to any cuboid $\mathbf{c}$ satisfying $\mathbf{c} \cap T \neq \phi$.*
- *A source S is* **sensitive** *with respect to a target T, if $Sensitive(S, T) = TRUE$ holds.*

7.4.2.2 A Special Case

First consider a special case where the s-specification r is a complete cuboid. The slice of r is then the data cube itself. The object $Object((r, S_l))$ is thus simply (the union of) protected cuboids in $Below(S_l)$ (we shall omit *the union* and simply say a set of cuboids whenever possible). That is, we simplify the discussion by only considering cuboid-level authorizations. Finer-grained authorizations at cell level will be delayed until next section. Example 7.14 describes such an object. Consider the set of protected cuboids $Below(S_l)$ as the target, and the set of unprotected cuboids $\mathcal{L} \setminus Below(S_l)$ as the source. Our objective is to find a subset of the source that is *free of m-d inferences* to the target and is at the same time *maximal* with respect to the number of cuboids it includes.

Example 7.14. Figure 7.4 shows part of the dependency lattice of a four-dimensional data cube in a Hasse diagram. Each integer denotes an attribute. The dot lines denote the dependency relation (those implied by the reflexivity and transitivity of the dependency relation are omitted). Let $S_l = \{< 1, 1, 2, 2 >, < 1, 2, 1, 2 >\})$, the lower curve in the solid line depicts an object $Below(S_l)$. All cuboids below the lower curve are protected, and those above are unprotected. Apparently, m-d inferences are possible from unprotected cuboids to protected ones. For instance, $\{< 1, 2, 2, 2 >$ and $< 2, 1, 2, 2 >\}$ are two non-comparable descendants of $< 1, 1, 2, 2 >$. The cells in the former may thus be combined to infer those in the latter, even if each of the cuboids alone does not cause any inference.

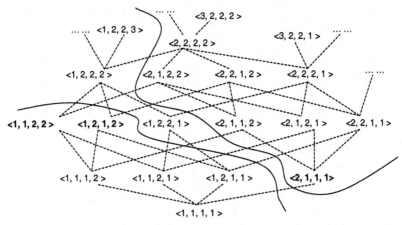

Fig. 7.4. An Example of Preventing m-d Inferences

First, considering the redundancy inherent to a data cube, our job can be simplified, since not all cuboids in the source contribute to the m-d inference of a cuboid in the target. According to the two conditions in Definition 7.13, for each cuboid c_t in the target $Below(S_l)$, we can reduce the source to a minimal subset without changing its sensitivity with respect to c_t by removing those cuboids that either carry only redundant information or are irrelevant to the inference of c_t.

Specifically, a cuboid can be ignored if it is either non-comparable to c_t or a descendant of other cuboids in the source. The first is due to the assumption that only descendants cause inferences, and the second is due to that derived cuboids are redundant. We thus have the minimal elements in the set of descendants of c_t, namely, the *basis* $Basis(S)$ of the source S with respect to the cuboid c_t, as formalized in Definition 7.15. An example of the basis is given in Example 7.16.

Definition 7.15. *In any data cube $\mathcal{L}$,*

- *We define a function $Basis(.) : 2^{\mathcal{L}} \times \mathcal{L} \to 2^{\mathcal{L}}$ as $Basis(S, c_t) = \{c : c \in S, c_t \preceq c, (c_1 \in S \wedge c_1 \preceq c) \text{ implies } c_1 = c\}$*
- *We say $Basis(S, c_t)$ is the **basis** of the source S with respect to a cuboid c_t in the target*

Example 7.16. From Example 7.14, we already have

$$Basis(\mathcal{L} \setminus Below(S_l), <1,1,2,2>) = \{<1,2,2,2>, <2,1,2,2>\}$$

That is, for inferences to the protected cuboid $<1,1,2,2>$, we only need to consider its two non-comparable descendants $<1,2,2,2>$ and $<2,1,2,2>$.

Because a basis only includes non-comparable cuboids, we can have the following conclusion. m-d inferences are possible from the source S to c_t only if the basis $Basis(S, c_t)$ includes more than one cuboid. That is, although a source may include many cuboids, effectively only those in its basis contribute to an m-d inference. For example, m-d inferences are possible in Example 7.16, because the basis includes two cuboids. The two cuboids also carry non-redundant information, which can be combined to bring adversaries with more knowledge about the cuboid in the target, making inferences possible.

Conversely, to prevent such a situation, we can construct a subset of the source that is free of m-d inferences to c_t by *growing* from a singleton basis, namely, a *root*. More precisely, we first choose an unprotected cuboid c_r satisfying $c_r \succeq c_t$, then we include all the descendants of c_r to form a set. The result must satisfy that its basis with respect to c_t includes only one cuboid, that is the root c_r. Hence, the result is free of m-d inferences to c_t. This process is formalized as a function $Above()$ in Definition 7.17 (this concept is known as an *ideal* in lattice theory [30]) and illustrated in Example 7.18.

Definition 7.17. *In any data cube $\mathcal{L}$,*

- *We define a function $Above(.) : \mathcal{L} \to 2^{\mathcal{L}}$ as $Above(c_r) = \{c : c_r \preceq c\}$*
- *We say the cuboid c_r is the* **root** *of $Above(c_r)$*

Example 7.18. In Figure 7.4, the cuboids above the upper curve in the solid line comprise $Above(c_r)$, where the root $c_r = <2,1,1,1>$ is an unprotected descendant of the core cuboid $<1,1,1,1>$. Clearly, no m-d inference is possible from $Above(<2,1,1,1>)$ to $<1,1,1,1>$, since the basis $Basis(Above(<2,1,1,1>), <1,1,1,1>)$ includes only the root itself.

However, we not only need to prevent m-d inferences to the cuboid c_t but also need to prevent them to other cuboids in the target. Consider another protected cuboid c_1 that is non-comparable to the root c_r. Then $Basis(Above(c_r), c_1)$ must be different from $Basis(Above(c_r), c_t)$, because at least the root c_r is not included by the former. A question thus arises: is $Basis(Above(c_r), c_1)$ also a singleton set? In another word, is the subset constructed for protecting c_t also sufficient for protecting other cuboids?

Lemma 7.19 answers the above question. It shows that the subset we have chosen does not cause any m-d inference to any cuboid in the target. Moreover, the cuboid included by $Basis(Above(c_r), c_1)$ happens to be the joint $c_1 \vee c_r$. We have thus successfully obtained a subset $Above(c_r)$ of the source $\mathcal{L} \setminus Below(S_l)$ that is free of m-d inferences to the target $Below(S_l)$. Finally, Lemma 7.19 extends the target from $Below(S_l)$ to $\mathcal{L} \setminus Above(c_r)$. This is important because inference is transitive. That is, m-d inferences may first compromise the unprotected cuboids between $Below(S_l)$ and $Above(c_r)$, and then continue to infer the protected cuboids in $Below(S_l)$.

Lemma 7.19. *In any data cube $\mathcal{L}$, given any l-specification S_l and a root $c_r \in \mathcal{L} \setminus Below(S_l)$, $Basis(Above(c_r), \{c_t\}) = \{c_r \vee c_t\}$ holds for any cuboid $c_t \in \mathcal{L} \setminus Above(c_r)$.*

Proof: By Definition 7.15, we have that any $c \in Basis(Above(c_r), \{c_t\})$ holds only if $c \in Above(c_r)$ and $c \succeq c_t$ are both true. Then by Definition 7.17, $c \succeq c_r$ must also be true. Hence, $Basis(Above(c_r), \{c_t\}) \subseteq S = \{c : c \succeq c_r, c \succeq c_t\}$ holds. Clearly, $c_r \vee c_t \in S$ holds. Moreover, any $c \in S$ must satisfy $c \succeq c_r \vee c_t$. Then again by By Definition 7.15, any $c \succ c_r \vee c_t$ must not satisfy $c \in Basis(Above(c_r), \{c_t\})$, because otherwise $c \succ c_r \vee c_t$ implies $c = c_r \vee c_t$, a contradiction. Consequently, $Basis(Above(c_r), \{c_t\}) \subseteq \{c_r \vee c_t\}$ is true. On the other hand, the definition of joint says that $c \in S$ and $c \preceq c_r \vee c_t$ implies $c = c_r \vee c_t$. That is, $c_r \vee c_t \in Basis(Above(c_r), \{c_t\})$ is also true. This implies $Basis(Above(c_r), \{c_t\}) = \{c_r \vee c_t\}$.   □

Example 7.20. In Figure 7.4, now consider the cuboids above the upper curve as the source, and those below the upper curve as the target. From any cuboid in the target, exactly one dot line goes into the source. Each such line points to the joint of this cuboid and the root $< 2, 1, 1, 1 >$. For example, a line goes from the leftmost cuboid $< 1, 1, 2, 2 >$ to its joint with the root, $< 2, 1, 2, 2 >$ (another line points to $< 1, 2, 2, 2 >$, which is not in the source). Similarly, from $< 1, 2, 2, 2 >$, a line points to $< 2, 2, 2, 2 >$ but other lines do not point to the source. Those observations indicate the absence of m-d inferences.

Next we consider the maximality aspect of this result. The maximality is achieved by choosing a minimal root. More precisely, we let c_r be a minimal element of the set of unprotected cuboids $\mathcal{L} \setminus Below(S_l)$. Lemma 7.21 then states that for any unprotected cuboid not included by $Above(c_r)$, its meet with the root must be a protected cuboid. Hence, this cuboid together with the root may cause m-d inferences to their meet. That is, $Above(c_r)$ is indeed maximal.

Lemma 7.21. *In any data cube $\mathcal{L}$, given any l-specification S_l and a minimal element of $c_r \in \mathcal{L} \setminus Below(S_l)$, $c_1 \wedge c_r \in Below(S_l)$ holds for any $c_1 \in \mathcal{L} \setminus (Below(S_l) \cup Above(c_r))$.*

Proof: Because c_r is a minimal element of $\mathcal{L} \setminus Below(S_l)$, $c_r \wedge c_1 \preceq c_r$ implies either $c_r \wedge c_1 = c_r$ or $c_r \wedge c_1 \notin \mathcal{L} \setminus Below(S_l)$ holds. However, $c_r \wedge c_1 = c_r$ must not hold, because otherwise $c_1 \succeq c_r$ implies the contradiction $c_1 \in Above(c_r)$. That is, $c_r \wedge c_1 \in Below(S_l)$ holds.   □

Example 7.22. As shown in Figure 7.5, we increase the size of the source $Above(< 2, 1, 1, 1 >)$ by redrawing the upper curve, such that the cuboid $< 1, 2, 2, 2 >$ is now above the new curve. Then we have that $< 1, 2, 2, 2 > \wedge < 2, 1, 1, 1 > = < 1, 1, 1, 1 >$, indicating potential m-d inferences from the former two cuboids to the latter.

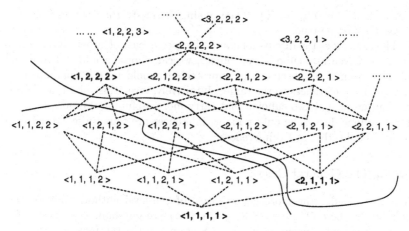

Fig. 7.5. An Example of Potential m-d Inferences

As the uniqueness of our result, $Above(c_r)$ is not arbitrary, but instead the only choice to satisfy both the prevention of m-d inferences and the maximality. This is formalized as the only if part in Theorem 7.23 (the if part is given by Lemma 7.19 and 7.21). Hence, $Above(c_r)$ is the best possible result with respect to the prevention of m-d inferences. Any further improvement of this result will require the detection of m-d inferences, which is possible in only a few special cases, as discussed in Section 7.4.1.

Theorem 7.23. *In any data cube $\mathcal{L}$, given any l-specification S_l, any set of unprotected cuboids $C \subseteq \mathcal{L} \setminus Below(S_l)$ satisfies the following two properties, if and only if $C = Above(c_r)$, where c_r is a minimal element of $\mathcal{L} \setminus Below(S_l)$.*

1. $| Basis(C, c) | = 1$, for any $c \in \mathcal{L} \setminus C$.
2. $| Basis(S, c) | > 1$, for any S satisfying $C \subset S \subseteq \mathcal{L} \setminus Below(S_l)$, and some $c \in Below(S_l)$.

Proof: The if part is given by Lemma 7.19 and Lemma 7.21. We only show the only if part. Any non-empty $C \subseteq \mathcal{L} \setminus Below(S_l)$ is a poset , and hence has a unique non-empty set of minimal elements C_m. We first show that $| C_m | > 1$ must not hold by contradiction. Let c be GLB of C_m. Then $c \in Below(S_l)$ must not hold. Otherwise, by Definition 7.15, $Basis(C, c) = C_m$ and hence $| Basis(C, c) | = | C_m | > 1$ is a contradiction to the first condition. Hence, $c \in \mathcal{L} \setminus Below(S_l)$ is true. Because c is the GLB of C_m, it is also the GLB of C. Then by Definition 7.17, $C \subseteq Above(c)$ holds. However, $| C_m | > 1$ implies $C = Above(c)$ must not hold, because $Above(c)$ has only one minimal element c. Hence, $C \subset Above(c)$. This contradicts the second condition of maximality, because $Above(c)$ clearly satisfies the first condition. Consequently, $| C_m | =$

1 must hold. Let $C_m = \{\mathbf{c}\}$. Then again, to satisfy the maximality, $C = Above(\mathbf{c})$ must be true. □

This concludes the discussion about the special case of cuboid-level authorizations. Given any cuboid-level object, we can choose a minimal root and compute from it a subset of the unprotected cuboid that is guaranteed to cause no m-d inferences to the target. Intuitively, given this subset, an adversary can never find two cuboids that carry more useful information than any of them alone does. The only possible inferences are thus those caused by a single cuboid, that is 1-d inferences.

7.4.2.3 The General Case

Next we consider the more general case of cell-level authorization objects $Object(O)$, where $O = \{(r_i, S_i) : 1 \leq i \leq n\}$ are any number of pairs of s-specification and l-specification. As in Section 7.3, the key issue in extending our results in the special case lies in the potentially exponential number of intersections between slices. Inference control will be prohibitive if it needs to deal with each such intersection in addition to the slices.

Fortunately, the result stated in Lemma 7.19 is distributive over set intersection. Without loss of generality, suppose neither $Below(S_1) \subseteq Below(S_2)$ nor $Below(S_2) \subseteq Below(S_1)$ holds, and $Object((r_1, S_1)) \cap Object((r_2, S_2)) \neq \phi$ (that is, some protected cells are included by the intersection). We divide $Slice(r_1)$ and $Slice(r_2)$ into three disjoint parts $Slice(r_1) \setminus Slice(r_2)$, $Slice(r_2) \setminus Slice(r_1)$ and $Slice(r_1) \cap Slice(r_2)$. Then by the conditions of Definiton 7.13, we can consider each part independently for inferences. By Theorem 7.23, we can prevent m-d inferences in $Slice(r_1) \setminus Slice(r_2)$ and $Slice(r_2) \setminus Slice(r_1)$ by choosing a root for each part respectively.

Now for the intersection $Slice(r_1) \cap Slice(r_2)$, we simply regard the joint of the two chosen roots as a new root. Lemma 7.24 then states two results. First, this new root is unprotected with respect to the closure $Below(S_1 \cup S_2)$. This means the root is indeed valid for preventing m-d inferences according to Lemma 7.19. Second, the function $Above()$ is *distributive* over set intersection. Hence, the intersection can be ignored in inference control, if the open policy is properly enforced. That is, the cells in the intersection are free of m-d inferences only if both slices say so.

Lemma 7.24. *In any data cube $\mathcal{L}$, given any two pair of s-specification and l-specification (r_1, S_1) and (r_2, S_2), let $\mathbf{c}_1 \in \mathcal{L} \setminus Below(S_1)$ and $\mathbf{c}_2 \in \mathcal{L} \setminus Below(S_2)$. Then we have the following both hold.*

- $\mathbf{c}_1 \vee \mathbf{c}_2 \in \mathcal{L} \setminus Below(S_1 \cup S_2)$
- $Above(\mathbf{c}_1 \vee \mathbf{c}_2) = Above(\mathbf{c}_1) \cap Above(\mathbf{c}_2)$

Proof: We first show $\mathbf{c}_1 \vee \mathbf{c}_2 \in Below(S_1 \cup S_2)$ must not hold by contradiction. Suppose it is true, then by Proposition 7.6, either $\mathbf{c}_1 \vee \mathbf{c}_2 \in Below(S_1)$ or $\mathbf{c}_1 \vee \mathbf{c}_2 \in Below(S_1)$ (or both) holds. However, if $\mathbf{c}_1 \vee \mathbf{c}_2 \in Below(S_1)$ is true, then $c_1 \preceq c_1 \vee c_2 \preceq c$ must hold for some $c \in S_1$. This leads to the contradiction $c_1 \in Below(S_1)$. Similarly, $c_1 \vee c_2 \in Below(S_1)$ implies $c_2 \in Below(S_2)$. This shows that $c_1 \vee c_2 \in \mathcal{L} \setminus Below(S_1 \cup S_2)$ must be true. Then we show $Above(c_1 \vee c_2) = Above(c_1) \cap Above(c_2)$ also holds. By Definition 7.17, $c \in Above(c_1 \vee c_2)$ holds if and only if $c \succeq c_1 \vee c_2$ and hence both $c \succeq c_1$ and $c \succeq c_1$ hold. This is equivalent to saying $c \in Above(c_1) \cap Above(c_2)$.   □

However, while intersections are free of m-d inferences, the maximality aspect stated in Lemma 7.21 is not guaranteed for them. When the two roots c_1 and c_2 are minimal elements of $\mathcal{L} \setminus Below(S_1)$ and $\mathcal{L} \setminus Below(S_2)$, respectively, their joint is not necessarily a minimal element of $\mathcal{L} \setminus Below(S_1 \cup S_2)$. In order to preserve the maximality for the intersection, we must coordinate the choice of both roots. In general, preserving maximality for all the intersections is difficult.

As we shall show, even a restricted case where the number of intersections is linear in that of slices is no easier than the *maximal independent set* problem, which is known as NP-complete [35]. Considering that intersections are usually not intentional, and the choices of roots also depend on other probably more important factors (such as the elimination of 1-d inferences discussed in Section 7.4.3), the maximality is not further pursued for intersections. We define the answerable set given by a set of roots in Definition 7.25. We also extend the function $Basis()$ defined in Definition 7.15.

Definition 7.25. *In any data cube $\mathcal{L}$, let $\mathcal{A}$ be the set of all cells, define*

- *a function $Answerable(.) : 2^{2^{\mathcal{A}} \times \mathcal{L}} \to 2^{\mathcal{A}}$ as: $Answerable(\{(r_i, c_i) : 1 \leq i \leq n\}) = \{t : for\ 1 \leq i \leq n, t \in Slice(r_i)\ implies\ t \in c\ holds\ for\ some\ c \in Above(c_i)\}$*
- *a function $gBasis(.) : 2^{\mathcal{A}} \times \mathcal{A} \to 2^{\mathcal{A}}$ as $gBasis(S, t_t) = \{t : t \in S, t_t \preceq t, (t_1 \in S \wedge t_1 \preceq t)\ implies\ t_1 = t\}$*

We say that

- *$Answerable(R)$ is the **answerable set** given by the set of roots $R = \{(r_i, c_i) : 1 \leq i \leq n\}$*
- *$t \in Answerable(R)$ is **answerable**, and each cell $t \in \mathcal{A} \setminus Answerable(R)$ **restricted***
- *$gBasis(S, t_t)$ is the **basis** of a set of cells S with respect to a cell t_t*

The answerable set is characterized in Theorem 7.26. The first claim says that an answerable set given by unprotected roots is always free of m-d inferences to any restricted cell. The second claim shows that an answerable set is maximal, if all the roots are minimal and no protected cells are included by intersections of slices. The third claim says that finding an appropriate set of roots to maximize the answerable set is NP-hard, if such disjoint slices are not the case. Notice that this NP-hardness result only states the infeasibility of maximizing the answerable set, but does not imply that of finding an answerable set.

Theorem 7.26. *In any data cube $\mathcal{L}$ with the set of all cells $\mathcal{A}$, given pairs of s-specification and l-specification $O = \{(r_i, S_i) : 1 \leq i \leq n)\}$, and a set of roots $R = \{(r_i, \mathbf{c}_i) : 1 \leq i \leq n, \mathbf{c}_i \text{ is a minimal element of } \mathcal{L} \setminus Below(S_i)\}$. The following conditions 1 and 2 hold, if $Object((r_i, S_i)) \cap Object((r_j, S_j)) = \phi$ is true for any $1 \leq i \neq j \leq n$; the following conditions 1 and 3 hold, otherwise.*

1. $\mid gBasis(Answerable(R), \mathbf{t}_t) \mid = 1$, *for any restricted cell* $\mathbf{t}_t \in \mathcal{A} \setminus Answerable(R)$.
2. $\mid gBasis(S, \mathbf{t}_t) \mid > 1$, *for any set of cells S satisfying $Answerable(R) \subset S \subseteq \mathcal{A} \setminus Object(O)$, and some protected cell* $\mathbf{t}_t \in Object(O)$.
3. *Finding the set R satisfying the above two conditions is NP-hard.*

Proof:

1. We first justify the first claim. Suppose $\mathbf{t}_t \in \mathbf{c}_t$ holds for some $\mathbf{c}_t \in \mathcal{L}$, and let $I = \{i : 1 \leq i \leq n, \mathbf{t}_t \in Slice(r_i)\}$. Then $\mathbf{t}_t \in \mathcal{A} \setminus Answerable(R)$ implies

$$\mathbf{c}_t \in \bigcup_{i \in I} Below(S_i) = Below(\bigcup_{i \in I} S_i)$$

First by Definition 7.25, we have

$$gBasis(Answerable(R), \mathbf{t}_t) \subseteq Answerable(R) \cap (\bigcup_{i \in I} Slice(r_i))$$

$$= (\bigcap_{i \in I} Above(\mathbf{c}_i)) \cap (\bigcup_{i \in I} Slice(r_i))$$

Then by Lemma 7.24, we have that

$$gBasis(Answerable(R), \mathbf{t}_t) \subseteq Above(\bigvee_{i \in I} \mathbf{c}_i) \cap (\bigcup_{i \in I} Slice(r_i))$$

and

$$\bigvee_{i \in I} 1\mathbf{c}_i \in \mathcal{L} \setminus Below(\bigcup_{i \in I} S_i)$$

Where $\bigvee_{i \in I} \mathbf{c}_i$ dentoes the LUB of $\{c_i : i \in I\}$. By Lemma 7.19 we then have

$$Basis(Above(\bigvee_{i \in I} \mathbf{c}_i), \mathbf{c}_t) = \{\mathbf{c}_t \cap \bigvee_{i \in I} \mathbf{c}_i\}$$

Denotes $\mathbf{c}_t \cap \bigvee_{i \in I} \mathbf{c}_i$ by $\mathbf{c}_r$. Because $\mathbf{c}_t \preceq \mathbf{c}_r$, there must exist one and only one $\mathbf{t}_r \in \mathbf{c}_r$ satisfying $\mathbf{t}_t \preceq \mathbf{t}_r$. Then $\mathbf{t}_r \in S$ holds, because the following are both true:

$$\mathbf{t}_r \in \mathbf{c}_r \in Above(\bigvee_{i \in I} \mathbf{c}_i) \text{ and } \mathbf{t}_r \in \bigcup_{i \in I} Slice(r_i)$$

For any $\mathbf{t} \in S$ satisfying $\mathbf{t}_t \preceq \mathbf{t}$, if $\mathbf{t} \in \mathbf{c}$ then $\mathbf{c}_r \preceq \mathbf{c}$ must hold, and $\mathbf{t}_r \preceq \mathbf{t}$ follows. Hence, $\mathbf{t} \preceq \mathbf{t}_r$ implies $\mathbf{t} = \mathbf{t}_r$ and $gBasis(Answerable(R), \mathbf{t}_t) = \{\mathbf{t}_r\}$ follows.

2. Next we justify the second claim by contradiction. Suppose some S satisfies both $Answerable(R) \subset S \subseteq \mathcal{A} \setminus Object(O)$ and $| gBasis(S, \mathbf{t}_t) | = 1$ for any $\mathbf{t}_t \in Object(O)$. Let $\mathbf{t}_s \in S \setminus Answerable(R)$, and $\mathbf{t}_s \in \mathbf{c}_s$ for some $\mathbf{c}_s \in \mathcal{L}$. Because $Object(\{(r_i, S_i)\}) \cap Object(\{(r_j, S_j)\}) = \phi$ is true for any $1 \leq i \neq j \leq n$, $| I = \{i : 1 \leq i \leq n, \mathbf{t}_s \in Slice(r_i)\} | = 1$ must be true. Without loss of generality, suppose $\mathbf{t}_s \in Slice(r_1)$ holds. Then $\mathbf{t}_s \in S \subseteq \mathcal{A} \setminus Object(O)$ implies $\mathbf{c}_s \in \mathcal{L} \setminus Below(S_1)$. Moreover, $\mathbf{t}_s \in Slice(r_1)$ and $\mathbf{t}_s \notin Answerable(R)$ implies $\mathbf{c}_s \notin Above(\mathbf{c}_1)$. By Lemma 7.21, $\mathbf{c}_s \wedge \mathbf{c}_1 \in Below(S_1)$. Denote $\mathbf{c}_s \wedge \mathbf{c}_1$ as $\mathbf{t}_t$, and suppose $\mathbf{t}_t \in \mathbf{c}_t \in Below(S_1)$. Then $\mathbf{t}_t \in Object(O)$ follows. Because $\mathbf{c}_t \preceq \mathbf{c}_1$, there must exist $\mathbf{t}_1 \in \mathbf{c}_1 \cap Slice(r_1) \subseteq Answerable(R)$ satisfying $\mathbf{t}_t \preceq \mathbf{t}_1$. Moreover, $\mathbf{c}_s \notin Above(\mathbf{c}_1)$ implies $\mathbf{c}_s$ and $\mathbf{c}_1$ are non-comparable, and hence $\mathbf{t}_1$ and $\mathbf{t}_s$ are also non-comparable. Consequently, $gBasis(S, \mathbf{t}_t) \supseteq \{\mathbf{t}_s, \mathbf{t}_1\}$, a contradiction to $| gBasis(S, \mathbf{t}_t) | = 1$.

3. Finally, we show the third claim holds by reducing the *maximal independent set* problem to a restricted case of our problem. Given any simple undirected graph $G(V, E)$, with the vertex set $V = \{i : 1 \leq i \leq n\}$, the edge set $E = \{\{i, j\} : 1 \leq i \neq j \leq n\}$, and the vertices i and j being incidenced by the edge $\{i, j\}$, we construct a new graph $G'(V', E')$ as the follows. First we let $G' = G$. Then for any isolated vertex $i \in V$, we add a new vertex $2i$ to V' and a new edge $\{i, 2i\}$ to E'. Then for any vertex $i \in V$ that is incidenced by only one edge, we add a new vertex $3i$ to V' and a new edge $\{i, 3i\}$ to E'. The new graph G' satisfies that $| V' | \leq 3n$, and each $1 \leq i \leq n$ in V' is incidenced by at least two edges, while each vertex $i > n$ in V' is incidenced by a single edge. For each vertex $1 \leq i \leq n$ in V', we use I_i for the set of its adjacent vertices $\{j : \{i, j\} \in E'\}$. We then construct a data cube $\mathcal{L}$, so a subset $S = \{\mathbf{c}_i : 1 \leq i \leq 3n\} \subseteq \mathcal{L}$ satisfies that any two cuboids in S are non-comparable, and their joint is the topmost cuboid $\mathbf{c}_{all} = < all, all, \ldots, all >$. For any edge $\{i, j\} \in E$, we let S_{ij} be the maximal elements of the set $\mathcal{L} \setminus \{\mathbf{c}_i, \mathbf{c}_j, \mathbf{c}_{all}\}$. Considering S_{ij} as an l-specification, then $\mathbf{c}_i$ and $\mathbf{c}_j$ are the two minimal elements of $\mathcal{L} \setminus Below(S_{ij})$, while $\mathbf{c}_h \in Below(S_{ij})$ holds for any $h \neq i$ and $h \neq j$. For each S_{ij}, we also choose one s-specification r_{ij}, such that for any $1 \leq i \leq n$, $J \subseteq I_i$, and $h \notin I_i$, the following both hold.

$$\bigcap_{j \in J} Object(\{(r_{ij}, S_{ij})\}) \neq \phi \text{ and } \bigcap_{j \in J \cup \{h\}} Object(\{(r_{ij}, S_{ij})\}) = \phi$$

That is, any two objects overlap if and only if the two corresponding edges incidence the same vertex. Let $O = \{(r_{ij}, S_{ij}) : \{i, j\} \in E\}$. Let $R = \{(r_{ij}, \mathbf{c}_{ij}) : \{i, j\} \in E, \mathbf{c}_{ij} \in \{\mathbf{c}_i, \mathbf{c}_j\}\}$.

We claim that if we can find an R such that $Answerable(R)$ is maximal, then we immediately have $V_s \subseteq V$ such that for any $i \in V_s$ and $j \in V_s$, $\{i,j\} \notin E$, and V_s is maximal. The latter is an instance of the maximal independent set problem, which is known as NP-complete [35], and hence finding an R to maximize $Answerable(R)$ is NP-hard. Now we justify the claim. Because for $1 \leq i \leq n$, each root $\mathbf{c}_{ij} \in \{\mathbf{c}_i, \mathbf{c}_j\}$ is a minimal element of $\mathcal{L} \setminus Below(S_{ij})$, $Answerable(R)$ is maximal if and only if the intersections are. Without loss of generality, consider the intersection at $\mathbf{c}_1$. That is,

$$(\bigcup_{i \in I_1} Slice(r_{1i})) \cap Answerable(R) = (\bigcup_{i \in I_1} Slice(r_{1i})) \cap Above(\bigvee_{i \in I_1} \mathbf{c}_{1i})$$

$Above(\bigvee_{i \in I_1} \mathbf{c}_{1i})$ is maximal if and only if $\mathbf{c}_{1i} = \mathbf{c}_1$ for all $i \in I_1$, and hence $(\bigvee_{i \in I_1} \mathbf{c}_{1i}) = \mathbf{c}_1$. Because if $\mathbf{c}_{lj} = \mathbf{c}_j$ holds for some j, then $(\bigvee_{i \in I_1} \mathbf{c}_{1i}) = \mathbf{c}_1 \wedge \mathbf{c}_j = \mathbf{c}_{all}$.

We know that $Above(\mathbf{c}_{all})$ includes only a single cell, which must be less than the number of cells in $Above(\mathbf{c}_1)$ (considering that $\mid \mathbf{c}_i \mid \gg 1$ for any i). However, by assigning $\mathbf{c}_{1i} = \mathbf{c}_1$ for all $i \in I_1$, the answerable set of the intersection at $\mathbf{c}_1$ is maximized, but those of the intersections at $\mathbf{c}_i$ for $i \in I_1$ are not maximized. Consequently, $Answerable(R)$ is maximal if and only if for most of i ($1 \leq i \leq n$), $\mathbf{c}_{ij} = \mathbf{c}_i$ holds for all $j \in I_i$. This is equivalent to finding a maximal subset $V_s \subseteq [1,n]$, so that for any $i \in V_s$ and $j \in V_s$, we can let $\mathbf{c}_{ih} = \mathbf{c}_i$ and $\mathbf{c}_{jk} = \mathbf{c}_j$ ($h \in I_i$ and $k \in I_j$). This is possible only if $\{i,j\} \notin E$ holds for all $i \in V_s$ and $j \in V_s$. That is, V_s is the maximal independent set of $V = [1,n]$.

$\square$

7.4.3 Eliminating One-Dimensional Inferences

In this section, we address the elimination of 1-d inferences. For a given set of specifications $O = \{(r_i, S_i) : 1 \leq i \leq m\}$, the answerable set $Answerable(R)$ given by a set of unprotected roots $R = \{(r_i, \mathbf{c}_i) : 1 \leq i \leq n\}$ is free of m-d inferences. However, $Answerable(R)$ may not be truly answerable, because some of its cells may still cause 1-d inferences, as illustrated in Example 7.9. Without loss of generality, consider the first slice $Slice(r_1)$. Let $r \subseteq Answerable((r_1, \mathbf{c}_1))$ be the set of cells in $Slice(r_1)$ that cause 1-d inferences according to a given sensitivity criterion $Sensitive()$. It may seem a viable solution to simply restrict r to remove 1-d inferences from $Slice(r_1)$. However, such basic access control is always vulnerable to inferences. Both m-d inferences and 1-d inferences are possible from the unrestricted cells in $Answerable((r_1, \mathbf{c}_1)) \setminus r$ to those in r (and then to the protected cells in $Slice(r_1) \cap Object(O)$).

On the other hand, considering r as a new object, then nothing prevents it from being protected by the same methods used to protect $Object(O)$.

Procedure *SeCube*
Input: a data cube $\mathcal{L}$ with the set of all cells $\mathcal{A}$, pairs of s-specification and
      l-specification $\{(r_i, S_i) : 1 \leq i \leq n\}$, and a sensitivity criterion $Sensitive()$
Output: $R = \{(u_i, \mathbf{w}_i) : 1 \leq i \leq l\}$ (each u_i is an s-specification and $\mathbf{w}_i$ a root)
Method:
    Let $\mathcal{L} = \mathcal{L} \cup \{\mathbf{c}_{nil}\}$ ($\mathbf{c}_{nil}$ satisfies $< all, all, \ldots, all > \preceq \mathbf{c}_{nil}$ and $R = \phi$)
    For $i = 1$ to n
        Let $R = R \cup \{(r_i, \mathbf{c}_i)\}$, where $\mathbf{c}_i \in \mathcal{L} \setminus Below(S_i)$
        Let $r = r_i$, $S = S_i$, and $\mathbf{c}_r = \mathbf{c}_i$
        While *TRUE*
            Let $Ans = Answerable((r, \mathbf{c}_r))$
                and $r = \{\mathbf{t} : \mathbf{t} \in Ans, Sensitive(\mathbf{t}, \mathcal{A} \setminus Ans) = TRUE\}$
            If $r = \phi$ **Break**
            Let $S = S \cup \{\mathbf{c} : \mathbf{c} \in Above(\mathbf{c}_r), \mathbf{c} \cap r \neq \phi\}$
            Let $\mathbf{c}_r \in Above(\mathbf{c}_r) \setminus Below(S)$
            Let $R = R \cup \{(r, \mathbf{c}_r)\}$
   Return R

Fig. 7.6. A Procedure for Inference Control in Data Cubes

Specifically, by the conditions of Definition 7.13, we can consider $Slice(r_1) \setminus Slice(r)$ and $Slice(r)$ separately for inferences. The former is now free of both m-d inferences and 1-d inferences. Let S be the union of S_1 and the set of cuboids with which r has a non-empty intersection. Then $Object((r, S))$ is a new object to be protected, if we consider r and S as the s-specification and l-specification, respectively. Now we have reached the same point as to protect $Object(O)$. That is, we first find a new root $\mathbf{c}_r$ to prevent m-d inferences from $Answerable((r_1, \mathbf{c}_1)) \setminus Object((r, S))$ to $Object((r, S))$. Then again, the result $Answerable((r, \mathbf{c}_r))$ is free of m-d inferences to $Object((r, S))$, but may cause 1-d inferences.

Hence, we repeat the above process until either no more 1-d inferences are detected, or there is no cuboid left to be chosen for the root. Then the root is set as a dummy cuboid $\mathbf{c}_{nil}$, which depends on the topmost cuboid $< all, all, \ldots, all >$ (hence $Above(\mathbf{c}_{nil}) = \phi$, causing no 1-d inferences). The process terminates in at most $| Above(\mathbf{c}_1) |$ steps, because in each round the root is chosen from fewer candidates, with the cuboids causing 1-d inferences excluded. The procedure *SeCube* shown in Figure 7.6 computes a set of roots as described above.

Proposition 7.27 states that the result of the procedure *SeCube* is provably secure. The first claim says the set of restricted cells is itself an object, and this new object is a superset of the originally specified object (that is, the set of protected cells). This result has two implications. First, the protection provided by inference control actually meets the requirements of the basic access control discussed at the end of Section 7.3 (notice that this is different from access control in general, which may go beyond the open policy we have assumed). Hence, unauthorized accesses to the specified object are eliminated by the inference control, if the authorizations are specified as in Section 7.3. Intuitively, any protected cells (explicitly specified so by administrators) will be restricted, although the reverse may not be true.

Second, the result of such inference control can be enforced through access control, since it is nothing but an object. The task of implementing inference control can thus be fulfilled using existing access control mechanisms. The second claim in Proposition 7.27 states that the answerable set is always free of inferences to restricted cells, regardless what sensitivity criterion is given, as long as it meets the requirements stated in Definition 7.13. This claim implies that sensitivity criteria can be implemented as customizable modules, in order to incorporate different requirements in different applications.

Proposition 7.27. *Taken as input a data cube $\mathcal{L}$ with the set of all cells $\mathcal{A}$, pairs of s-specification and l-specification O, and any sensitivity criterion $Sensitive()$, then*

1. *The procedure* SeCube *in Figure 7.6 returns $R = \{(u_i, \mathbf{w}_i) : 1 \leq i \leq l\}$ satisfying that*
   - $\mathcal{A} \setminus Answerable(R) = Object(O_a)$
   - $Object(O_a) \supseteq Object(O)$

   both hold, where $O_a = \{(u_i, W_i) : 1 \leq i \leq l\}$ and each W_i is the set of maximal elements of $\mathcal{L} \setminus Above(\mathbf{w}_i)$
2. *$Sensitive(Answerable(R), Object(O_a)) = FALSE$ is true.*

Proof:

1. We justify the first claim. In order to show that $\mathcal{A} \setminus Answerable(R) \subseteq Object(O_a)$ holds, for any $\mathbf{t} \in \mathcal{A} \setminus Answerable(\{(u_i, \mathbf{w}_i) : 1 \leq i \leq l\})$, suppose $\mathbf{t} \in \mathbf{c}_t$ for some $\mathbf{c}_t \in \mathcal{L}$. Let $I = \{i : 1 \leq i \leq l, \mathbf{t} \in Slice(u_i)\}$. By Definition 7.25, $\mathbf{c}_t \notin Above(\mathbf{w}_j)$ holds for some $j \in I$. Equivalently, $\mathbf{c}_t \in \mathcal{L} \setminus Above(\mathbf{w}_j)$ holds. Then $\mathbf{c}_t \preceq \mathbf{c}_w$ holds for some $\mathbf{c}_w \in W_j$, and hence $\mathbf{c}_t \in Below(W_j)$ and $\mathbf{c}_t \in Below(\bigcup_{i \in I} W_i)$ both follow. Consequently we have

$$\mathbf{t} \in (\bigcup_{i \in I} Slice(u_i)) \cap Below(\bigcup_{i \in I} W_i) \subseteq Object(O_a)$$

This shows $\mathcal{A} \setminus Answerable(R) \subseteq Object(O_a)$ is true. In order to show that $\mathcal{A} \setminus Answerable(R) \supseteq Object(O_a)$ also holds, for any $\mathbf{t} \in Object(O_a)$, suppose $\mathbf{t} \in \mathbf{c}_t$ for some $\mathbf{c}_t \in \mathcal{L}$. Let $I = \{i : 1 \leq i \leq l, \mathbf{t} \in Slice(u_i)\}$. Then $\mathbf{c}_t \in Below(\bigcup_{i \in I} W_i)$ implies that $\mathbf{c}_t \notin Above(W_j)$ must hold for some $j \in I$. Consequently, $\mathbf{c}_t \notin Answerable(R)$ is true and $\mathcal{A} \setminus Answerable(R) \supseteq Object(O_a)$ follows.

Next we show $Object(O_a) \supseteq Object(O)$ holds. For any $\mathbf{t} \in Object(O)$, suppose $\mathbf{t} \in \mathbf{c}_t$ for some $\mathbf{c}_t \in \mathcal{L}$. Let $I = \{i : 1 \leq i \leq n, \mathbf{t} \in Slice(r_i)\}$.

By Definition 7.7, $\mathbf{c}_t \in Below(\bigcup_{i \in I} S_i)$ holds. According to the procedure *SeCube* in Figure 7.6, $(r_i, \mathbf{c}_i) \in R$ holds for all $1 \le i \le n$. Hence, $I \subseteq J = \{i : 1 \le i \le l, \mathbf{t} \in Slice(u_i)\}$ is true. Then we have

$$\mathbf{c}_t \in Below(\bigcup_{i \in I} W_i) \subseteq Below(\bigcup_{i \in J} W_i)$$

Consequently we have

$$\mathbf{t} \in (\bigcup_{i \in J} Slice(u_i)) \cap Below(\bigcup_{i \in J} W_i) \subseteq Object(O_a)$$

2. We justify the second claim by contradiction. First, by Theorem 7.26, we have that $Sensitive(Answerable(R), Object(O_a)) = TRUE$ holds only if $Sensitive(\mathbf{t}, Object(O_a)) = TRUE$ is true for some $\mathbf{t} \in Answerable(R)$. That is, m-d inferences are impossible. Then according to the procedure *SeCube* in Figure 7.6, for some $1 \le j \le l$, $\mathbf{t} \notin Above(\mathbf{w}_j)$ must hold. Hence, $\mathbf{t} \notin Answerable((u_j, \mathbf{w}_j))$ must be true, as $Answerable((u_j, \mathbf{w}_j)) = Above(\mathbf{w}_j) \cap Slice(u_j)$. By Definition 7.25, $\mathbf{t} \in Answerable(R)$ cannot hold, either, which is a contradiction.

$\square$

7.5 Implementation Options and Complexity

The methods proposed in previous sections provably eliminate both unauthorized accesses and inferences in data cubes. In this section, we discuss the implementation options and the computational and storage requirements. The implementation options largely depend on the existing security capability of an OLAP system. Most ROLAP systems have access control mechanisms in their relational backend. Such mechanisms can check incoming queries and deny any request for protected cells. However, the access control mechanisms are not aware of inferences. Our methods can enhance those existing mechanisms with the capability of inference control. Proposition 7.27 states that the result of inference control is simply a *larger* object containing restricted cells, which encloses the originally specified object containing protected cells.

Therefore, once the result of inference control is computed off-line by the Procedure *SeCube*, it can be enforced by existing access control mechanisms, in the same way as the specified object is enforced. That is, the request for any restricted cell will be denied. Ideally, such an *inference control-through access control* approach brings no additional on-line performance overhead to the OLAP system with access control already in place. Because a query needs to be checked by access control mechanisms anyway. The distributivity stated in Proposition 7.6 and Lemma 7.24 also implies that the result of inference control can be incrementally maintained, when new specifications arrive. Hence, old specifications do not need to be kept once the result is computed, meaning no additional storage is required, either.

For an OLAP system with no existing access control mechanisms, the implementation can adopt a *query-modification* approach [59]. The core cuboid c_c is materialized in most data cubes [40]. Hence, the answerable set can be encoded by attaching the root to each cell in c_c. The root can be implemented as a new attribute of the size $O(k)$, for a k-dimensional data cube. The storage requirement is thus $O(|c_c| \cdot k)$. After a request for a set of cells S in a cuboid c is received, the system modifies the request by appending to it a simple restriction. The restriction says that a cell in the core cuboid c_c is aggregated by the answer only if its root is an ancestor of the requested cuboid c (in ROLAP this will be a simple *WHERE* clause, which is appended to the SQL command formed by the front-end).

The above restriction ensures that all aggregated cells are included by the answerable set, and hence lead to neither inferences nor unauthorized accesses. The dependency relationship between any two cuboids can be checked in $O(k)$ time (by comparing two k-tuples), and hence the on-line delay is $O(|S| \cdot k)$. Additional processing may be necessary to inform the subject about the restricted cells. This approach causes on-line performance delay and also requires modifications of existing OLAP systems. However, the cost of our solution is comparable to that of the basic access control (that is, denying any request for protected cells).

In contrast to the on-line performance overhead, the off-line complexity of our solution is not trivial. It depends on the implementation and optimization of the procedure *SeCube* shown in Figure 7.6. In the worst case, the complexity of *SeCube* is bounded by the number of specifications, the size of the data cube, and the size of the dependency lattice. The outer loop of the procedure runs n times, where n is the number of specification pairs. The inner loop of the procedure runs at most $|Above(c_i)|$ times for the ith round of the outer loop. 1-d inferences are detected once for each protected cell t_t (against its single descendant in the basis $gBasis(Answerable(R), t_t)$, according to Theorem 7.26) in the slice $Slice(r_i)$, whose results are stored and reused. The total number of detections is thus bounded by $O(|A|)$.

The above detection of 1-d inferences can be carried out by a customizable module that implements the function $Sensitive()$ in Definition 7.13. Each such detection usually takes constant time (such as checking whether a requested cell has less than two ancestors in a specific cuboid). In practice, the likelihood of 1-d inferences can usually be estimated based on statistics such as cuboid sizes [25]. Hence, the choice of roots can be optimized to reduce both the number of 1-d inferences in the initial answerable set, and the number of rounds in eliminating 1-d inferences. In most OLAP systems, materializations and precomputations are extensively adopted, and off-line computational complexity is usually not a major concern in those systems. Our approach also reflects such an effort in achieving less on-line delay through more off-line processing.

7.6 Summary

This chapter has shown a lattice-based solution to protecting sensitive data in OLAP data cubes from both unauthorized accesses and inferences. We first devised a flexible framework for specifying authorization objects. We then proposed a method for controlling inferences. The result is provably secure in that both inferences and unauthorized accesses are eliminated. In contrast to previous sections where only the core cuboid is regarded as sensitive, this chapter allows basically any subset of the core cuboid to be an object. The method proposed in this chapter is applicable to any aggregation functions, external knowledge, and sensitivity criteria, given that they satisfy clearly stated algebraic properties. This leads inference control one step closer to practice. The technique is efficient in terms of on-line delays to answering queries, and its implementation requires little modifications to existing OLAP systems, since its result can be directly enforced by existing access control mechanisms.

8

Query-driven Inference Control in Data Cubes

8.1 Introduction

Chapter 7 describes a novel way of controlling inferences in data cubes. That is, we prevent, instead of detecting, complex inferences through restrictions on queries, and then we remove the remaining simpler inferences. This approach reduces the on-line complexity of inference control to a practical level. It also eliminates the needs for impractical assumptions by supporting a customizable criteria of sensitive information. However, the method is *static*, in the sense that the restrictions on queries are computed once and for all. Such a static approach may lead to unnecessary denials of queries and hence reduce the usefulness of an OLAP system, because optimal restrictions usually depend on actual incoming queries and the queries a user will eventually ask cannot always be predicted.

The contribution of this chapter is two-fold. First, we complete the framework for specifying and incrementally updating authorization objects in data cubes. Although the previous chapter has already discussed how to specify objects in data cubes, issues such as how to represent the specified objects and how to incrementally update them have not been addressed. Second, we propose a query-driven solution to minimize the impact of inference control upon the availability of an OLAP system. Similar to the Audit Expert (which was discussed in Chapter 3), we keep a profile of data disclosed by previously answered queries either directly or indirectly through inferences. This profile is then used to determine whether an incoming query can be safely answered without disclosing any sensitive data. The profile is incrementally updated upon answering each new query. This approach is able to answer a query whenever it is safe to do so, maximizing the availability. Moreover, we shall show that the additional performance overhead caused by the method is reasonable. Hence, a balance between security, availability, and performance has been achieved.

The rest of the chapter is organized as follows. Section 8.2 reviews the specification of authorization objects and introduces our model for queries in data cubes. Section 8.3 discusses the limitation of the static method proposed in the previous chapter to motivate further discussions. Section 8.4 proposes a query-driven approach to inference control in data cubes. Section 8.5 concludes the chapter.

8.2 Authorization Objects and Queries in Data Cubes

The previous chapter has discussed the specification of authorization objects in data cubes. We briefly review the relevant concepts here. Analogous to the spectrum of objects in relational tables including tables, records of a table, and fields of a record, objects in a data cube can define partitions along one or more dimensions. In addition, objects in a data cube can also partition it along the dependency lattice, which gives data cubes an additional opportunity of refining authorizations.

For example, referring to Figure 7.1, the security requirement may say that any access to the commissions in year Y_1 and the book department should be prohibited. This object thus partitions the data cube along both the time and the organization dimension. More specifically, it includes all the cells whose first attribute value is comparable to Y_1 and whose second attribute value comparable to $Book$. For instance, the cell $< Q_1, Bob >$, $< ALL, Bob >$, and $< Q_1, Branch_1 >$ are all members of the object, but $< Q_5, Bob >$ is not.

At the same time, there may exist a second requirement saying that no access should be given to the yearly commissions, either specified together with the above requirement or specified separately. This requirement not only protects the cuboid $< year, employee >$ but also implies the protection of its ancestor $< quarter, employee >$, since the latter can be computed from the former if not protected. Instead of depending on administrators in ensuring their specification to be complete, we define objects based on ancestor closures, such that any object will automatically include all the cuboids from which the specified ones can be computed.

Objects indicate what to be protected from unauthorized subjects. Dually, queries describe what are requested by a subject. Considering that some cells in a data cube can be computed from others, queries should also include not only the explicitly requested cells but also the cells that can be computed from the requested ones. Similar to an object, a query can select part of a data cube through selections along one or more dimensions. Hence, a query is essentially the dual concept of objects, as formally stated in Definition 8.1 and illustrated in Example 8.2.

Definition 8.1. *In a data cube $< \mathcal{L}, \mathcal{A} >$, define*

- *a function $Above(.) : 2^{\mathcal{L}} \to 2^{\mathcal{L}}$ as $Above(S) = \{\mathbf{c} : \text{ there exists } \mathbf{c}_s \in S, \text{ such that } \mathbf{c}_s \preceq \mathbf{c} \text{ holds}\}$.*
- *a function $Query(.) : 2^{\mathcal{L}} \times 2^{\mathcal{A}} \to 2^{\mathcal{A}}$ as $Query(r, S) = \{\mathbf{t} : \mathbf{t} \in Slice(r), \mathbf{t} \in \mathbf{c} \text{ for some } \mathbf{c} \in Above(S)\}$*

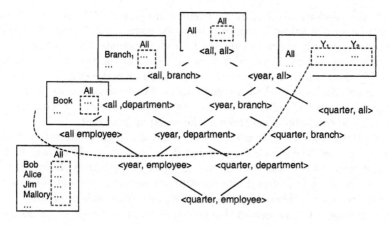

Fig. 8.1. An Example of Queries

We say that

- *Above(S) is the* **descendant closure** *of S.*
- *Query(r, S) is a* **query** *specified by the pair (r, S)*
- *any cell* **t** ∈ *Object(r, S) is* **requested**.

Example 8.2. In Figure 8.1, Eve asks for the total commission of each employee and the yearly commission of each department, both within the book department. The corresponding query can be specified as follows. First, a set of two cuboids {< *all, employee* >, < *year, department* >} stands for *the total commission of each emplyee and the yearly commission of each department.* Their descendants, such as < *all, department* > and < *all, branch* >, should also be included by the query. Second, a slice can limit the requested cells to be *within the book department.*

8.3 The Static Approach and Its Impact on Availability

The key observation in Chapter 7 is that detecting m-d inferences is generally infeasible as evidenced by the high complexity of most on-line inference control methods in statistical databases. Hence, we choose to prevent m-d inferences from emerging, instead of detecting then removing them. This approach provides provable security while reducing the on-line complexity of inference control to a practical level. It also allows the proposed method to remain effective for different aggregation functions, external knowledge and sensitivity criteria. This section first briefly reviews this approach and then indicates its limitation.

In the previous chapter, m-d inferences are prevented by restricting subjects to a special subset of unprotected cells, namely, an *answerable set*. For simplicity, we only consider cuboid-level authorizations. First, while considering inferences from a source S to a cuboid c_t in the target, the function $Basis()$ described in Definition 7.15 gives the minimal descendants of c_t in S, namely, the basis of S with respect to c_t. The basis allows us to focus on a smaller number of cuboids, because other cuboids are either redundant (if they can be computed from those in the basis) or irrelevant.

An answerable set is the descendant closure of a single unprotected cuboid, namely, a *root*. The cuboids not included by an answerable set are said to be *restricted*. Our discussions in the previous chapter have shown that an answerable set is free of m-d inferences to any restricted cuboid. The lack of m-d inferences is indicated by the following fact. The basis of an answerable set with respect to any restricted cuboid is always a singleton set, as formally stated in Lemma 7.19.

Hence, an answerable set is always free of m-d inferences. An iterative procedure is given in the previous chapter to eliminate remaining 1-d inferences, and hence to obtain a final result free of any inferences. The complement of the answerable set (with respect to the data cube), that is the set of restricted cells, is shown to be a superset of the original object. Hence any protected cell will be restricted, although the converse is not necessarily true due to potential inferences. This result guarantees that the answerable set is not subject to unauthorized accesses, either.

One of the advantages of the above approach is that answerable sets can be pre-computed regardless of what queries the subject might ask, since there is no longer a need for worrying about the combination of multiple queries. This simplifies the implementation of the method, since once the answerable sets are computed off-line, queries can be authorized with existing access control mechanisms. This approach also reduces on-line performance overhead, because the most computationally expensive task of computing the answerable set has been shifted to off-line processing.

However, while this *static* approach helps in terms of security and performance, it hurts availability in the sense that predetermined answerable sets may cause desirable queries to be denied. The previous chapter gives maximality results, which ensure that the answerable set cannot be increased without introducing potential m-d inferences. However, there are usually more than one maximal answerable set available, while only one of these can be chosen to prevent m-d inferences. The optimal choice, however, will depend on actual queries posed by users at a later time.

In Example 8.3, all the roots are optimal, since the answerable set cannot be further enlarged without introducing potential m-d inferences. Nevertheless, in each case the result will be unsatisfactory to the subject. Suppose $<all, employee>$ has been chosen as the root and Eve wants to know the total commission in each quarter or year, then she will be denied on both requests. Similarly, she will be rejected if she asks for the total commission of

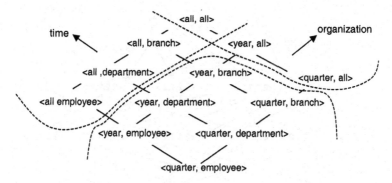

Fig. 8.2. An Example of Multiple Choices of Root

each employee, department, or branch, while $< quarter, all >$ has been chosen (this situation is somehow analogous to that of the Chinese Wall policy, where a subject can access one and only one of the conflicting classes [25]).

Example 8.3. In Figure 8.2, suppose the cuboids in $Below(< year, branch >)$ are to be protected. Hence, either $< all, employee >$ or $< quarter, all >$ can be chosen as the root. The answerable set is then $\{< all, all >, < all, branch >$, $< all, department >, < all, employee >\}$ in the first case, and $\{< all, all >$, $< year, all >, < quarter, all >\}$ in the second.

The actual sequence of queries in an OLAP system usually cannot be predicted, because the next query to be posed by a subject not only depends on the outcome of the current query, but also depends on subjective decisions of human users (this is different from data mining where pre-defined queries are compiled into a procedure). Hence, it may not be possible to choose an answerable set that is universally optimal. Therefore, the above-mentioned effect of inference control on the availability is usually unavoidable for a static approach like the one described in the previous chapter.

8.4 Query-Driven Prevention of Multi-Dimensional Inferences

The previous section motivates us to introduce a query-driven approach to control inferences in data cubes while maximizing the availability of queries. Similar to the Audit Expert described in Chapter 3, we do not predetermine the answerable set. Instead, we compute and upate it based on actual incoming queries. First, Section 8.4.1 considers the special case of cuboid-level authorizations. Section 8.4.2 then generalizes the results to cell-level authorizations. Section 8.4.3 dicusses the implementation of the method. Finally, Section 8.4.4 analyzes the performance overhead and storage requirement.

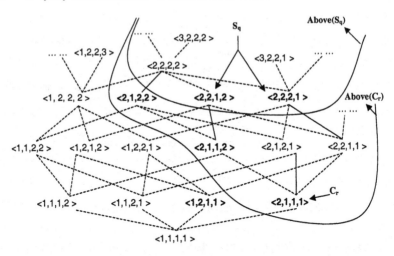

Fig. 8.3. An Example of Query-driven Prevention of m-d Inferences

8.4.1 A Special Case

To simplify the discussion, this section considers the special case of cuboid-level authorizations and queries. That is, we assume all queries are given with the slice specified by a complete cuboid. The slice is then simply the data cube, and its intersection with any cuboid is equal to that cuboid itself. Hence, we can disregard slices for the time being and consider queries as descendant closures. Specifically, a query $Query(r_q, S_q)$ is now simply (the union of the cuboids in) $Above(S_q)$. We shall directly refer to $Above(S_q)$ as a query, as illustrated in Example 8.4.

Example 8.4. Figure 8.3 shows the dependency lattice of a four-dimensional data cube. Each 4-tuple denotes a cuboid. For example, $< 1, 1, 1, 1 >$ can be interpreted as $< quarter, employee, ... >$. The dotted-lines denote the dependency relation. A set of two cuboids $S_q = \{< 2, 2, 1, 2 >, < 2, 2, 2, 1 >\}$ defines (the descendant closure of) a query $Above(S_q)$, as illustrated by the upper curve in the solid line.

If we would use the static approach described in Section 8.3, an answerable set must have already been computed. Determining whether a query is free of m-d inferences is then equivalent to determining whether it is a subset of the answerable set, according to Lemma 7.19. However, in the query-driven approach, we do not pre-compute any answerable set beforehand. Instead, we look at the converse problem. That is, given any query and a protected cuboid, *does there exist a superset of the query, such that the superset is free of m-d inferences to the cuboid ?* If the answer is *yes*, then we know that the query does not cause m-d inferences to the cuboid since it discloses less information than its superset does, and vice versa.

First, we show how to find a superset of any given query that is free of m-d inferences to a given cuboid, by assuming that such a superset does exist. By Lemma 7.19, an answerable set suffices the prevention of m-d inferences to a cuboid, if it does not include that cuboid. On the other hand, to ensure the answerable set to be a superset of the query, we can take advantage of the dependency relation as follows. In order to find a root c_r satisfying that $Above(c_r)$ is a superset of the query $Above(S_q)$, we let c_r be any lower bound of S_q. Then $Above(S_q) \subseteq Above(c_r)$ must hold, because c_r is an ancestor of each cuboid in S_q and hence it must also be an ancestor of each cuboid in $Above(S_q)$, by the transitivity of the dependency relation. This is illustrated in Example 8.5 and formally stated in Lemma 8.6.

Example 8.5. Suppose we want to show that the query $Above(S_q)$ in Example 8.4 does not cause m-d inferences to a given cuboid $c = < 1, 2, 1, 1 >$. We can let $c_r = < 2, 1, 1, 1 >$ be the root, since it is a lower bound of S_q and hence $Above(S_q) \subseteq Above(c_r)$ holds. Moreover, $Above(c_r)$ is an answerable set satisfying $c \notin Above(c_r)$, and thus is free of m-d inferences to c by Lemma 7.19. In Figure 8.3, $Above(c_r)$ is illustrated by the lower curve in the solid line. It can be observed that from c only one dotted-line points into $Above(c_r)$. That is, the basis of $Above(c_r)$ with respect to c is a singleton set.

Lemma 8.6. *In a data cube* $< \mathcal{L}, \mathcal{A} >$, *given any* $S_q \subseteq \mathcal{L}$ *and* $c \in \mathcal{L}$, *let* $c_r \in \mathcal{L}$ *be any lower bound of* S_q. *Then* $Above(c_r)$ *satisfies that*

- $Above(c_r) \supseteq Above(S_q)$, *and*
- $| Basis(Above(c_r), c) |= 1$,

    if $c \notin Above(c_r)$ *holds.*

Proof:
$| Basis(Above(c_r), c) |= 1$ holds for any $c \in \mathcal{L} \setminus Above(c_r)$ due to Lemma 7.19. Hence, we only need to show that $Above(c_r) \supseteq Above(S_q)$ is true. For any $c \in Above(S_q)$, Definition 8.1 implies that $c_1 \preceq c$ holds for some $c_1 \in S_q$. Because c_r is a lower bound S, $c_r \preceq c_1$ is true. Then $c_r \preceq c$ follows from the transitivity of $\preceq$. Hence, $c \in Above(c_r)$ is true and $Above(c_r) \supseteq Above(S_q)$ follows.   □

Next we look at the other side of the problem. That is, if no superset of the given query exists to be free of m-d inferences to a given cuboid, how can we determine this fact. The condition given by Lemma 8.6 is sufficient but not necessary. That is, $c \in Above(c_r)$ does not necessarily mean that $Above(S_q)$ causes m-d inferences to c. Hence, Lemma 8.6 can prove that $Above(S_q)$ does not cause any m-d inferences to c but cannot disprove it when $Above(S_q)$ does so. Following Example 8.5, a counterexample can be found by letting the core cuboid $< 1, 1, 1, 1 >$ be the root c_r. Clearly, the core cuboid is a lower bound of S_q, and $c \notin Above(c_r)$ no longer holds, failing the condition of Lemma 8.6. However, this does not change the fact that $Above(S_q)$ is free of m-d inferences to c, which is already established in Example 8.5.

In order to fix this, we restrict the root c_r to be the GLB (greatest lower bound) of S_q, instead of an arbitrary lower bound of it. Intuitively, such a c_r gives the *smallest* superset of the query that can be an answerable set. If the given cuboid is included by such a smallest superset, then it cannot be excluded from any other supersets of the query. Specifically, with c_r being the GLB of S_q, any lower bound of S_q must be an ancestor of c_r. This implies that if c is a descendant of c_r, then it must be a descendant of all lower bounds of S_q, too. Hence, if $c \in Above(c_r)$ holds, then no superset of $Above(S_q)$ can be found to be an answerable set. That is, the query $Above(S_q)$ causes m-d inferences to c. This is illustrated in Example 8.7 and formally stated in Lemma 8.8.

Example 8.7. In Figure 8.3, now let $S_q = \{< 2,1,2,2 >, < 2,2,1,2 >, < 2,2,2,1 >\}$, and $c = < 2,1,1,2 >$. The GLB of S_q is $c_r = < 2,1,1,1 >$. Clearly the two cuboids $< 2,1,2,2, >$ and $< 2,2,1,2 >$ together may cause m-d inferences to c.

Lemma 8.8. *In a data cube* $< \mathcal{L}, \mathcal{A} >$, *given any* $S_q \subseteq \mathcal{L}$ *and any* $c \in \mathcal{L}$. *Let* c_r *be the GLB of* S_q. *Then there does not exists an* $S \subseteq \mathcal{L}$ *satisfying that*

- $S \supseteq Above(S_q)$, *and*
- $| Basis(S, c) | = 1$,

  if $c \in Above(c_r) \setminus Above(S_q)$ *is true.*

Proof:
First of all, if S_q has a single minimal element, then it must be the unique GLB c_r, and hence $Above(c_r) \setminus Above(S_q) = \phi$ implies the lemma trivially holds. Hence, we only consider the case when S_q has a set of more than one minimal elements S_m. Then c_r is also the GLB of S_m. For any $c \in Above(c_r) \setminus Above(S_q)$, $| Basis(Above(S_q), c) | > 0$ holds because $c \notin Above(S_q)$ is true. Because $Above(c_r)$ is a sub-lattice, it must include the meet of any two cuboids in it [30]. Hence, c_r must be the GLB of a set of more than one cuboids in S_m. Let this set be S'_m. Now suppose there does exist a set S satisfying that $S \supseteq Above(S_q)$ and $| Basis(S, c) | = 1$ both hold. Then $S'_m \subseteq S_q \subseteq S$ is true. Let c_1 be the only member of $Basis(S, c)$. Then c_1 must be a lower bound of S'_m, and $c \prec c_1$ must hold. However, this contradicts the fact that c is the GLB of S'_m, and hence $c_1 \preceq c$ holds. The contradiction justifies the claim. $\square$

We combine the descendant closure $Above(c_r)$ with the slice $Slice(r)$ by taking the intersection, where c_r is the GLB of S_q. The result is named the *inferable set* of the query $Query(r_q, S_q)$, as given in Definition 8.9. We extend the function $Basis()$ to its more general form $gBasis()$ in order to deal with slices. By Lemma 8.6 and Lemma 8.8, the inferable set of any query includes all the cells that are subject to m-d inferences from the query. Moreover, because the inferable set is also a superset of the query, it also includes all the requested cells. Conversely, a cell is neither requested nor subject to m-d inferences from a query, if it is not included by the inferable set of that query. Intuitively, we can then consider that cell *safe* from being disclosed by the query. Those are illustrated in Figure 8.4 and formally stated in Theorem 8.10.

Definition 8.9. *In a data cube* $< \mathcal{L}, \mathcal{A} >$, *define*

- *a function Inferable(.)* : $2^{\mathcal{A}} \times 2^{\mathcal{L}} \to 2^{\mathcal{A}}$ *as* $Inferable(r_q, S_q) = \{\mathbf{t} : \mathbf{t} \in Slice(r_q), \mathbf{t} \in \mathbf{c}$ *for some* $\mathbf{c} \in Above(\mathbf{c}_r)$, *where* $\mathbf{c}_r$ *is the GLB of* $S_q\}$
- *a function gBasis(.)* : $2^{\mathcal{A}} \times \mathcal{A} \to 2^{\mathcal{A}}$ *as* $gBasis(T, \mathbf{t}_t) = \phi$ *if* $\mathbf{t}_t \notin Slice(T)$, *and* $gBasis(T, \mathbf{t}_t) = \{\mathbf{t} : \mathbf{t} \in T, \mathbf{t}_t \prec \mathbf{t}, (\mathbf{t}_1 \in T$ *and* $\mathbf{t}_t \prec \mathbf{t}_1$ *and* $\mathbf{t}_1 \preceq \mathbf{t})$ *implies* $\mathbf{t}_1 = \mathbf{t}\}$, *otherwise.*

We say that

- $Inferable(r_q, S_q)$ *is the* **inferable set** *of the query* $Query(r_q, S_q)$
- $gBasis(T, \mathbf{t}_t)$ *is the* **basis** *of* T *with respect to* $\mathbf{t}_t$

Theorem 8.10. *In a data cube* $< \mathcal{L}, \mathcal{A} >$, *given any* $r_q \subseteq \mathcal{A}$ *and* $S_q \subseteq \mathcal{L}$, *any* $\mathbf{t} \in Slice(r_q)$ *satisfies*

- *either* $\mathbf{t} \in Query(r_q, S_q)$, *or*
- *there does not exist a* $T \supseteq Query(r_q, S_q)$ *satisfying* $\mid gBasis(T), \mathbf{t}) \mid = 1$,

if and only if $\mathbf{t} \in Inferable(r_q, S_q)$ *is true.*

Proof:
We justify the claim in three steps.

1. We first show the if part of the claim. If $\mathbf{t} \in Inferable(r_q, S_q)$ holds, then either $\mathbf{t} \in Query(r_q, S_q)$ or $\mathbf{t} \in Inferable(r_q, S_q) \setminus Query(r_q, S_q)$ must be true. The claim holds trivially for the former. For $\mathbf{t} \in Inferable(r_q, S_q) \setminus Query(r_q, S_q)$, suppose $\mathbf{t} \in \mathbf{c}$ for some $\mathbf{c} \in \mathcal{L}$. Then $\mathbf{c} \in Above(\mathbf{c}_r) \setminus Above(S_q)$ must hold by Definition 8.9, where $\mathbf{c}_r$ is the GLB of S_q. , Suppose there does exist a $T \supseteq Query(r_q, S_q)$ satisfying $\mid gBasis(T), \mathbf{t}) \mid = 1$ holds, and let $gBasis(T), \mathbf{t}) = \{\mathbf{t}_t\}$ and assume $\mathbf{t}_t \in \mathbf{c}_t$ for some $\mathbf{c}_t \in \mathcal{L}$. Let $S = \{\mathbf{c}_1 : \mathbf{c}_1 \in \mathcal{L}, \mathbf{c}_1 \cap T \cap Slice(\mathbf{t}) \neq \phi\}$. Then $S \supseteq Above(S_q)$ must hold because $T \supseteq Query(r_q, S_q)$ is true. Moreover, $Basis(S, \mathbf{c}) = \{\mathbf{c}_t\}$ must be true. Hence, S satisfies both $S \supseteq Above(S_q)$ and $\mid Basis(S, \mathbf{c}) \mid = 1$ for a $\mathbf{c} \in Above(\mathbf{c}_r) \setminus Above(S_q)$, contradicting the established result of Lemma 8.8. That is, such an S does not exist, and this justifies the if part of the claim.

2. Next we show that $Inferable(r_q, S_q) \supseteq Query(r_q, S_q)$ holds, and hence $\mathbf{t} \in Query(r_q, S_q)$ only if $\mathbf{t} \in Inferable(r_q, S_q)$ is true. By Definition 8.1, any $\mathbf{t} \in Query(r_q, S_q)$ satisfies $\mathbf{t} \in Slice(r_q)$ and $\mathbf{t} \in \mathbf{c}$ for some $\mathbf{c} \in Above(S_q)$. That is, $\mathbf{c}_1 \preceq \mathbf{c}$ holds for some $\mathbf{c}_1 \in S_q$. By Definition 8.9, $\mathbf{c}_r \preceq \mathbf{c}_1 \preceq \mathbf{c}$ must hold, where $\mathbf{c}_r$ is the GLB of S_q. Hence, $\mathbf{c} \in Above(\mathbf{c}_r)$ is true. Then $\mathbf{t} \in Slice(r_q)$ and $\mathbf{t} \in \mathbf{c} \in Above(\mathbf{c}_r)$ indicates that $\mathbf{t} \in Inferable(r_q, S_q)$ holds.

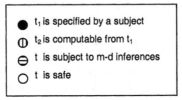

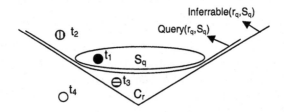

Fig. 8.4. A Query and Its Inferable Set

3. Finally, we show that for any $t \in Slice(r_q) \setminus Inferable(r_q, S_q)$, there exists a $T \supseteq Query(r_q, S_q)$ satisfying that $\mid gBasis(T), t) \mid = 1$ holds. Specifically we let $T = Inferable(r_q, S_q)$. Suppose $t \in c$ for some $c \in \mathcal{L}$. Then $c \in \mathcal{L} \setminus Above(c_r)$ holds by Definition 8.9, where c_r is the GLB of S_q. By Lemma 8.6, $Basis(Above(c_r), c) = \{c_1\}$, for some $c_1 \in Above(c_r)$. Let t_1 be the cell in c_1 that depends on t. Then $t_1 \in gBasis(Inferable(r_q, S_q), t)$ is true. For any $t_2 \in Slice(r_q)$ satisfying $t \prec t_2$ and $t_2 \in c_2 \in Above(c_r)$, $c_1 \preceq c_2$ must hold. Hence, $t_1 \preceq t_2$, and $t_2 \in gBasis(Inferable(r_q, S_q), c)$ cannot be true unless $t_2 = t_1$. That is, $gBasis(Inferable(r_q, S_q), t) = \{t_1\}$, and $\mid gBasis(Inferable(r_q, S_q), t) \mid = 1$ is true. This concludes the proof of the theorem.

□

8.4.2 The General Case

We extend the results of Section 8.4.1 to the general case of cell-level authorizations and queries. Again, the main difficulty in such an extension is that slices *overlap* with each other (that is, having a non-empty intersection). Hence, whether the cells inside the intersection of objects(queries) are protected (requested) need to be clarified.

Because queries and objects are dual concepts, we only need to consider objects. First of all, slices always overlap, even if the sets of cells used to specify them are disjoint. The intersection includes at least one cell, that of the top-most cuboid in the dependency lattice (such as $< all, all >$ in Figure 8.1). Intuitively, slices eventually merge into one cell while going up in the

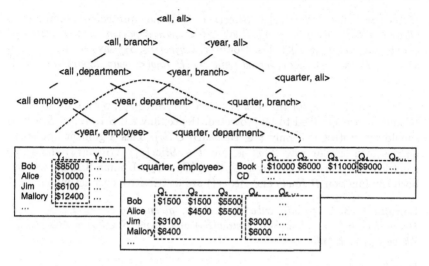

Fig. 8.5. An Example of Overlapping Objects

dependency lattice. On the other hand, two objects may or may not overlap, because the cells in the intersection of two slices are not always included by the ancestor closure. Example 8.11 illustrates overlapping slices and overlapping objects.

Example 8.11. In Figure 8.5, suppose we are given two sets of cells as $r_1 = \{< q,d >: q \in quarter, d \in department, q \leq Q_3, d = Book\}$ (assuming the attribute values in *quarter* are ordered by subscripts) and $r_2 = \{< q,d >: q \in quarter, d \in department, q \geq Q_4, d = Book\}$. The two slices r_1 and r_2 overlap, with their intersection including cells such as $< Y_1, Bob >$ (because Y_1 depends on both Q_3 and Q_4), $< all, Bob >$, $< Y_1, Book >$, and $< all, Book >$. Let S_1 be $\{< quarter, department >\}$, then $Object(r_1, S_1) \cap Object(r_2, S_1) = \phi$ holds. That is, the two objects are disjoint. However, as illustrated by the dotted lines in Figure 8.5, with $S_2 = \{< year, department >\}$, the two objects $Object(r_1, S_2)$ and $Object(r_2, S_2)$ overlap, and their intersection $Object(r_1, S_2) \cap Object(r_2, S_2)$ includes cells such as $< Y_1, Book >$.

In Example 8.11, the two objects have the same ancestor closure, and hence any cell in the intersection of the two slices are either protected by both objects, or protected by none of them. Hence, no ambiguity is possible. However, two objects may be defined with different ancestor closures, and hence the cells in the intersection of the two slices may be protected by one object, but not by the other, as illustrated in Example 8.12.

Example 8.12. Following Example 8.11, let the two objects be $Object(r_1, S_1)$ and $Object(r_2, S_2)$. Consider the cell $< Y_1, Book >$ in the intersection of the two slices $Slice(r_1) \cap Slice(r_2)$. It is not protected according to $Object(r_1, S_1)$, because $< Y_1, Book > \in < year, department > \notin Below(< quarter, department >)$ holds. However, $Object(r_2, S_2)$ says it is protected, as $< Y_1, Book > \in < year, department > \in Below(< year, department >)$ is true.

In Example 8.12, for the cells in $Slice(r_1) \cap Slice(r_2)$, both the cuboids in S_1 and S_2 are specified to be protected. Hence, any $t \in Slice(r_1) \cap Slice(r_2)$ should be protected if only $t \in Below(S_1 \cup S_2)$. This argument applies to queries in a similar way. That is, any $t \in Slice(r_1) \cap Slice(r_2)$ should be regarded as requested, if only $t \in Above(S_1 \cup S_2)$. Lemma 8.13 shows that both the function $Below()$ and $Above()$ are distributive over set union.

Lemma 8.13. *In a data cube* $< \mathcal{L}, \mathcal{A} >$, *given any* $S_1 \subseteq \mathcal{L}$, $S_2 \subseteq \mathcal{L}$, $Below(S_1 \cup S_2) = Below(S_1) \cup Below(S_2)$ *and* $Above(S_1 \cup S_2) = Above(S_1) \cup Above(S_2)$ *both hold.*

Proof:
It has been shown that $Below(S_1 \cup S_2) = Below(S_1) \cup Below(S_2)$ holds in the last chapter, and dually $Above(S_1 \cup S_2) = Above(S_1) \cup Above(S_2)$ is also true.   □

Therefore, the concept of object (or query) naturally extends to multiple overlapping objects (or queries), and are interpreted as the union of those objects (or queries). That is, any cell is protected (or requested), if only one of the objects (or queries) indicates so. This allows multiple objects (and queries) to be handled independently, without having to worry about their interplay. Hence, we extend the concept of objects and queries to the general case with multiple slices in Definition 8.14. When we say an object, whether it is defined by $Object()$ or $gObject()$ will be clear from context.

Definition 8.14. *In a data cube* $< \mathcal{L}, \mathcal{A} >$, *define*

- *a function* $gObject(.) : 2^{2^{\mathcal{A}} \times 2^{\mathcal{L}}} \to 2^{\mathcal{A}}$ *as*

$$gObject(\{(r_i, S_i) : 1 \leq i \leq n\}) = \bigcup_{i=1}^{n} Object(r_i, S_i)$$

- *a function* $gQuery(.) : 2^{2^{\mathcal{A}} \times 2^{\mathcal{L}}} \to 2^{\mathcal{A}}$ *as*

$$gQuery(\{(r_i, S_i) : 1 \leq i \leq m\}) = \bigcup_{i=1}^{m} Query(r_i, S_i)$$

We say that

- *$gObject(O)$ is an* **object** *specified by the set of pairs* $O = \{(r_i, S_i) : 1 \leq i \leq n\}$, *and any* **t** $\in gObject(O)$ *is* **protected**.

- $gQuery(Q)$ *is a* **query** *specified by the set of pairs* $Q = \{(r_i, S_i) : 1 \leq i \leq m\}$, *and any* $\mathbf{t} \in gQuery(Q)$ *is* **requested**.

The distribuitivity over set union, which objects and queries exhibit, does not apply to inferable sets. That is, even though a cell is not included by the inferable set of each slice, it may still appear in the inferable set of the intersection between slices, and hence is subject to m-d inferences. In Example 8.15, the cells in the cuboid $< year, employee >$, such as $< Y1, Bob >$, are not included by either of the two inferable sets. Hence, if the distribuitivity hold for inferable sets, they would not be included by the inferable set of the query $gQuery(\{(r_1, S_1), (r_2, S_2)\})$, either.

However, this is untrue. For cells in the intersection of the two slices $Slice(r_1) \cap Slice(r_2)$, the descendant closure is $Above(S_1 \cup S_2)$ according to Definition 8.14. Hence, the inferable set should be defined with the GLB of $S_1 \cup S_2$, that is the cuboid $c_r =< year, employee >$. Consequently, the cells in $(Slice(r_1) \cap Slice(r_2)) \cap < year, employee >$, such as $< Y1, Bob >$, should be included by the inferable set of the query $gQuery(\{(r_1, S_1), (r_2, S_2)\})$. Indeed, a cell like $< Y1, Bob >$ is subject to m-d inferences from the query, because the basis of the query with respect to $< Y1, Bob >$ is a set of two cells $\{< all, Bob >, < Y_1, Book >\}$.

Example 8.15. In Figure 8.5, let $r_1 = \{< q, e >: q \leq Q_3, q \in quarter, e \in employee\}$, $r_2 = \{< q, e >: q \in quarter, e \in employee, q \geq Q_4\}$, $S_1 = \{< all, employee >\}$, and $S_2 = \{< year, department >\}$. Because S_1 (or S_2) is a singleton set, its GLB is equal to its only member. Hence, the inferable set of $Query(r_1, S_1)$ (or that of $Query(r_2, S_2)$) is equal to the query itself. The cuboid $< year, employee >$ is included by neither $Above(S_1)$ nor $Above(S_2)$, none of its cells is included by the two inferable sets, either.

The discussion of Example 8.15 can be extended to more than two slices. Consider queries $Query(r_1, S_1)$, $Query(r_2, S_2)$, $\ldots, Query(r_n, S_n)$. Without loss of generality, suppose the slices $Slice(r_1), Slice(r_2), \ldots, Slice(r_m)$ overlap, for some $m \leq n$. Also let c_r be the GLB of $\bigcup_{i=1}^{m} S_i$. Then those m queries together may cause m-d inferences to the cells in a cuboid in $Above(c_r)$. Hence, the inferable set should be the intersection of $Above(c_r)$ with the slices. This discussion extends the concept of inferable set given in Definition 8.9 to the general case with multiple slices, as given in Definition 8.16.

Definition 8.16. *In a data cube* $< \mathcal{L}, \mathcal{A} >$, *define a function* $gInferable(.)$: $2^{2^{\mathcal{A}} \times 2^{\mathcal{L}}} \to 2^{\mathcal{A}}$ *as* $gInferable(\{(r_i, S_i) : 1 \leq i \leq n\}) =$

$$\{\mathbf{t} : \mathbf{t} \in \bigcap_{i \in I \subseteq [1,n]} Slice(r_i) \text{ implies } \mathbf{t} \in \mathbf{c} \text{ for some } \mathbf{c} \in Above(GLB(\bigcup_{i \in I} S_i))\}$$

With proper definition of an inferable set, we are now ready to extend the result of Theorem 8.10 to the general case of cell-level authorizations and queries. That is, any cell included by an inferable set will either be requested by queries, or be subject to m-d inferences from those queries. Conversely, any cell outside of an inferable set will be guaranteed to be safe. This is stated in Theorem 8.17. Later when we refer to an inferable set, whether it is defined by $Inferable()$ or $gInferable()$ will be clear from context.

Theorem 8.17. *In a data cube $< \mathcal{L}, \mathcal{A} >$, given an object $gObject(O)$ and a query $gQuery(Q)$, where $O = \{(r_i, S_i) : 1 \leq i \leq n\}$ and $Q = \{(u_i, V_i) : 1 \leq i \leq m\}$, any $\mathbf{t} \in \bigcup_{i=1}^{m} Slice(u_i)$ satisfies*

- *either $\mathbf{t} \in gQuery(Q)$, or*
- *there does not exist a $T \supseteq gQuery(Q)$ satisfying $\mid gBasis(T), \mathbf{t} \mid= 1$,*

  if and only if $\mathbf{t} \in Inferable(Q)$ is true.

Proof:
We justify the claim by applying Theorem 8.10 as follows.

- For the if part of the claim. If $\mathbf{t} \in gInferable(Q)$ holds, then either $\mathbf{t} \in gQuery(Q)$ or $\mathbf{t} \in gInferable(Q) \setminus gQuery(Q)$ must be true. The claim trivially holds for the former case. For $\mathbf{t} \in gInferable(Q) \setminus gQuery(Q)$, let $I = \{i : 1 \leq i \leq m, \mathbf{t} \in Slice(u_i)\}$, $r = \bigcup_{i \in I} u_i$, and $S = \bigcup_{i \in I} V_i$. Then $gQuery(Q) = Query(r, S)$, and $gInferable(Q) = Inferable(r, S)$. By Theorem 8.10, there does not exist a $T \supseteq Query(r, S)$ satisfying $\mid gBasis(T), \mathbf{t} \mid= 1$ holds. This justifies the if part of the claim.
- For the only if part of the claim. We first justify that $gInferable(Q) \supseteq gQuery(Q)$ holds. For any $\mathbf{t} \in gQuery(Q)$, suppose $\mathbf{t} \in \mathbf{c}$ holds for some $\mathbf{c} \in \mathcal{L}$. Let $I = \{i : 1 \leq i \leq m, \mathbf{t} \in Slice(u_i)\}$. Then $\mathbf{t} \in gQuery(Q)$ implies that $\mathbf{c} \in Above(\bigcup_{i \in I} V_i)$ by Definition 8.14. Hence, $\mathbf{c}_r \preceq \mathbf{c}$ holds, where $\mathbf{c}_r$ is the GLB of $\bigcup_{i \in I} V_i$. Then $\mathbf{c} \in Above(\mathbf{c}_r)$ is true, and $\mathbf{t} \in gInferable(Q)$ follows. and hence $\mathbf{t} \in Query(r_q, S_q)$ only if $\mathbf{t} \in Inferable(r_q, S_q)$ is true. Finally, we show that for any $\mathbf{t} \in \bigcup_{i=1}^{m} Slice(u_i) \setminus gInferable(Q)$, there exists a $T \supseteq gQuery(r_q, S_q)$ satisfying that $\mid gBasis(T), \mathbf{t} \mid= 1$ holds. Let $I = \{i : 1 \leq i \leq m, \mathbf{t} \in Slice(u_i)\}$, $r = \bigcup_{i \in I} u_i$, and $S = \bigcup_{i \in I} V_i$. Then $gQuery(Q) = Query(r, S)$, and $gInferable(Q) = Inferable(r, S)$. By Theorem 8.10, $\mid gBasis(Inferable(r, S), \mathbf{t} \mid= 1$ is true. This concludes the proof of the theorem.

$\square$

8.4.3 Authorizing Queries

In this section we apply the results obtained in previous sections to authorize incoming queries. The first issue to be addressed is to properly encode the objects and inferable sets in a data cube. In most data cubes, the core cuboid is materialized. The result of a query is computed from cells that the requested cells depend on. Other cuboids may or may not be materialized [40]. Hence, we encode objects and inferable sets in the core cuboid. It is easy to extend the results to encode objects and inferable sets in other materialized cuboids.

Intuitively, the object and inferable set of a subject are encoded using their *projections* on the core cuboid. Two relations, R_o and R_q, map each cell t of the core cuboid to a pair $(S, \mathbf{c}_r)$, where S is a set of cuboids and $\mathbf{c}_r$ is a cuboid. S can be considered as a projection of the object on the cell $\mathbf{t}$, in the sense that if any cuboid $\mathbf{c}$ includes a protected descendant of $\mathbf{t}$, then $\mathbf{c}$ must be an ancestor of some cuboid in S. Similarly, $\mathbf{c}_r$ is the projection of the inferable set, as any cuboid $\mathbf{c}$ must be a descendant of $\mathbf{c}_r$ if it overlaps with the inferable set. Those are formalized in Definition 8.18.

Definition 8.18. *In a data cube $< \mathcal{L}, \mathcal{A} >$ with the core cuboid $\mathbf{c}_c$, given any object $gObject(O)$ and query $gQuery(Q)$, define*

- *a relation $R_o \subseteq \mathbf{c}_c \times 2^{\mathcal{L}}$, such that $(\mathbf{t}, S) \in R_o$ iff S is the set of maximal elements of $\{\mathbf{c} : \mathbf{c} \in \mathcal{L}, \mathbf{c} \cap gObject(O) \cap Slice(\mathbf{t}) \neq \phi\}$, and*
- *a relation $R_q \subseteq \mathbf{c}_c \times \mathcal{L}$, such that $(\mathbf{t}, \mathbf{c}_r) \in R_q$ iff $\mathbf{c}_r$ is the minimal element of $\{\mathbf{c} : \mathbf{c} \in \mathcal{L}, \mathbf{c} \cap gInferable(Q) \cap Slice(\mathbf{t}) \neq \phi\}$.*

*We call R_o and R_q the **projection relation** of $gObject(O)$ and that of $gQuery(Q)$, respectively.*

With the two dependency relations R_o and R_q, it is easy to determine whether the inferable set overlap with a given object. That is, if for any cell $\mathbf{t}$ of the core cuboid, $R_q(\mathbf{t})$ is an ancestor of some cuboid in $R_o(\mathbf{t})$, then the inferable set overlaps the object. This means that some of the protected cells are either requested or subject to m-d inferences, and hence the query should not be answered, according to Theorem 8.17. On the other hand, if this is not the case for any cell of the core cuboid, then the query is guaranteed to be free of of m-d inferences. This is summarized in Proposition 8.19.

Proposition 8.19. *In a data cube $< \mathcal{L}, \mathcal{A} >$, given any object $gObject(O)$ and query $gQuery(Q)$, where $O = \{(r_i, S_i) : 1 \leq i \leq n\}$ and $Q = \{(u_i, V_i) : 1 \leq i \leq m\}$. Let R_o and R_q be the projection relation of $gObject(O)$ and $gQuery(Q)$, respectively. Then some cells of $gObject(O)$ are either requested or subject to m-d inferences from $gQuery(Q)$, if and only if there exists a cell $\mathbf{t} \in \mathbf{c}_c$ and a cuboid $\mathbf{c} \in R_o(\mathbf{t})$ satisfying $R_q(\mathbf{t}) \preceq \mathbf{c}$.*

Proof:

- We first show the if part of the claim by contradiction. Suppose some $\mathbf{t} \in gObject(O)$ is subject to m-d inferences from $gQuery(Q)$. Then by Theorem 8.17, we have that $gObject(O) \cap gInferable(Q) \neq \phi$ holds. Let $\mathbf{t} \in gObject(O) \cap gInferable(Q)$. Suppose $\mathbf{t} \in \mathbf{c}$ and $\mathbf{t}_c \preceq \mathbf{t}$ both hold for some $\mathbf{c} \in \mathcal{L}$ and $\mathbf{t}_c$ in the core cuboid $\mathbf{c}_c$. Let $I = \{i : 1 \leq i \leq m, \mathbf{t} \in Slice(u_i)\}$. Then $\mathbf{t} \in gInferable(Q)$ implies that $\mathbf{c}_r \prec \mathbf{c}$ holds, where $\mathbf{c}_r$ is the GLB of $\bigcup_{i \in I} V_i$. Next let $J = \{i : 1 \leq i \leq n, \mathbf{t} \in Slice(r_j)\}$.

Then $t \in gObject(O)$ implies that $c \prec c_1$ holds for at least one $c_1 \in \bigcup_{i \in I} S_i$. Consequently, $c_r \prec c \preceq c_1$ implies that $c_r \prec c_1$ holds. Moreover, both $c_r \cap Slice(t) \subseteq gObject(O)$ and $c_1 \cap Slice(t) \subseteq gInferable(Q)$ hold. Hence, $c_1 \in R_o(t_c)$ and $R_q(t_c) = \{c_r\}$ are true, and $c_r \prec c_1$ implies a contradiction.

- Next we justify the only if part of the claim. Suppose for some $t_c \in c_c$ and $c_o \in R_o(t)$ we have that $R_q(t) \preceq c_o$ holds. Let $R_q(t) = \{c_q\}$. Then by Definition 8.18, $Slice(t_c) \cap c_o \neq \phi$ and $Slice(t_c) \cap c_q \neq \phi$ must both hold, and let them be $\{t_o\}$ and $\{t_q\}$, respectively. Because $c_q \preceq c_o$ holds, $c_q \in Below(c_o)$ is true. Moreover, $t_q \in Slice(t_o)$ also holds. Then by Definition 8.14, $t_q \in gObject(O)$ must be true. That is, $gObject(O) \cap gInferable(Q) \neq \phi$ holds, and by Theorem 8.17, $gInferable(O)$ cannot be free of m-d inferences to $gObject(O)$.

$\square$

Next we show how to incrementally update the projection relation of objects and queries. Objects can be added or removed, when an authorization is specified or revoked, respectively. Adding an object requires more cells to be protected, but those cells may have already been disclosed by queries. In such a case, the request for adding the object should be denied. Otherwise, adding (or removing) an object $Object(r, S)$ updates the projection relation R_o as follows. For each cell t of the core cuboid that the object depends on, we compute the set of maximal elements of the set union $S \cup R_o(t)$ (or the set difference $R_o(t) \setminus S$ if the object is to be removed), and then update $R_o(t)$ with the result. The procedure $Update\_Object$ given in Figure 8.6 summarizes the above discussion to process a request for adding or removing an object. Initially when no object is specified, we let $R_o(t) = \phi$ for any t in the core cuboid.

For queries, information cannot be withdrawn once they are revealed to subjects. Hence we only consider adding new queries. It may be suspected that a new query can be processed similarly as a new object is, because the objects and queries are dual concepts. However, one issue arises. That is, overlapping slices may appear to be disjoint in the core cuboid. Hence, the inferable set cannot be correctly updated based on the core cuboid, like the object is. This is illustrated in Example 8.20. The two slices in the example overlap in some protected cuboid, but are disjoint in the core cuboid. This leads to wrong results if we update the projection relation of queries in the same way as we do for objects.

Example 8.20. In Figure 8.7, the pair $O = (< all, all >, < year, employee >)$ specifies the object, and all the cells in $< year, employee >$ and $< quarter, employee >$ are thus protected. Let $r_1 = \{< q, e >: q \in quarter, e \in employee, q \leq Q_3\}$ and $r_2 = \{< q, e >: q \in quarter, e \in employee, q \geq Q_4\}$. Suppose the query $Query(r_1, < all, employee >)$ (illustrated in dotted lines) is already answered, and a new query $Query(r_2, < year, department >)$ (illustrated in solid lines) is posed. The two queries seem to be disjoint by

Procedure *Update_Object*
Input: a data cube $< \mathcal{L}, \mathcal{A} >$ with the core cuboid $\mathbf{c}_c$;
       the object $Object(O)$; the projection relations R_o and R_q;
       an object $Object(r, S)$ to be added (or removed)
Output: the updated O and R_o if the request is granted, FALSE if it is denied
Method:
   1. **If** $Object(r, S)$ is to be added
      For each $\mathbf{t} \in Slice(r) \cap \mathbf{c}_c$
         If $\mathbf{c} \preceq R_q(\mathbf{t})$ holds for some $\mathbf{c} \in S$
         //the object cannot be safely added
         Return FALSE
   2. **For each** $\mathbf{t} \in Slice(r) \cap \mathbf{c}_c$ //updating the project relations
      If $Object(r, S)$ is to be added
         Let $R_o(\mathbf{t})$ be the set of maximal elements of $R_o(\mathbf{t}) \cup S$
      Else
         Let $R_o(\mathbf{t})$ be the set of maximal elements of $R_o(\mathbf{t}) \setminus S$
   3. **If** $Object(O)$ is to be added //updating the object
      Let $O = O \cup (r, S)$
   Else
      Let $O = O \setminus (r, S)$
   4. **Return** $Object(O)$ and R_o

Fig. 8.6. A Procedure for Updating Objects in Data Cubes

observing the intersection of the two slices with the core cuboid, because r_1 and r_2 are disjoint. This may lead to the wrong conclusion that the second query is safe to answer (assuming it causes no 1-d inferences). However, the two slices $Slice(r_1)$ and $Slice(r_2)$ actually overlap in the protected cuboid $< year, employee >$. Its protected cells such as $< Y1, Bob >$ is thus subject to m-d inferences from the two queries, and hence the second query should indeed be rejected.

The above difficulty can be removed by enforcing the following restriction on the specification of queries. In specifying a query, the slice is required to be specified in the descendants of the cuboids used to specify the descendant closure. More specifically, in any $Query(r, S)$, if r overlaps any cuboid $\mathbf{c}$, then $\mathbf{c}$ must be an upper bound of S. Example 8.20 does not meet this requirement, because in both queries, the slice is specified in an ancestor (the core cuboid) of the cuboid used to specify descendant closures.

The above restriction ensures that slices overlap in some cuboids in the inferable set if and only if they overlap in the core cuboid. More precisely, given any two queries $Query(r_1, S_1)$ and $Query(r_2, S_2)$ satisfying the stated restriction, let $\mathbf{c}_r$ be the GLB of $S_1 \cup S_2$. Then the two slices $Slice(r_1)$ and $Slice(r_2)$ overlap in any cuboid $\mathbf{c} \in Above(\mathbf{c}_r) \setminus Above(S_1 \cup S_2)$, if and only

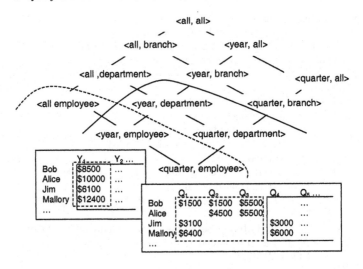

Fig. 8.7. An Example of Overlapping Queries With Disjoint Projections

they do so in all ancestors of c, which certainly include the core cuboid. This is formally stated in Proposition 8.21.

Proposition 8.21. *In a data cube $< \mathcal{L}, \mathcal{A} >$, suppose any two given queries $Query(r_1, S_1)$ and $Query(r_2, S_2)$ satisfy the following condition. That is, $r_1 \cap c \neq \phi$ implies c is an upper bound of S_1, and $r_2 \cap c \neq \phi$ implies c is an upper bound of S_2, for any $c \in \mathcal{L}$. Then for any $c_2 \in Above(c_r) \setminus Above(S_1 \cup S_2)$ and $c_1 \in \mathcal{L}$ satisfying $c_1 \prec c_2$, $Slice(r_1) \cap Slice(r_2) \cap c_2 \neq \phi$ holds if and only if $Slice(r_1) \cap Slice(r_2) \cap c_1 \neq \phi$ is true, where c_r is the GLB of $S_1 \cup S_2$.*

Proof:

1. If $Slice(r_1) \cap Slice(r_2) \cap c_1 \neq \phi$, let $t_1 \in Slice(r_1) \cap Slice(r_2) \cap c_1$. Then because $c_1 \prec c_2$, there must exist a $t_2 \in c_2$ satisfying $t_1 \prec t_2$. Suppose the core cuboid is c_c, and $t_c \in c_c$ satisfies $t_c \preceq t_1$. Then by the transitivity of $\preceq$, $t_c \preceq t_2$ also holds. Hence, by definition of an object, $t_2 \in Slice(r_1) \cap Slice(r_2)$ holds, and $Slice(r_1) \cap Slice(r_2) \cap c_2 \neq \phi$ follows.

2. Next we justify the converse. Suppose $Slice(r_1) \cap Slice(r_2) \cap c_2 \neq \phi$, and let $t_2 \in Slice(r_1) \cap Slice(r_2) \cap c_2$. Because $c_2 \in Above(c_r) \setminus Above(S_1 \cup S_2)$, there must exist c to satisfy $c_2 \preceq c$ and either $c \in S_1$ or $c \in S_2$. Without loss of generality, suppose $c \in S_1$ holds. Then $t_2 \in Slice(r_1)$ implies that $t_2 \preceq t_a$ holds for some $t_a \in r_1$. Suppose $t_a \in c_a$ holds for some $c_a \in \mathcal{L}$. Then by the restriction stated in the proposition, c_a is an upper bound of S_1, and hence is also a descendant of c_2 because $c_2 \preceq c \in S_1$ is true. Then any t_c in the core cuboid c_c satisfying $t_c \preceq t_2$ must also satisfy $t_c \preceq t_a$, and hence $t_c \in Slice(r_1)$ holds. This implies that any $t_1 \in c_1$ satisfying $t_1 \preceq t_2$ must also satisfy $t_1 \in Slice(r_1)$. On the other hand, $t_2 \in Slice(r_2)$

Procedure *Authorize_Query*
Input: a data cube $< \mathcal{L}, \mathcal{A} >$ with the core cuboid $\mathbf{c}_c$;
      the object $Object(O)$; the projection relations R_o and R_q;
      a query $Query(r, S)$ to be authorized
Output: the updated R_q if the query is answered, FALSE if it is rejected
Method:
    1. Let c_r be the GLB of S
    2. For each $\mathbf{t} \in Slice(r) \cap \mathbf{c}_c$
        If $(c_r \wedge R_q(\mathbf{t})) \preceq \mathbf{c}$ holds for some $\mathbf{c} \in R_o(\mathbf{t})$
            Return FALSE //the query may cause m-d inferences
    3. **If** $Query(r, S)$ causes 1-d inferences
        Return FALSE //the query causes 1-d inferences
    4. For each $\mathbf{t} \in Slice(r) \cap \mathbf{c}_c$ //updating the project relation
        Let $R_q(\mathbf{t}) = c_r \wedge R_q(\mathbf{t})$
    5. **Return** R_q

Fig. 8.8. A Procedure for Query Authorization

implies that there must exist at least one $\mathbf{t}_b \in Slice(r_2)$ satisfying $\mathbf{t}_b \preceq \mathbf{t}_2$. But then $\mathbf{t}_b \in Slice(r_1)$ must also hold. That is, $Slice(r_1) \cap Slice(r_2) \cap \mathbf{c}_1 \neq \phi$ is true.

$\square$

By Proposition 8.21, the projection relation of queries can now be updated similarly to that of objects, upon answering a query. Specifically, for a new query $Query(r, S)$, we first compute the GLB of S as $\mathbf{c}_r$. Then for each cell $\mathbf{t}$ of the core cuboid that the new query depends on, we compute the meet $R_q(\mathbf{t}) \wedge \mathbf{c}_r$. If the result is an ancestor of $R_o(\mathbf{t})$, then by Proposition 8.19 the new inferable set causes m-d inferences. That is, inferences may be possible if the new query were answered. Hence, the query is rejected and nothing is updated. If this is not the case for any of the $\mathbf{t}$, then the query is answered if only it is free of 1-d inferences, too.

Upon answering the query, $R_q(\mathbf{t}) \wedge \mathbf{c}_r$ becomes the new value of $R_q(\mathbf{t})$. The procedure *Authorize_Query* given in Figure 8.8 implements the above process. Initially when no query has been answered, we let $R_q(\mathbf{t}) = nil$ for any $\mathbf{t}$ in the core cuboid, where nil is a special cuboid that depends on all other cuboids (and hence $\mathbf{c} \wedge nil = \mathbf{c}$ holds for any $\mathbf{c} \in \mathcal{L}$).

8.4.4 Complexity Analysis

Authorizing queries on the fly brings more performance overhead than the static approach does. However, this reflects the inherent tradeoff among security, availability and performance. We analyze the complexity of our methods, and show that it is reasonable with respect to normal query processing of OLAP.

Specifically, we show that the time complexity of inference control is comparable to that of computing the result of a query, and the storage requirement is linear in the size of the core cuboid.

Let c_c be the core cuboid. We call the number of cells of c_c that a query depends on, $n = | Slice(r) \cap c_c |$, the *size of the query* $Query(r, S)$. Because the result of the query is normally computed from those cells in $Slice(r) \cap c_c$ (If some other cuboids are also materialized to speed up query-processing, then our method benefits accordingly). We assume the number of dimensions k, the number of cuboids $| \mathcal{L} |$ are constants compared to n (in data cubes the number of cells is large, but those of dimensions, attributes, and cuboids are relatively small).

Given a new query $Query(r, S)$ to be processed, the procedure *Authorize_Query* has four tasks. First, it computes the GLB of S as c_r. Second, it computes the meet of c_r and $R_q(t)$, for each $t \in Slice(r) \cap c_c$. Third, for each such t, it also needs to determine whether the result of the second step is an ancestor of some cuboid $c \in R_o(t)$. Finally it detects 1-d inferences. The complexity of the first step can be considered as a constant, and 1-d inferences can be detected in $O(n)$. Hence, next we only consider the second and third steps.

Computing the meet of c_r and $R_q(t)$ requires k comparisons for each t. Hence, the second step requires totally $k \cdot n$ comparisons in the worst case (when no two results of $R_q(t)$ are identical). Determining whether such a meet is the ancestor of some $c \in R_o(t)$ requires at most $k \cdot | R_o(t) | \leq k \cdot | \mathcal{L} |$ comparisons. Hence, the third step needs totally $k \cdot | \mathcal{L} | \cdot n$ comparisons. The total run time of authorizing a query is thus $k \cdot | \mathcal{L} | \cdot n = O(n)$. That is, a new query can be authorized in the time comparable to that is required for computing its result.

Now we consider the storage requirement. Notice that for each query $Query(r, S)$, we do not store the pair (r, S), once the query is processed (If the query needs to be recorded for other reasons like auditing, then the overhead is not due to inference control). That is, the inference control is *stateless* with respect to queries (the information required by inference control is actually encoded by the projection relation R_q).

Although the authorizations $Object(O)$ need to be stored, its size is usually a constant compared to the number of cells in the data cube. Hence, the storage requirement depends on the size of the projection relations R_o and R_q. For each $t \in c_c$, $| R_q(t) | = 1$ and $| R_o(t) | \leq | \mathcal{L} |$. Hence, the total size of R_o and R_q is at most $| c_c | \cdot (| \mathcal{L} | + 1)$. By considering the number of cuboids as a constant compared to the number of cells, the total storage requirement of R_o and R_q is $O(| c_c |)$.

8.5 Summary

This chapter has studied preventing m-d inferences in data cubes based on actual incoming queries, such that sensitive data can be protected while not adversely decreasing the availability of an OLAP system. We described potential limitations of the static approach discussed in the previous chapter, which may cause desirable queries to be rejected due to the static nature of the approach. We then proposed a query-driven alternative for preventing complex inferences caused by combinations of queries. We showed that the result is provably secure, and a query is answered if only it can be determined as free of inferences. We discussed encoding the result in data cubes and authorizing queries based on such an encoding. Our analysis of complexity indicates that preventing inferences at the run time is practical with the proposed method, even though additional performance overhead is unavoidable as the cost of improved availability.

9

Conclusion and Future Direction

This book has addressed the following issue: *How can we achieve the seemingly conflicting goals of keeping private data secret and answering aggregate data cube queries about the private data?*

The above issue is important to many data applications that demand both the confidentiality of private data and the availability of private data for useful analyses. For example, details of electronic transactions are being collected on a daily basis. The data are then stored in the enterprise's data warehouses and analyzed through decision support systems, such as OLAP. Inappropriate disclosures of the collected sensitive information may breach an individual's privacy and consequently harm the enterprise's interests. At the same time, the analysis of transactional data is important for the enterprise to evaluate its past performance and to improve future business practices.

The key challenge of the study has been to meet the seemingly conflicting goals of security (of private data) and availability (of data cube queries) under the performance constraints of on-line analytical processing applications. Security of sensitive data can be breached not only through unauthorized accesses due to lack of access control but also through indirect inferences using results of legitimate queries. OLAP systems are especially vulnerable to the latter, since they typically rely on aggregated data to hide insignificant details from users and hence accentuate global patterns and trends. On the other hand, the interactive nature of OLAP systems implies both stringent performance requirement and the demand for versatile queries. A security measure proposed for OLAP systems must meet these requirements while guaranteeing security.

This book reviewed some existing techniques in traditional database applications, such as statistical databases. These techniques have been shown to be impractical if directly applied to OLAP systems. They suffer from high on-line complexity and poor adaptability. The most common approach is to check queries for inferences and to grant queries only if no inference can be detected. The checking for complex inferences is expensive. Moreover, the checking can only be done after the queries have arrived the system, causing delays to the user. A more serious problem is that different checking methods are required for different type of queries, and effective methods do not exist for checking many combinations of queries. Although existing techniques do not directly comprise a valid solution to our problem, understanding these techniques has provided us with a solid foundation for further investigation of the problem.

The book then discussed four solutions for protecting sensitive data in data cubes from unauthorized accesses and malicious inferences. First, inspired by the result of Dobkin et al. on the cardinality-based inference control, Chapter 5 derived a tight upper bound on empty cells (i.e., previously known values) for data cubes to remain free of inferences. Second, inspired by Chin's result on sum-two queries, Chapter 6 developed a method for checking inferences of multi-dimensional range queries. The result is an improvement over Chin's result on Audit Expert. Although both results still inherit certain limitations of previous techniques, and are thus not fully satisfactory, they nonetheless provided us with a thorough understanding of the problem and key insights.

Based on such insights, Chapter 7 strived to propose a more practical solution to protecting private data while answering data cube-style queries. We adopted a novel approach of preventing complex inferences instead of detecting them. Such an approach can provide provable security and at the same time reduce the complexity to a practical level. The approach also removed the limitation on aggregation types by supporting generic sensitivity criteria. The proposed methods can guarantee security through restrictions on queries, which can be pre-computed. Existing security mechanisms can easily enforce the computed restrictions, leading to a readily deployable solution.

The above approach is static in the sense that restrictions on queries are computed once and for all. This fact implies that the result is not always optimal with respect to actual needs of the user. Chapter 8 showed that there usually exist many options in computing the restrictions, and the optimal choice depends on queries that are posed to the system. Therefore, we proposed to let the actual sequence of queries drive the computation of security restrictions. This enabled us to always make the optimal choice with respect to all answered queries. While availability is improved, dynamically computing restrictions on queries would certainly bring more performance overhead. We thus justified the approach by showing such additional overhead is reasonable in comparison to the cost of computing the answers to queries.

There are many open problems left for further investigations. For example, the collusion between different users may result in undetected inferences. Currently we can only address this issue by grouping users that tend to collude into a single subject so they always have the same authorizations. However, in practice we do not always know about collusions in advance, so better solutions for tolerating collusions should be pursued. As another example, it may be desirable to pursue less conservative query specification than what discussed in this book. For example, in this book, if Bob's commission in the first quarter is requested, then his commission in the first year is also considered as requested, since the latter is a descendant of the former. However, it is possible to keep the latter secret while disclosing the former. How to prevent inferences in this case is not addressed in the current approach and worth additional investigation. Finally, the effectiveness of the query-driven approach depends on the assumption that users will first ask the queries that are most desired, which may not always hold in practice since users may accidentally ask meaningless queries first. It is thus desirable to combine the approach with some statically determined restrictions, leading to a hybrid approach.

References

1. N.R. Adam and J.C. Wortmann. Security-control methods for statistical databases: a comparative study. *ACM Computing Surveys*, 21(4):515–556, 1989.
2. S. Agarwal, R. Agrawal, P.M. Deshpande, A. Gupta, J.F. Naughton, R. Ramakrishnan, and S. Sarawagi. On the computation of multidimensional aggregates. In *Proceedings of the Twenty-Two Conference on Very Large Data Base (VLDB'96)*, pages 506–521, 1996.
3. R. Agrawal and R. Srikant. Privacy-preserving data mining. In *Proceedings of the Nineteenth ACM SIGMOD Conference on Management of Data (SIGMOD'00)*, pages 439–450, 2000.
4. R. Agrawal, R. Srikant, and D. Thomas. Privacy-preserving olap. In *Proceedings of the Twenty-fourth ACM SIGMOD Conference on Management of Data (SIGMOD'05)*, pages 251–262, 2005.
5. D. Barbara and X. Wu. Using approximations to scale exploratory data analysis in datacubes. In *Proceedings of the Fifth ACM SIGKDD International Conference on Knowledge Discovery and Data Mining (KDD'99)*, pages 382–386, 1999.
6. J. Beck and V.T. Sós. Discrepancy theory. In R.L. Graham, M. Grötschel, and L. Lovász, editors, *Handbook of combinatorics*, pages 1405–1446. Elsevier Science, 1995.
7. L.L. Beck. A security mechanism for statistical databases. *ACM Trans. on Database Systems*, 5(3):316–338, 1980.
8. B. Bhargava. Security in data warehousing (invited talk). In *Proceedings of the 3rd Data Warehousing and Knowledge Discovery (DaWak'00)*, 2000.
9. L. Brankovic, M. Miller, P. Horak, and G. Wrightson. Usability of compromise-free statistical databases. In *Proceedings of the Ninth International Conference on Scientific and Statistical Database Management (SSDBM '97)*, pages 144–154, 1997.
10. Electronic Privacy Information Center. http://www.epic.org.
11. L. Chang and I. S. Moskowitz. Parsimonious downgrading and decision trees applied to the inference problem. In *Workshop on New Security Paradigms*, pages 82–89, 1998.
12. F.Y. Chin. Security in statistical databases for queries with small counts. *ACM Transaction on Database Systems*, 3(1):92–104, 1978.
13. F.Y. Chin. Security problems on inference control for sum, max, and min queries. *Journal of the Association for Computing Machinery*, 33(3):451–464, 1986.

174   References

14. F.Y. Chin, P. Kossowski, and S.C. Loh. Efficient inference control for range sum queries. *Theoretical Computer Science*, 32:77–86, 1984.
15. F.Y. Chin and G. Özsoyoglu. Statistical database design. *ACM Trans. on Database Systems*, 6(1):113–139, 1981.
16. F.Y. Chin and G. Özsoyoglu. Auditing and inference control in statistical databases. *IEEE Trans. on Software Engineering*, 8(6):574–582, 1982.
17. V. Ciriani, S. De Capitani di Vimercati, S. Foresti, and P. Samarati. Microdata protection. In Y. Ting and J. Jajodia, editors, *Security in Decentralized Data Management*. Springer-Verlag, To Appear.
18. E.F. Codd, S.B. Codd, and C.T. Salley. Providing olap to user-analysts: An IT mandate. White Paper, 1993. E.F. Codd Associates.
19. WWW Consorortium. Platform for privacy preferences (p3p) project. http://www.w3.org/P3P/.
20. Microsoft Corporation. Microsoft sql server olap services cell-level security white-paper. White Paper, 1999.
21. L.H. Cox. Suppression methodology and statistical disclosure control. *Journal of American Statistical Association*, 75(370):377–385, 1980.
22. L.H. Cox. On properties of multi-dimensional statistical tables. *Journal of Statistical Planning and Inference*, 117(2):251–273, 2003.
23. K. Coyle. P3p: Pretty poor privacy? a social analysis of the platform for privacy preferences (p3p). http: //www.kcoyle.net/ p3p.html, 1999. June.
24. R.A. DeMillo, D. Dobkin, and R.J. Lipton. Even data bases that lie can be compromised. *IEEE Transactions on Software Engineering*, 4(1):73–75, 1978.
25. D.E. Denning. *Cryptography and data security*. Addison-Wesley, Reading, Massachusetts, 1982.
26. D.E. Denning, P.J. Denning, and M.D. Schwartz. The tracker: A threat to statistical database security. *ACM Trans. on Database Systems*, 4(1):76–96, 1979.
27. D.E. Denning and J. Schlörer. A fast procedure for finding a tracker in a statistical database. *ACM Transactions on Database Systems*, 5(1):88–102, 1980.
28. D.E. Denning and J. Schlörer. Inference controls for statistical databases. *IEEE Computer*, 16(7):69–82, 1983.
29. D. Dobkin, A.K. Jones, and R.J. Lipton. Secure databases: protection against user influence. *ACM Trans. on Database Systems*, 4(1):97–106, 1979.
30. T. Donnellan. *Lattice Theory*. Pergamon press, Oxford, 1968.
31. The end of privacy. The Economist, 1999. May.
32. P. Erdös. On some extremal problems in graph theory. *Isarel Journal of Math.*, 3:113–116, 1965.
33. L.P. Fellegi. On the question of statistical confidentiality. *Journal of American Statistic Association*, 67(337):7–18, 1972.
34. L.P. Fellegi and A.B. Sunter. A theory for record linkage. *Journal of American Statistic Association*, 64(328):1183–1210, 1969.
35. M.R. Garey and D.S. Johnson. *Computers and Intractability: A guide to the Theory of NP-Completeness*. W.H. Freeman and Company, San Francisco, 1979.
36. R. Gellman. How the lack of privacy costs consumers and why business studies of privacy costs are biased and incomplete. http://www.epic.org /reports/dmfprivacy.html, 2002.
37. J. Gray, A. Bosworth, A. Bosworth, A. Layman, D. Reichart, M. Venkatrao, F. Pellow, and H. Pirahesh. Data cube: A relational aggregation operator generalizing group-by, cross-tab, and sub-totals. *Data Mining and Knowledge Discovery*, 1(1):29–53, 1997.

38. P. Griffiths and B.W. Wade. An authorization mechanism for a relational database system. *ACM Transactions on Database Systems*, 1(3):242–255, September 1976.

39. J. Han. OLAP mining: Integration of OLAP with data mining. In *IFIP Conf. on Data Semantics*, pages 1–11, 1997.

40. V. Harinarayan, A. Rajaraman, and J.D. Ullman. Implementing data cubes efficiently. In *Proceedings of the Fifteenth ACM SIGMOD international conference on Management of data (SIGMOD'96)*, pages 205–227, 1996.

41. D.T. Ho, R. Agrawal, N. Megiddo, and R. Srikant. Range queries in olap data cubes. In *Proceedings Sixteenth ACM SIGMOD International Conference on Management of Data (SIGMOD'97)*, pages 73–88, 1997.

42. K. Hoffman. *Linear Algebra*. Prentice-Hall, Englewood Cliffs, New Jersey, 1961.

43. S. Jajodia, P. Samarati, M.L. Sapino, and V.S. Subrahmanian. Flexible support for multiple access control policies. *ACM Transactions on Database Systems*, 26(4):1–57, dec 2001.

44. J.B. Kam and J.D. Ullman. A model of statistical databases and their security. *ACM Transactions on Database Systems*, 2(1):1–10, 1977.

45. J. Kleinberg, C. Papadimitriou, and P. Raghavan. Auditing boolean attributes. In *Proceedings of the Ninth ACM SIGMOD-SIG ACT-SIGART Symposium on Principles of Database System*, pages 86–91, 2000.

46. Y. Li, H. Lu, and R.H. Deng. Practical inference control for data cubes (extended abstract). In *Proceedings of the IEEE Symposium on Security and Privacy*, 2006.

47. Y. Li, L. Wang, X.S. Wang, and S. Jajodia. Auditing interval-based inference. In *Proceedings of the Fourteenth Conference on Advanced Information Systems Engineering (CAiSE'02)*, pages 553–568, 2002.

48. F.M. Malvestuto. A universal-scheme approach to statistical databases containing homogeneous summary tables. *ACM Transactions on Database Systems*, 18(4):678–708, 1993.

49. F.M. Malvestuto and Moscarini M. An audit expert for large statistical databases. In *Proceedings of the Conference on Statistical Data Protection*, 1998.

50. F.M. Malvestuto and M. Moscarini. Query evaluability in statistical databases. *IEEE Transactions on Knowledge and Data Engineering*, 2(4):425–430, 1990.

51. F.M. Malvestuto and M. Moscarini. Censoring statistical tables to protect sensitive information: Easy and hard problems. In *Proceedings of the Eighth International Conference on Scientific and Statistical Database Management*, pages 12–21, 1996.

52. F.M. Malvestuto and M. Moscarini. Computational issues connected with the protection of sensitive statistics by auditing sum-queries. In *Proceedings of Tenth IEEE Scientific and Statistical Database Management (SSDBM'98)*, pages 134–144, 1998.

53. F.M. Malvestuto, M. Moscarini, and M. Rafanelli. Suppressing marginal cells to protect sensitive information in a two-dimensional statistical table. In *Proceedings of the Tenth ACM SIGACT-SIGMOD-SIGART Symposium on Principles of Database Systems (PODS'96)*, pages 252–258, 1996.

54. J.M. Mateo-Sanz and J. Domingo-Ferrer. A method for data-oriented multivariate microaggregation. In *Proceedings of the Conference on Statistical Data Protection'98*, pages 89–99, 1998.

55. G. Miklau and D. Suciu. A formal analysis of information disclosure in data exchange. In *Proceedings of the 23th ACM SIGMOD Conference on Management of Data (SIGMOD'04)*, 2004.

56. H.B. Newcombe, J.M. Kennedy, S.J. Axford, and A.P. James. Automatic linkage of vital records. *Science*, 130(3381):954–959, 1959.
57. N. Pendse. The olap report - database explosion. OLAP Report Technical Report, 2001. http:// www.olapreport.com / DatabaseExplosion.htm.
58. N. Pendse. The olap report - what is olap. OLAP Report Technical Report, 2001. http:// www.olapreport.com / fasmi.htm.
59. S. Rizvi, A.O. Mendelzon, S. Sudarshan, and P. Roy. Extending query rewriting techniques for fine-grained access control. In *Proceedings of the 23th ACM SIGMOD Conference on Management of Data (SIGMOD'04)*, 2004.
60. P. Samarati. Protecting respondents' identities in microdata release. *IEEE Transactions on Knowledge and Data Engineering*, 13(6):1 010–1027, 2001.
61. P. Samarati and L. Sweeney. Generalizing data to provide anonymity when disclosing information (abstract). In *PODS*, 1998.
62. R.S. Sandhu, E.J. Coyne, H.L. Feinstein, and C.E. Youman. Role-based access control models. *IEEE Computer*, 29(2):38–47, 1996.
63. J. Schlörer. Disclosure from statistical databases: Quantitative aspects of trackres. *ACM Transactions on Database Systems*, 5(4):467–492, 1980.
64. J. Schlörer. Security of statistical databases: multidimensional transformation. *ACM Trans. on Database Systems*, 6(1):95–112, 1981.
65. A. Shoshani. OLAP and statistical databases: Similarities and differences. In *Proceedings of the Sixteenth ACM SIGACT-SIGMOD-SIGART Symposium on Principles of Database Systems (PODS'97)*, pages 185–196, 1997.
66. G. Pernul T. Priebe. Towards olap security design - survey and research issues. In *Proceedings of 3rd ACM International Workshop on Data Warehousing and OLAP (DOLAP'00)*, pages 114–121, 2000.
67. Pedersen T.B. and Jense C.S. Multidimensional database technology. *IEEE Computer*, 34(12):40–46, 2001.
68. R.P. Tewarson. *Sparse Matrices*. Academic Press, New York, 1973.
69. J.F. Traub, Y. Yemini, and H. Woźniakowski. The statistical security of a statistical database. *ACM Trans. on Database Systems*, 9(4):672–679, 1984.
70. European Union. Directive on privacy protection, 1998. October.
71. J. Vaidya and C. Clifton. Privacy preserving association rule mining in vertically partitioned data. In *Proceedings of the eighth ACM SIGKDD international conference on Knowledge discovery and data mining (KDD'02)*, pages 639–644, 2002.
72. V.S. Verykios, A.K. Elmagarmid, E. Bertino, Y. Saygin, and E. Dasseni. Association rule hiding. *IEEE Transactions on Knowledge and Data Engineering*, 16(4):434–447, 2004.
73. L. Wang, S. Jajodia, and D. Wijesekera. Securing OLAP data cubes against privacy breaches. In *Proceedings of the 2004 IEEE Symposium on Security and Privacy (S&P'04)*, pages 161–175, 2004.
74. L. Wang, Y.J. Li, D. Wijesekera, and S. Jajodia. Precisely answering multidimensional range queries without privacy breaches. In *Proceedings of the Eighth European Symposium on Research in Computer Security (ESORICS'03)*, pages 100–115, 2003.
75. L. Wang, Y.J. Li, D. Wijesekera, and S. Jajodia. Precisely answering multidimensional range queries without privacy breaches. Technical Report ISE-TR-03-03, 2003.

76. L. Wang, D. Wijesekera, and S. Jajodia. Cardinality-based inference control in sum-only data cubes. In *Proceedings of the Seventh European Symposium on Research in Computer Security (ESORICS'02)*, pages 55–71, 2002.

77. L. Wang, D. Wijesekera, and S. Jajodia. Cardinality-based inference control in sum-only data cubes (extended version). Center for Secure Information Systems Technical Report, 2002.

78. L. Wang, D. Wijesekera, and S. Jajodia. Cardinality-based inference control in data cubes. *Journal of Computer Security*, 12(5):655–692, 2004.

79. L. Wang, D. Wijesekera, and S. Jajodia. Query-driven privacy preserving in data cubes. Center for Secure Information Systems Technical Report, 2004.

80. L. Willenborg and T. de Walal. *Statistical disclosure control in practice*. Springer Verlag, New York, 1996.

81. C.T. Yu and F.Y. Chin. A study on the protection of statistical data bases. In *Proceedings of the ACM SIGMOD International Conference on Management of Data (SIGMOD'77)*, pages 169–181, 1977.

Index